EMPOWERED INVESTING

EMPOWERED INVESTING

Strategies for Proactive Investors

Joseph F. LoPresti

iUniverse, Inc.
New York Lincoln Shanghai

Empowered Investing
Strategies for Proactive Investors

Copyright © 2007 by Joseph F. LoPresti

iUniverse books may be ordered through booksellers or by contacting:

iUniverse
2021 Pine Lake Road, Suite 100
Lincoln, NE 68512
www.iuniverse.com
1-800-Authors (1-800-288-4677)

The views expressed in this work are solely those of the author and do not necessarily reflect the views of the publisher, and the publisher hereby disclaims any responsibility for them.

ISBN-13: 978-0-595-37177-8 (pbk)
ISBN-13: 978-0-595-67469-5 (cloth)
ISBN-13: 978-0-595-81575-3 (ebk)
ISBN-10: 0-595-37177-9 (pbk)
ISBN-10: 0-595-67469-0 (cloth)
ISBN-10: 0-595-81575-8 (ebk)

Printed in the United States of America

To Angela, my wife, and Christina, Marissa, and Breanna, my incredible daughters—you are my inspiration.

CONTENTS

INTRODUCTION

The argument can be made that too many books have been written about investing. So why, you ask, should anyone read this one? The best reason is that this may very well be the last investment book you will ever have to read. Period.

If you bought this book expecting to read and learn about a get-rich-quick system, you can return it, and I'll refund your money. You won't find it here.

If, on the other hand, you learn what I have to teach you (it isn't difficult; it's easy) and if you master it and apply the knowledge you gain, you will take control of your financial destiny with confidence and will do it better than most professionals can.

This book will provide you with the tools you need for developing effective investment strategies and for making confident and profitable decisions. It will help eliminate indecision, self-doubt, and guesswork. You will grow your investments confidently and safely with a simple but disciplined approach and reap the rewards that are possible because of it. And you will even enjoy the process.

How do I know this? Because I've worked with thousands of investors for over twenty-one years, and I know how individual investors think, how people decide which stocks and mutual funds to buy, and how hope and prayers enter into financial decisions rather than investment strategies that work. I know the mistakes people make that lead not only to disappointing results but also to a lower quality of life.

I know extremely bright, well-educated, and very talented people who have lost huge sums of money in the stock market. You may know some, too. As an investment manager, I, too, suffered through some stressful times. However, in 1994, I was introduced to a different way of analyzing the markets, and it changed my life. Learning this way of viewing the markets and making investment decisions can do the same for you.

The financial seas are riddled with overturned boats whose owners are barely hanging on or making little to no financial progress. These are confusing

1

times for investors. More than ever, you need an independent, unbiased, and accurate analysis of the forces driving the markets. Whether you are a new or an experienced investor, you will benefit from this book—even in turbulent markets when many professional investors are struggling. Even if you are thoroughly confused by all things financial, you will be amazed at what you can accomplish if you consistently apply my methods and principles.

Many investors trust themselves to make financial decisions. After all, you work hard for your money and want to maintain control over your financial life. The sad reality is that most investors do not know how to combine pertinent information with consistent discipline and make positive investment decisions consistently. My hope is that this book will provide the road map you need to be a successful investor, which will help you enjoy life.

After working with so many individuals, I know people view their investments as personal statements about who they are and what they are trying to accomplish in life. Being able to enjoy security in retirement, having more time to spend with their families, and ultimately enriching their lives are very real goals for the people I've worked with. I share those goals, and I enjoy sharing my experiences as an educator and an investment manager.

SECTION 1

BACKGROUND

CHAPTER 1

INFLUENCE OF WALL STREET AND THE MEDIA

Most individual investors rely too heavily on:
Wall Street Research
The Media
A Buy-and-Hold (Hope) Strategy
Blind Diversification

Before delving into my approach to disciplined portfolio management and investment selection, it is beneficial to understand how most investors make decisions. This discussion will help you determine what kind of information leads to making informed versus uninformed decisions. It will also provide perspective on the difference between a disciplined approach and one I will call "emotion based."

If I've learned one thing in the past twenty-plus years counseling investors, it is that most investors rely heavily on Wall Street research and on the media for their investment information. This is not surprising, considering that both Wall Street reports and media information are readily available twenty-four hours a day to time-strapped investors. Sadly, information from these sources is often inaccurate and works to the detriment of the individual investor.

Additionally, most individuals rely on two investment strategies: the buy-and-hold strategy (I refer to as the "buy-and-hope" strategy) and the blind-diversification strategy. Neither strategy alone or in combination will maximize returns over the long haul, yet many investment firms promote buying and holding because it is easy and requires less time and fewer resources for them to manage portfolios. Financial-planning professionals, in particular, advocate a buy-and-hold or blind-diversification approach.

I also advocate diversification, but, in reality, your portfolio must be diversified in a focused way, or it could result in mediocre results at best.

Let's explore in more detail how each of these factors plays a role in shaping an individual's way of investing and ultimately his or her success.

Wall Street Research

Wall Street research is slow to notice changing market conditions. An accurate analysis of the past is no guarantee of anything going forward. In my investment experience, I have found little value in an accurate explanation of past events. In fact, projecting the past into the future can lead to disastrous results. Think about how many fortunes were lost as Wall Street led investors to believe that the favorable conditions of technology stocks in the 1990s would continue into the 2000s.

More importantly, the information provided by Wall Street is often inaccurate and cannot be trusted. When reading Wall Street research, keep in mind these reports are often written with hidden agendas. Wall Street brokerage firms do not profit from holding your investment portfolio. Instead, their "big" money is made by catering to the large institutions, such as pension funds, banks, mutual funds, hedge funds, and insurance companies. After all, institutions buy large blocks of stocks; individuals usually buy small blocks. There are even times when research reports are expressly written to get the small investor to act counter to institutional clients. For example, if an institutional client needs to sell a large block of stock, a brokerage house might issue a positive report on the stock, or the firm's analyst might raise the company's earnings estimates. These actions create demand for the stock on the part of individuals, who buy the stock based on the reports, and provide the liquidity necessary for the institutional client to sell its holdings without negatively affecting their sale price.

Further fueling a brokerage firm's loyalty to its institutional clients are the significant profits they earn by providing institutions investment-banking services (i.e., raising capital and providing advice on merger and acquisition deals). Understanding the role of sell-side analysts helps one understand the conflicting nature of Wall Street research. The sell-side analyst's role at a brokerage firm is to represent the firm's institutional clients and to sell their stock to the public or to the firm's individual clients. Brokerage firms are paid multimillion-dollar fees for raising capital for their institutional clients. In contrast, commissions from an individual's transactions constitute a much smaller part of their earnings. If you were a sell-side analyst or a chief executive of a large brokerage firm, where would you direct your efforts?

As long as intentions are pure, all parties benefit. Companies get the needed capital to grow their business, the public buys stock in a strong business, and the brokerage firm is paid to bring the parties together. However, intentions are often not what they seem, and a transaction is "created" by the institution's insiders or Wall Street investment bankers. They know a company's stock is greatly overvalued and, therefore, want to sell the stock to the public quickly. Similarly, Wall Street bankers want to collect their fees while the stock appears strong. In these situations, the brokerage firm's analysts create a "good story." The firm's brokers call their clients to sell the story, and the individual investor buys stock from an inventory owned by insiders. Word spreads that the stock is in demand, which fuels more demand by other individual investors who buy it. Sadly, when the share price drops, the individual investor is left owning stock that he or she bought at a significantly higher price.

Does this whole process sound unethical, even illegal? Well, it is, and regulatory authorities to help protect the public against such fraud have established safeguards. However, they also established safeguards some seventy years ago to prevent similar schemes, and the Wall Street Machine found a way to get around the law. One thing you can count on is that as long as the markets are around, there will be attempts to take advantage of the uninformed investor. To avoid being taken advantage of, you need to make sure you are not one of the uninformed.

The Internet and telecom bubble in the late 1990s through early 2000 is a real example of a misleading story. Wall Street convinced many uninformed investors that the new companies would be successful for years to come and that their stock prices would only go higher. As a result, individual investors sometimes paid hundreds of dollars per share for a stock. The "story" and the story's spin were so promising that buyers often disregarded weak or deteriorating fundamentals. Yet, at the same time, inside investors were cashing out millions of shares. Many of these companies are no longer in business or are trading for a fraction of the price they once fetched. Consider the amount of money lost in companies like WorldCom, Lucent Technologies, Cisco Systems,

Sun Microsystems, JDS Uniphase, and Nortel Networks (just to name a few). Insiders cashed out their millions, and individual investors lost theirs.

Overall, Wall Street research can be very confusing. What does it mean when an analyst "downgrades" a stock to "buy" from "strong buy" or from "overweight" to "market neutral"? This terminology can leave an investor confused and unsure of what action, if any, to take. What you need is an objective way of reading the markets that either substantiates what you are told by Wall Street or that gives you concrete information to refute any hidden agendas within the investment community. You need a strategy that provides you clear and concise information, so you can make confident and informed decisions.

The Media and How It Influences Investors

Emotional Investing

The media is not in the business of selling investment advice, yet it profoundly influences people's thinking about investments. It can be argued that the media, whether business oriented or for a general audience, makes money by creating emotions. In today's sensationalist society, emotion is, in part, what causes people to tune into the news, subscribe to magazines, read Internet articles, or support other forms of media. Even what is considered "hard news" is sometimes slanted toward an emotional perspective, and thus it affects people's judgment because we're emotional animals. I have repeatedly seen how investment decisions based on emotions rather than from objective, accurate, and pertinent information are nearly always wrong.

Furthermore, the media reports ongoing and past business and economic conditions. The inevitable delay between events and media coverage means that the news is already old, and that an investor is responding to it in an "after-the-fact" manner. Stock prices have already adjusted to the event and, in fact, may have already peaked. Using the media for your source of investment information assures that you are making reactive, not proactive, decisions.

The media tends to play on two key investor emotions: greed and fear. By the time positive or negative news is reported, stock prices have already adjusted to the news. People who react to media reports by buying or selling stock are in for unfortunate losses. This happens far too frequently to otherwise intelligent people.

When world, national, or business situations are positive, the media's reporting is positive. When events are negative, the media's reporting is negative. People naturally want to benefit from positive news but make "after-the-fact" decisions that result in buying near market highs. This is a greed-based reaction. Negative news, on the other hand, causes investors to sell their holdings; yet, stock prices have already adjusted to the event. This is a fear-based reaction stemming from a desire to sell before "things get worse." In these cases, the individual sells after the price has already dropped. Reacting to either positive or negative news in this fashion leads investors to buy and sell at inappropriate times.

Herd Mentality

A different problem arising out of media-influenced investor decisions is that one is inevitably making the same decision as the masses. It is a fact that the minority of investors make the majority of the profits whereas the crowd settles for less than average returns. If you follow the crowd, you will end up with mediocre returns. If the masses have sold, the large amount of supply is already discounted in the market price of the stock. If you sell with the masses, you stand a strong chance of selling near a low. If the masses are buying, the individual investor stands a very strong chance of buying near a high price. The market has a way of fooling the masses. Yet not following the herd isn't enough by itself; you must follow an investment approach that offers an accurate and detailed examination of any investment.

In order to make sound investment decisions consistently, you need to put the media and emotions aside and rely on indicators that speak to the two, true forces that move prices: supply and demand. You need to rely on indicators that reflect current market conditions, not on media reports, which, by their nature, are delayed or historic. To be successful, you have to think a few steps ahead of the crowd. The best time to buy, for example, is often when the news is at its worst. Similarly, the best time to sell is often when the news is at its best. The proactive approach taught in this book will reveal these opportunities.

Buy-and-Hold (Hope) Strategy

Those who follow a buy-and-hold strategy take a passive approach to investing. These individuals purchase an investment and hold on, riding out changing market conditions. Such an investor assumes there is no value in market analysis. I refer to these individuals as "buy-and-hope" investors: they buy stocks and hope the market will take care of them.

During long periods of generally rising equity prices, which we enjoyed in the 1980s and 1990s, a buy-and-hold strategy can work. Little knowledge or experience is needed to make money during strong bull markets. Even so, one's returns will be far from optimized.

More importantly, during long periods of declining or stagnant equity prices, a buy-and-hold strategy results in significant lost returns and opportunities. It can take years to recover losses generated from passively holding on through an extended stagnant period or a significant market decline. During most market conditions, you cannot afford to act passively. You must take on a proactive approach and apply that knowledge to your benefit. When the market is declining, an investor must be actively looking for windows of opportunity, that is, specific situations where prices are rising. An active approach is your best choice.

By understanding the supply and demand relationships of individual stocks, within specific industries and of the market as a whole, you are able to maximize returns in bull markets and find windows of opportunity in bear markets.

Blind Diversification

Diversification is a protection against ignorance.
It makes very little sense for those that know what they are doing.
—*Warren Buffet*

Warren Buffet said it best. However, a large percentage of investors, including many professionals, believe the key to successful investing is to build a diversified portfolio that includes different asset categories (large cap, small cap, growth, value, international stocks, and various bonds) to protect against market risk. I call this the "pie chart" strategy; I'm sure you have seen such charts. They allocate a certain percentage of your portfolio to various asset categories, depending on your financial situation, age, years until retirement, and so forth. Usually, this strategy will suggest the purchase of various mutual funds that invest in the various asset classes suggested in the strategy. Maybe you have had a financial plan drawn up that takes this approach.

Diversification is important to a certain extent, but *blind diversification* is uneducated and counterproductive. One very popular diversification strategy, called Modern Portfolio Theory, goes so far as to suggest that it is desirable to diversify your portfolio to the extent that you intentionally hold different asset classes that are highly uncorrelated. In other words, while one asset goes up in value, the other goes down, and vice versa. To me, this strategy virtually guarantees your returns to be anything but great.

I am an advocate of diversification; however, your portfolio diversification must be focused. *Focused diversification* is part of a greater investment strategy. After reading this book, I hope that you will understand what focused diversification is and will be able to apply it to your own portfolio.

Secular (Long-Term) Market Trends

Financial markets experience extended periods of generally rising prices followed by extended periods of stagnant prices. These trends are referred to as secular market trends, which I'll cover in depth later in the *Market Analysis* section of this book. It is worthy of mention right now because an understanding of secular market trends is critical as background for you to develop disciplined and proactive strategies.

Secular market trends are best described after you look at the 102-year chart of the Dow Jones Industrial Average in chapter 19, *figure 19.1*. Looking at that chart, you can clearly see very long-term periods when stock prices rise, called secular *bull* trends. Inevitably, stock prices rise too much toward the end of secular bull trends, which leads to an extended period when they consolidate the advance. During these consolidation periods, referred to as secular *bear* trends, stock prices are generally stagnant for extended periods. Why do you care about secular market trends? Because strategies that work during secular bull trends do not work during secular bear trends. The strategies I teach in this book will help you maximize opportunities during secular bull trends, but they are imperative during secular bear trends.

11

The last secular bull trend occurred during 1982–2000 in the U.S. stock market. Toward the end of that period, stock prices became overvalued, and the secular trend turned bearish. Following the 1982–2000 advance, stock prices became generally stagnant. At the end of 2006, many stock-market averages, such as the S&P 500 and the NASDAQ Composite, are near the same levels at which they traded in 1999. Seven years of no further progress indicates stock prices consolidated the huge advance experienced during the 1982–2000 secular bull trend, meaning the U.S. stock market was back in a secular bear trend. Most of today's investors gained their experience during the bull market of the 1980s and 1990s when stock prices were generally rising. The strategies that worked during the '80s and '90s do not work during secular bear trends. For example, the last completed secular bear trend occurred from 1966–1982. During this period, successful investors used different strategies than investors who were successful in the '80s and '90s.

Let's get a better picture of the type of investor you are and of your strengths and weaknesses.

CHAPTER 2

INVESTOR STYLES

> **Informed or Uninformed (Unemotional or Emotional)**
> **Active or Passive**
>
> **Which Are You?**

Some people actively engage in life. They take advantage of opportunities, engage in thoughtful analysis, and easily adjust to new situations. Others take a more passive approach. They watch without action, allow others to make important decisions for them, and only react when encountering drastic changes or situations. These behaviors can be seen in many aspects of life: how one handles social situations, new job opportunities, personal relationships, and even in one's financial investments.

People become more actively engaged whenever they are comfortable with their surroundings and have confidence in their knowledge. My goal is to help you develop the knowledge needed to be comfortable and confident with your investment decisions by using a disciplined approach that works.

While working with investors over the last twenty-plus years, I've observed that people generally share certain behaviors that will either lead to their success or be detrimental to them as investors. As a starting point in learning how to become a disciplined investor, I would like you to think about your own investment style. In the previous chapter, I covered some common misconceptions about good investment practices. What type of investor are you? Be honest. What do you consider when you make investment decisions? What behaviors reflect your overall investment style? Working through the following yes-or-no statements may help you better define your current investment style:

1. I regularly adjust my investments to reflect current market trends.

2. I prefer to invest in individual securities rather than managed mutual funds.

3. Other than an occasional adjustment to my asset allocation to reflect lifestyle changes, I rarely make changes to my portfolio.

4. I believe buying and holding a diversified portfolio of good stocks and bonds or mutual funds will lead to desirable results.

5. I believe the market will generally rise over time, and, if I hold fundamentally sound investments over time, my portfolio will rise with it. Any market downturns should be temporary.

6. I base my investment decisions primarily on a company's fundamental information (i.e., their products and services, sales and earnings trends, price to earnings ratio, dividends, balance-sheet data, quality of management, and leadership in the industry).

7. I make better *buy* decisions than I do *sell* decisions.

8. I tend to use information I hear or read about in the news, analysts' research reports, or conversations with other investors to make my decisions.

9. I believe it is as important to know *when* to buy a stock, as it is to know *what* stock to buy.

10. I have a well-defined discipline to know when to sell, and I adhere to it.

11. I base my investment decisions on both market and industry trends as well as on a company's fundamental information.

12. I never change my investments, regardless of information available.

   ➢ If you answered Yes to statements 1 and 2, you tend to be what I call an *active investor*.

   ➢ If you answered Yes to statements 3 through 5, you tend to be what I consider a *passive investor*.

   ➢ If you answered Yes to statements 5 through 8, you tend to fall into the category of what I consider to be *emotional* or *uninformed* in your investing style.

> ➤ If you answered Yes to statements 9 through 11, you are an *unemotional* or *informed* investor.

> ➤ If you answered Yes to statement 12, you tend to be a *passive* (*inactive*) but *unemotional* investor.

What does this mean for you as an investor? These questions will help you better understand your strengths and weaknesses as an investor. They focus on characteristics shared by investors that may or may not be beneficial to successful investing: (1) whether an investor is actively or passively involved, (2) whether an investor is informed or uninformed, and (3) whether one's emotions dictate one's decisions.

Figure 2.1 shows how combinations of the above three variables define four approaches to investing: (1) reactive, (2) periodic passive, (3) inactive, and (4) proactive. Every investor falls into one of these categories or shares overlapping characteristics. More detail about each approach will make it easier for you to see where you fit in.

Before I go over each investor style, it is important to point out that many investors will fall into more than one category or may answer the twelve questions differently for different accounts. For example, you might regularly adjust your position in one account while applying a buy-and-hold approach in another account.

Even as an investment manager, I find it appropriate to manage a client's assets differently based on the type, size, and custodian of the account. For example, a client may have a larger IRA rollover and trust account along with a smaller Roth IRA account. Although each account is managed individually as a complete investment portfolio, one may be managed slightly different from the others. The value of this exercise to help you determine the type of investor that *best* describes your current style. As you learn the strategies taught in this book, my goal is to help you apply a *proactive* approach to your overall portfolio.

Reactive investors enjoy making their own decisions. Some reactive investors consider investing a hobby: they like to choose individual stocks rather than let a mutual fund manager handle these selections. Reactive investors tend to make frequent changes to their portfolio; however, their decisions are based on emotions, gut feelings, or media coverage, causing their decisions to be either uninformed or "after the fact." They hear about a "hot opportunity" in the news, from a research report, or from a tip. The success of others drives them to change their investments. People in this group tend to "follow the herd" and adjust stocks because of media reports or information about the market or the economy.

Reactive investors tend to view themselves as informed because they follow news about the economy and the stock market. They believe the information to be true but have no way to validate its worthiness through their own research. They gather information about the market, but their decisions are largely driven by emotional reactions and occur *after* significant market events. Reactive investors are active but use the wrong sources to gather the information from which they make their decisions. They will greatly improve their results if they change the sources of their information from the media, Wall Street research, or tips to understanding market, sector, and stock trends.

	Uninformed	Informed
Active	**REACTIVE** Majority	**PROACTIVE** IDEAL/GOAL
Passive	**PERIODIC PASSIVE** Majority	**INACTIVE** Rare
	Emotional	Unemotional

figure 2.1

Periodic passive investors tend to establish a portfolio and "weather it out" for a period. They set a course and intend to stick to it though good times and bad. These individuals are the "buy and hope" investors I mentioned earlier. Periodic passive investors do not enjoy making investment decisions, so they tend to adjust their portfolios slowly. Only when market conditions are extremely volatile do they decide to make changes. These ultimate decisions are usually reactive and occur *after* significant market events. Like reactive investors, fear and greed drive most decisions they make.

Many investors followed this style during the 1990s. Given the bull market, many investors held a passively managed, diversified portfolio and enjoyed good returns. These investors only studied investment information when they felt other investors' portfolios were outperforming theirs or when they felt their portfolios were starting to decline. Investment information was available, but these individuals usually chose to change their portfolio to match the investments and allocations of those whose returns were better. In other words, changes were made to mirror the results of other investors and were not based on detailed investment analyses.

Inactive investors establish a portfolio and "ride it out" regardless of the media, the economy, or market indicators. Their portfolios are based on recommended asset allocations and are rarely adjusted. Inactive investors in the purest sense are rare since fear of monetary loss will eventually cause most to make some type of portfolio change.

The most successful investors out there are *proactive* investors who actively review the conditions and trends of the markets, industry sectors, and individual companies. Emotions, media reports, or tips do not drive their investment decisions. Individual investment selection is made with an understanding of current supply-demand trends with regard to stocks, to sectors, and to the market as a whole. In other words, these investors use all the information available to make informed decisions about allocations and individual investments.

Proactive investors understand that consistent returns lead to the best long-term results. These investors consistently evaluate both their positions and market conditions. Proactive investors know that market trends are more important than information provided by the media or analysts. These individuals follow a disciplined approach to managing their portfolios, yet they are flexible and respond to change. Their investment decisions are not based on what has happened or what they hope will happen but on what *is* happening.

Most people are reactive or periodic passive investors—exactly the *opposite* of how I would like to see people as investors. Interestingly, most people will tell you they are actively informed; however, as we further understand proactive investment strategies, it will become apparent that most people are not following a proactive approach at all.

Helping you become an active and informed (proactive) investor is the goal of this book. It requires that you be willing to view markets and approach your decisions in a new light. It requires that you learn the importance of analyzing sector and market trends as well as supply-demand relationships in individual stocks. It requires that you learn to adapt and change your investments as these important trends change, helping you be a dynamic investor and keeping your portfolio harmonious with prevailing market conditions. Such an approach will be the foundation for implementing effective investment strategies, making confident investment decisions, and allowing you to be a proactive investor for the rest of your life.

SECTION 2

SELECTING STOCKS

CHAPTER 3

THE TECHNICAL ANALYSIS EDGE

> **Technical analysis provides direction regarding when to buy and sell investments.**

Up to this point, we have been looking at general and conceptual elements of investing. While these elements help lay the groundwork for being a disciplined and proactive investor, they do not give you anything concrete for making better investment decisions. So now, the real fun begins!

Most investors analyze the fundamental strength of a company to determine if the stock is worth owning. In this chapter, I intend to show you that it is technical analysis—a study of the supply and demand relationship of a company's shares—that will pave the way to better investment decisions. Technical analysis helps a proactive investor decide when to buy and when to sell.

Technical analysis is quite different from fundamental analysis. Through fundamental analysis, one studies various financial statements, such as income statements and balance sheets, to analyze the quality of a company's financial position. Financial ratios such as P/E (price/earnings) ratios, price/book value, and current assets/current liabilities, are commonly used in fundamental analysis. The strength of a company's management, products and services, position in the industry, and other information about its strength is also considered in this form of analysis.

Although it is important to know which companies have sound fundamentals, knowing when to buy or sell is the more difficult aspect for most investors. Just because fundamental analysis has revealed some strong companies, it does not mean the time is right to buy stock in the company.

Fundamental analysis is more widely used and accepted among Wall Street analysts. Most analysts at brokerage firms are fundamentalists, as are most analysts for mutual fund companies. According to the Chartered Financial Analyst

Institute, an organization that provides certification and ethical standards for financial analysts, more than seventy-one thousand investment professionals in 120 countries are Chartered Financial Analysts (CFA) (accessed April 7, 2005, http://www.cfainstitute.org).[1] To earn the CFA designation, an analyst has to pass rigorous examinations, most of which are based on fundamental analysis. Comparatively, according to the Market Technicians Association, a national organization of technical market analysts, professionals who carry the Certified Market Technician designation number less than twenty-four hundred (accessed April 7, 2005, http://www.mta.org).[2]

Ask yourself, "What makes a good company's stock price go up?" Is it the strength of its balance sheet? Is it a low P/E ratio? Is it the company's position within the industry? No! What makes the price of the stock move up is *demand*. Here's the bottom line. If there are more investors buying a stock (demand) than there are sellers (supply), the price will move higher. The price will continue to move higher until shareholders feel it is a good price to sell. At that time, supply will balance out the demand, causing the price to stop moving higher.

Conversely, when a company's stock goes down, supply is greater than demand. If there are more sellers than buyers, the price will move lower. The price will continue to decline until more investors believe the stock has once again reached a good purchase price. At that time, demand will balance out supply, causing the price to stop moving lower.

The challenge for you is two-fold: (1) when will demand for a stock increase relative to the amount of supply and generate the opportunity for price appreciation, and (2) when will supply for a stock increase relative to the amount of demand and signal the time to sell the investment? Although both questions are equally important, the second proves to be more difficult for most investors.

Investors need a tool to know when demand and supply of a stock is out of balance because shifts in the balance between demand and supply provide the key times for buying and selling. Finding these supply-demand imbalances is what gives technical analysis the edge over fundamental analysis for making sound investment decisions.

THE TECHNICAL ANALYSIS EDGE

Fundamental analysis does not provide all of the information needed for confident investment decisions.

Supply and demand (technical analysis) alone causes the movement in stock prices; technical analysis addresses supply and demand.

Regardless of how fundamentally sound a company may be, the stock price will only advance when there is more demand than supply.

Using what I have already covered about influences on investment decisions, as well as what drives stock prices, technical analysis has an edge over fundamental analysis for several reasons:

1. Fundamental analysis relies largely on the information provided by the company's management and Wall Street's research, neither of which can be trusted as objective or completely accurate. Most fundamental analysts spend the majority of their time meeting with management teams of the companies they follow. Management provides the analysts with guidance as to trends in their business, revenues, earnings, etc. Often, the guidance fundamental analysts receive from management is slanted toward scenarios management wants the public to perceive. The analyst, often having a financially vested interest in supporting this perspective, passes the information on to the individual investors. Obviously, as an individual investor, you do not have access to the management teams of most companies and must rely on information produced by Wall Street's analysts. The challenge for the average investor lies in not knowing if the analyst is providing the "real" picture about a company or the "story" desired by the company's management. History shows us we cannot completely trust the information provided from management teams or the analysis results provided from Wall Street's research.

2. Supply and demand alone causes the movement in stock prices. Only technical analysis deals with a detailed evaluation of supply and

demand. Fundamental analysis attempts to understand why a stock may advance or decline, but the market does not reward you to be correct about *why* something might happen. The market only rewards those who can correctly anticipate the direction that a stock will trend. Being correct about *why* does not pay any extra profit.

3. A stock price will not advance unless there is more demand than supply. The price will decline if supply is stronger than demand. As I mentioned earlier, if there are more buyers than there are sellers, the price will move higher. The stock price will continue to move higher until investors feel the stock's price is no longer attractive and until they no longer want to purchase it at the offered price. Similarly, if there are more sellers than buyers, the price will move lower. The price will continue to decline until more investors believe the stock has once again reached a good purchase price.

If technical analysis is superior to fundamental analysis, why is the fundamental method more commonly used among individual and professional investors alike? This is a fair question and one that I am asked frequently. In my view, the main reason fewer investors gravitate toward the technical analysis method is that knowing when to buy is more difficult than knowing if a company has solid fundamentals. Most people will follow the path of least resistance; therefore, fundamental analysis is more popular.

Human beings are curious creatures. We want to know *why* events will occur. Our curiosity drives most people to fundamental analysis. If you told someone you had information that will likely cause a particular stock to increase in price, logically that person's curiosity will cause him or her to ask you *why*. If you responded, "because there are more buyers than sellers," they will likely walk away from you, thinking you are nuts! However, this is the very reason any stock increases—more buyers than sellers. Still, this reason is not enough for most investors. Maybe it's too simple. Maybe most people need to know *what* will cause the increased demand relative to supply. As I wrote earlier, you do not get paid extra to know *why* there is more demand than supply or *what* is causing the imbalance. You just are paid for knowing when the imbalance exists.

Fundamental analysis alone does not provide all the answers regarding an investment's value. Market history is loaded with cases in which a stock suffers a tumultuous decline well ahead of any public knowledge of deterioration in the company's fundamentals. Only after the damage was done did it become obvious to the investing public that the fundamentals had changed for the worse. We need only think of WorldCom, Lucent Technologies, Enron, Nortel Networks, and Cisco Systems to come up with examples. An accurate interpretation of the *technical* position (supply and demand relationship) of these same stocks would have given investors a timely indication to sell. (Later in this section, I will outline several case studies that will prove how using charts to understand that the *technical* position of stocks in companies, such as, Lucent Technologies, clearly would have shown that supply was overwhelming demand, creating a high probability these shares would have declined. An accurate interpretation of the *technical* position of these shares would have led an investor to the conclusion to sell rather early—before significant damage was done.)

Meanwhile, the fundamental analysis was focused on the information each company was providing. Fundamental analysts continued to recommend Lucent Technologies and Cisco Systems even as the shares declined from $60 per share and $80 per share (or more), respectively, into the single digits.

In this section, I am going to show you how to select stocks using technical analysis. The stock selection methodology will employ two different charts: *Point & Figure* charts and *Relative Strength* charts. In the next chapter, I will show you how to construct a Point & Figure chart and interpret the information on the chart to gain insight to a stock's supply-demand relationship. Later in this section, I will show you how to use valuable Relative Strength charts. Ultimately, we will combine the use of both charts, empowering you to have the knowledge to make proactive decisions.

CHAPTER 4

POINT & FIGURE CHARTING

Point & Figure charting fits the most critical criteria for analysis.

Point & Figure charting has been used more than one hundred years.

The Point & Figure approach is based on the supply and demand law of economics.

There are hundreds of different technical analysis methods, ranging from the very basic to the more complicated. Rather than learning the basics about many different technical analysis methods, focusing on one and learning it in detail will provide more clarity in your investment conclusions.

Over my twenty-year career, I have been exposed to many of these forms of technical analysis, both the basic and the more advanced. In my view, the Point & Figure charting approach is superior to all others. The reasons Point & Figure charting is superior are numerous. First and foremost, Point & Figure charting fits the critical criteria for analysis; it makes sense, it works, and it is easy to apply and understand. Second, this form of analysis eliminates second-guessing, leading you to make decisions with confidence. Third, it helps reduce, even eliminate, harmful, emotional influences on your decisions. Fourth, Point & Figure charting removes insignificant price movements that often create confusion in other forms of technical analysis. Fifth, Point & Figure charting reflects easily identifiable patterns and trends. Finally, this type of charting helps you strategize future decisions with any investment. Should I sell, or should I hold? The Point & Figure chart gives you the answer.

To lay some basic groundwork, let me present the background and general principles of Point & Figure charting:

➢ The name *Point & Figure* comes from the process used to track stock prices and from the pricing patterns revealed on the charts. *Point* comes from the fact that each full point movement is recorded. No fractions or decimals are used (except in stocks below $20). *Figure* comes from the fact that the charts have the tendency to create meaningful patterns or figures as price trends develop.

➢ Although not widely known by individual investors, the Point & Figure charting methodology has history dating back some 120 years. Charles H. Dow, founder of Dow Jones & Company and one of the most successful investors in history, was the father of technical analysis.

➢ Point & Figure charting offers a simple and effective method of analysis. Although simplicity and effectiveness are two of the reasons for using the approach, its simplicity resulted in Point & Figure charting losing popularity when computers provided an easy way to create flashy bar charts. Sadly, during this time, flashy was confused with effective.

➢ Point & Figure charting records the supply and demand relationship in a stock. The only activity that really makes a stock move is an imbalance in the supply and demand relationship, that is, more buyers than sellers (demand) or more sellers than buyers (supply). At times, these two forces, supply and demand, are in balance and a stock will trade without a strong trend. The pivotal points are, however, when the balance shifts in one direction and a trend is emerging. Point & Figure charts help investors identify new trends as they emerge and participate in the early stages of the new trend.

➢ Point & Figure charting eliminates much of the guesswork and emotional influence in investment decisions. In my view, eliminating the guesswork and emotion is the best feature of the charts. Whenever you reduce or eliminate emotion from your investment decisions, you will make better decisions. Point & Figure charts help provide the needed objectivity in investment decisions to eliminate emotion.

➢ Point & Figure charting creates patterns or figures that are easily recognized. These patterns identify changes in supply and demand, therefore reducing the subjective interpretation that occurs with both fundamental analysis and other types of technical analysis charts.

➢ Point & Figure charting focuses solely on price movements and the probability of future price movements based on *current* supply and demand relationships. The method ignores the media, Wall Street research, and the reasons for price movements.

➢ Point & Figure charting provides information to make confident buy *and* sell decisions.

How to Construct a Point & Figure Chart

> **Point & Figure charting includes:**
> **Recording of significant price movements**
> **Recording of price reversals**
> **Identifying significant changes in supply and demand**

Before I define the rules for constructing a Point & Figure chart, let me give you a general picture of what a Point & Figure chart looks like. Below is a very simple version:

50					X
49					5
48	X		X		X
47	X	O	X	O	X
46	3	O	X	O	X
45	X	O	X	O	X
44	X	4	X	O	X
43	X	O		O	
42	X				
41	2				
40	X				

figure 4.1

Having taught this information to investors for over eight years, I know you will have questions about constructing a Point & Figure chart after reading the rules. Later in this section, I will construct a Point & Figure chart, using actual data for AT&T. While this exercise will help solidify your understanding, we must start with the basic rules.

When first learning how to construct a Point & Figure chart, it is helpful to picture a sheet of graph paper. With Point & Figure charts, each horizontal row on the sheet represents a specific price level.

The vertical columns on a Point & Figure chart represent movement in stock price. In *figure 4.1*, notice that the stock price moves between $40 and $50 in $1 increments. Here is the standard scale used:

> $.25 for stocks trading under $5 per share

> $.50 for stocks trading between $5 and $20 per share

> $1 for stocks trading between $20 and $100 per share

> $2 for stocks trading over $100 per share

Given that the investment price ranged between $40 and $50 in *figure 4.1*, the price-level scale was based on $1 price changes.

Recording Stock-Price Movements

The combination of a price movement and a price level creates a box on the graph paper. We will record the price movement of a stock as it moves to new price levels (i.e., as it moves into a different box). We will record all $1 price movements for a stock that trades between $20 and $100. We only make a record on the chart if the stock moves through whole numbers. For example, if a stock moves from $40 up to $41 or from $48 down to $47, the movement is recorded on the chart. If a stock price moves from $40.95 down to $40.15, we do not round, and we do not make a recording. Remember, the scale changes for some price levels. As a result, if a stock price falls below $20, we will record every $.50 movement. If a stock price rises above $100, we will record every $2 movement.

Price changes are recorded with the use of two letters of the alphabet. X's are used when the price is rising, and O's are used when the price is falling. Each X or O occupies a "box" on the chart. (Note: The term "box" is often used when discussing price movement on Point & Figure charts.)

No recording is made unless a price moves into the next box. Do not round up to get to the next higher box when a stock is advancing. Do not round down to get to the next lower box when a stock is declining. The high or low has to reach the actual box level. For example, if the last recording on the chart is an X (meaning it is moving up) at the $40 level, and the stock moved up to $40.95 the next day, the increase is not high enough to record an X in the $41 box. In this example, the high would have to reach $41 or higher to record an X in the $41 box. Conversely, if the last recording was an O at the $43 level, and the stock moved down to $42.15 the next day, the change is not enough to record an O in the $42 box. In this example, the low would have to reach $42 or lower before you would place an O in the $42 box.

While the horizontal rows represent specific price levels on the chart, vertical columns represent price movement continuing in the same direction. In the abbreviated chart shown in *figure 4.2*, you can see that the horizontal rows represent a price range from $40 to $45. Each box represents $1 ($40, $41, $42, $44, and $45). The vertical column shows a column of X's. This column of X's tells you the price trend is up as the stock moved from $40 up to $44.

45		
44	X	
43	X	
42	X	
41	X	
40	X	

figure 4.2

Here is an important point: the daily high and low, not the opening or closing price, are used to determine the price movements on the chart. If a stock's price movement is up (in a column of X's), then first look at the daily high to see if the price reached the next higher box (price) level. In *figure 4.2*, the last entry was an X at $44. The next trading day, we need to first look at the high to determine if the price reached the next higher box, in this case, $45. For example, if the daily high reached a high of $45.63, an X would be recorded in the $45 box. The chart would then look like *figure 4.3*.

45	X
44	X
43	X
42	X
41	X
40	X

figure 4.3

Now, let's assume the high not only went above $45 but also penetrated the $46 level; in this scenario, X's would be placed in both the $45 and $46 box. See *figure 4.4*.

46	X
45	X
44	X
43	X
42	X
41	X
40	X

figure 4.4

Recording of Price Reversal

To identify a change in price direction, we use the three-box reversal method. In other words, in order for the chart to change from a column of X's (rising) to a column of O's (declining) it would take a price decline of three boxes to reverse the chart. Similarly, to reverse from O's up to X's, it would take a price advance of three boxes.

Going back to *figure 4.2*, let's assume the next day's high was not able to reach at least $45. If so, no additional X's are recorded in the current column. When the chart reflects a rising price trend, and the next daily high has not reached the necessary level to place an X in the next higher box, we then look at the low to see if the price trend reversed down into a column of O's. Given that we are using the three-box reversal method, we need to look for a decline of three boxes from $44 to $41. In this case, the daily low would have to be $41 or lower. Let's assume the daily low was $40.68. This price decrease is enough to record a reversal into a column of O's. *Figure 4.5* shows this reversal.

45			
44	X		
43	X	O	
42	X	O	
41	X	O	
40	X		

figure 4.5

The reversal is recorded by moving to the next vertical column on the right and recording a column of O's in the $43, $42, and $41 boxes. *A move to the next column must be in a diagonal direction*, either one square higher if the reversal in price is up, or one square lower if the reversal in price is down. Looking at *figure 4.5*, you can see the reversal down into a column of O's is recorded by moving diagonally down from $44 and recording the first O in the next column to the right at $43.

Here's another important point: a vertical column can only contain X's or O's; it cannot have both. If a stock price is being recorded in a column of X's, the price has been increasing, or there is demand for the stock. If the stock price is being recorded in a column of O's, the price has been decreasing, or there is a growing supply of stock. If the trend changes, you must move to the next column to the right to record the change in price direction and trend.

Timing of Price Movements

There will be days when no recording occurs. This period with no recordings is okay and very common. Again, using *figure 4.2* as an example, an additional X is only recorded if a daily high of $45 or higher occurs. Similarly, a reversal down into a column of O's can only occur if the price declines to $41 or lower. If neither the high of $45 nor the low of $41 occurs, there will not be a recording on the chart for that particular day. In fact, there may not be a recording on the chart for multiple days, even weeks, if neither of the two price levels is reached.

This approach of not recording insignificant price changes seems odd to most chartists. Most technical-analysis charting methods make a recording every single day. In my opinion, however, the fact that Point & Figure charts only record *significant* changes is one of the main benefits in using these charts. If a price movement is just minor and irrelevant, why should we be concerned with tracking the change? This minor price movement may just be market noise and not important to the trend (or change) in the stock. By eliminating meaningless trading activity, Point & Figure charts help you focus on only the price movements that are important (i.e., the price movements that will impact your investment decisions).

Charting methods that make daily recordings force the chartist to try to interpret what the recording means. Sometimes the recording doesn't mean anything, and the chartist is trying to read something that just isn't there. The Point & Figure chart helps you keep the recording process simple. The less energy you direct toward the process of charting, the more energy you will have available for interpretation of the charts.

Getting back to the rules, and as I mentioned earlier, you cannot record X's and O's in the same column. Either the chart can continue in the current column, or there is a reversal. First, you look to see if the chart can continue in the same column. If so, you record the price movement in the next box. If the price movement does not continue, then you check if the price has reversed direction and by what amount.

Again, looking at *figure 4.2*, if the next day's high and low were $45.56 and $40.84, respectively, the only recording on the chart that day would be adding an X in the current column in the $45 box. While the daily low did fall below $41, which would imply a three-box reversal, the fact that the daily high could move up to $45 offsets the reversal. There would *not* be another X added to the current column *and* a reversal down into a column of O's in the same day. When charting and looking at daily highs or lows, you always first look in the direction the chart is currently headed. In *figure 4.2*, the chart is in a column of X's and headed up; therefore, you first look at the daily high and only record an X at $45.

Eventually, the daily low will be reflected on the chart if it consistently remains below $41. In our example, if you go out one additional day and the stock does not reach a high of $46 on that day, but the stock continued to trade with a daily low below $42, the reversal will be accounted for on that day. The table reflected in *figure 4.6* helps with determining what price direction to check first.

Column Direction	First Check ...	Price Movement Needed	If You Cannot Add Another Box, Then Check ...	Price Movement Reversal Needed
X/Up	Daily High	One box	Daily Low	Three boxes
O/Down	Daily Low	One box	Daily High	Three boxes

figure 4.6

When starting a chart for a newly issued stock, simply begin recording the price movement based on the direction the stock's price begins trending. If the price begins moving higher, begin the chart by recording X's. If it begins moving lower, record O's.

Point & Figure charts do not record the passage of time, only price trend movements. Although the passage of time does not change the chart, it is helpful to have a time reference. To account for time, the first entry made each month uses the month's number in place of the X or O. On some charts, the numbers one through twelve represents January through December.

When you first learn how to construct Point & Figure charts, it is easy to get caught up in the details of adding an X or an O, reversing columns, etc. I don't want you to lose sight of the most important information contained in the chart—X's on the chart indicate a higher level of buying than selling (demand); O's indicate a higher level of selling than buying (supply).

Simple Examples and Interpretations

I have presented a lot of information, and, at this point, I'm sure Point & Figure charting appears more complex than it really is. So let's break down the fundamental purpose and interpretation of Point & Figure charting with a few examples and explanations. To do so, I will go through a series of daily highs and lows and construct a simple chart. Following this simple process, I will construct a chart, using actual daily highs and lows for

AT&T. These two exercises should help clear up any confusion you might currently have.

It is important to note that X's and O's on a Point & Figure chart are not enough information to buy or sell a stock. Other considerations need to be included, also, such as the industry or sector condition, the overall market condition, the major trend for the stock, and the relative strength of the stock. All of these considerations will be addressed in later chapters. The Point & Figure chart patterns and signals are just one piece of the bigger picture in becoming a proactive investor.

In *figure 4.7*, you see a column of X's, so you know the price of the stock is rising. Since there are no O's recorded on this abbreviated chart, you also know the price steadily rose from $40 up to $44. The column of X's shows that demand pushed the stock up to $44.

45		
44	X	
43	X	
42	X	
41	X	
40	X	

Column of X's denotes a rising stock price.

The price increased from $40 to $44 without any intermittent declines (three-box reversal).

figure 4.7

When the price reached $44, a slight change in the supply and demand relationship occurred. The demand began to weaken, the supply began to strengthen, or some combination of the two scenarios occurred. Regardless, the price stopped moving up. The price never reached $45 and eventually began declining to $41. As you have learned, when this change happens, you move over to the next column to the right, go down one box from the highest X at $44, and record a column of O's. There would be an O recorded at $43, $42, and $41. The chart would then look like *figure 4.8*.

45			
44	X		
43	X	O	
42	X	O	
41	X	O	
40	X		

Reversal to column of O's.

The price is unable to reach $45 as supply surfaces. It begins declining to $41, creating a three-box reversal.

figure 4.8

So far, this example looks like the original chart shown in *figure 4.5*. The column of O's shows supply pushing the price down to $41, but the price is not able to decline to $40. At this point, the demand meets the supply, and the price decline ends. In our example, we are going to assume demand surfaces again, and the price begins to rise. When the price rises to $44, the chart would reverse back up into a column of X's. To record the reversal, you would again move over to the next column to the right, go up one box from the lowest O at $41, and record a column of X's. There would be X's recorded in the $42, $43, and $44 boxes. The chart would look like *figure 4.9*

45			
44	X		X
43	X	O	X
42	X	O	X
41	X	O	
40	X		

Reversal to column of X's.

The price is unable to drop to $40; demand pushes it back up to $44, creating a three-box reversal.

figure 4.9

The chart now shows that demand pushed the price back up to $44. We now have a little history to look at, as brief as it may be. The history shows us that the last time the price reached $44, supply and demand came into balance, and the price was unable to reach $45. This balance is an important stage on our abbreviated chart; when the price reached $44 a second time, supply again met the demand, and the price began to decline. Once the price again declined to $41, the chart reversed down into a column of O's again. This reversal is recorded by moving over one column to the right and recording O's in the $43, $42, and $41 boxes. At this point, the chart would look like *figure 4.10*.

45				
44	X		X	
43	X	O	X	O
42	X	O	X	O
41	X	O		O
40	X			

figure 4.10

Another reversal down to O's.

Similar to the last reversal down, supply overtakes demand at $44 and begins a column of O's.

We now have even more history recorded on the chart. We now know that the price reached $44 two times and that demand was unable to push the price up to $45. What does this tell us? The information tells us that at the $44 price level, either fewer investors are willing to buy this stock or more shareholders are willing to sell the stock. Most likely, it is some combination of these two scenarios. The inability to push the price up to $45 also means there is a resistance level at $44.

As the second column of O's appears on the chart, we can see that the price movement reaches the same level as the previous column of O's. The last time the price traded down to $41, demand showed up to meet the supply, and the price began to rise. What does this tell us? The information tells us that at the $41 price level, either fewer shareholders are willing to sell this stock or more investors are willing to buy the stock. Again, most likely, it is some combination of these two scenarios. The $41 level is also important. The inability to push the price down to $40 means we have a support level at $41.

In looking at the patterns in *figure 4.10*, we now can step back and see that there are two important price levels on this chart—$44 and $41. Whenever the price advances to $44, supply meets the demand, and the price stops increasing. Whenever the price declines to $41, demand meets the supply, and the price stops declining. We now have resistance and support levels for this stock at $44 and $41, respectively. Since neither of these levels can be penetrated, the conclusion to draw from this four-column pattern is that the supply and demand relationship is in balance. The balance occurs between $44 and $41. Balance patterns are important to identify for two reasons:

1. First, during these patterns, there is no action you should take because there is no clear trend in place for the stock.

2. Second, and more importantly, you know that the balance will eventually be broken and that the price will either move below $41 or above $44. Once the balance is broken, there is a tendency for a strong follow-through in the direction of the break, providing you a good entry or exit point. Now, the uncertainly of knowing if the price is increasing or decreasing is greatly reduced. I will discuss balance patterns and entry/exit points in more detail in a later section.

Back to the progression of our chart. Let's assume that similar to earlier times, when the price reaches $41, demand holds the stock in check, and the price is unable to decline to $40. If so, the price will start to move higher and, once the price advances to $44, the chart will reverse up into a column of X's. At this point, we have a third time that demand pushes the price up to $44.

The more often a stock's price reaches a price level, the more important the specific price level becomes for the stock. The chart in *figure 4.11* shows all three columns of X's rising to the $44 level. The first two times the stock price reached this price level, supply met the demand, and the price was not able to advance to $45. When a stock price hits the same price level for a third time, a pattern known as a **triple top** occurs. This pattern is indicated in *figure 4.11* by the three X columns at $44.

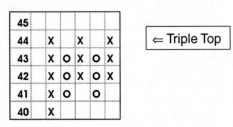

figure 4.11

In this example, the third time the price reaches $44, something changes in the supply and demand relationship; the demand becomes stronger, or the supply fades away, or both occur. As you will note in *figure 4.12*, more investors are willing to buy this stock, or the shareholders who want to sell the stock have already sold, or both. As a result, demand is finally able to push the stock past

$44 to reach $45. When this push occurs, another X is recorded in the current column at $45, breaking the triple top.

46					
45					X
44	X		X		X
43	X	O	X	O	X
42	X	O	X	O	X
41	X	O		O	
40	X				

⇐ Triple Top Broken

figure 4.12

When a triple top is broken, an important development occurs on the Point & Figure chart. The break indicates the balance in the supply and demand relationship of this stock was broken in favor of demand. The probability is good that a new trend has emerged and that the price will continue to rise. The increase will continue until more shareholders feel the stock has reached a good selling price. In our simple example, we do not know when demand and supply will come back into balance again. Many other factors will determine the extent of the advance, especially the strength of the industry sector this stock is in. I will cover sector analysis in a later section.

For now, let's again look at *figure 4.12*. Notice how clearly the break of a triple-top pattern is shown on a Point & Figure chart. The clarity of patterns is one of the main benefits of using these charts over many other charting methods. The patterns are clear. They are black-and-white; there is very little gray on this chart. You can't look at this chart and say, "Yeah, that's a triple top, but …" Other charts aren't as clear-cut with their patterns, and they leave open the possibility for subjective interpretation. Point & Figure charts provide objective conclusions and reduce the amount of subjectivity in your decisions. The less subjectivity you have when making decisions, the less emotion will play a role in your decision-making process. The less you let emotions enter into the picture, the better your investment decisions and the better your financial results.

The opposite of a triple-top pattern is a *triple bottom.* In a triple-bottom pattern, supply will emerge as the major force controlling price trends. Let's quickly go through a scenario when a triple bottom is formed and eventually broken.

Figure 4.13 shows a triple-bottom pattern. The pattern can be noted by all three columns of O's stopping at the $40 price level. This price level is where demand meets the supply and where the price stops declining. On this chart, you can also see that both X columns stop when the price reaches $44. At this point, supply meets the demand, and the price stops rising at $44. Similar to the earlier chart shown as *figure 4.11*, the general conclusion to be drawn is that there is no strong supply or demand trend in place. The most apparent pattern is a balance between $44 and $40, but we know that eventually one of these two price levels will be broken, and a trend will emerge.

45	O				
44	O	X		X	
43	O	X	O	X	O
42	O	X	O	X	O
41	O	X	O	X	O
40	O		O		O
39					

⟸ Triple Bottom

figure 4.13

Let's assume that the third time the price declines to $40, something changes in the supply and demand relationship. Let's assume that either the supply is stronger or that the demand fades away. If this change occurs, more shareholders are now willing to sell this stock, or every investor who wants to buy at $40 has bought. When supply is able to push the stock price below $40, an important development occurs. The balance between supply and demand has been broken in favor of supply, and the triple bottom has been broken. At this time, an O is recorded in the last column at $39.

45	O				
44	O	X		X	
43	O	X	O	X	O
42	O	X	O	X	O
41	O	X	O	X	O
40	O		O		O
39					O

⟸ Triple Bottom Broken

figure 4.14

The break also means the probability is good that a new trend is emerging. The trend will push the price lower until more investors feel the price is low enough to buy. In our simple example, we do not know when enough demand will surface to meet the supply. All we know is that when demand does surface, the stock price will stop declining.

The triple top and the triple bottom are just two of many buy and sell signals that form on a Point & Figure chart. Although we have only briefly touched on buy and sell signals, you probably have ascertained that the signals typically occur when a stock breaks out of a balance pattern. Further discussion on breaking out of balance patterns, greater detail about when to buy and sell, and further evaluation of other buy and sell patterns are covered in later chapters. First, to help solidify our understanding of Point & Figure charting, let's practice constructing a Point & Figure chart with actual stock data.

Point & Figure Charting: Real-Life Example with AT&T

I'm sure you still have several questions about constructing a Point & Figure chart. To help answer those questions, let's go through an exercise of recording a chart, using actual daily high and low data. The stock I will chart is AT&T. The starting point of the chart is shown in *figure 4.15*. Daily high and low data is shown in *figure 4.16*. Please note that you will be referring to the data in *figure 4.16* frequently, so you may want to bookmark the page.

AT&T Point & Figure Chart

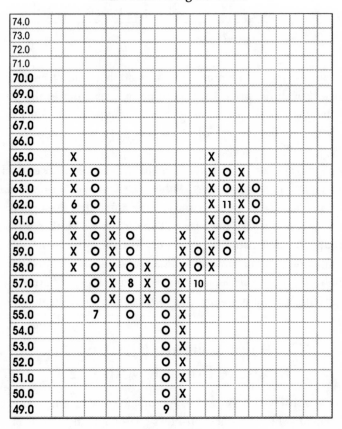

figure 4.15

AT&T CORP		
DATE	HIGH	LOW
11/16/1998	62.13	60.13
11/17/1998	61.88	60.31
11/18/1998	61.31	60.56
11/19/1998	63.31	61.56
11/20/1998	63.88	62.56
11/23/1998	64.00	63.06
11/24/1998	64.25	62.53
11/25/1998	63.75	62.56
11/27/1998	63.38	62.94
11/30/1998	63.94	62.19
12/1/1998	62.50	61.69
12/2/1998	62.81	61.69
12/3/1998	62.75	61.75
12/4/1998	63.69	62.06
12/7/1998	64.75	63.50
12/8/1998	68.50	65.50
12/9/1998	71.13	67.81
12/10/1998	72.25	70.63
12/11/1998	70.88	69.88
12/14/1998	70.19	68.25
12/15/1998	70.00	68.56
12/16/1998	71.44	68.50
12/17/1998	72.00	69.75
12/18/1998	73.00	71.44
12/21/1998	76.50	73.06
12/22/1998	74.19	72.56
12/23/1998	75.00	73.50
12/24/1998	74.94	73.56
12/28/1998	76.44	74.50
12/29/1998	79.00	74.94
12/30/1998	79.00	75.50
12/31/1998	76.88	74.38
1/4/1999	79.88	76.88
1/5/1999	80.38	78.00
1/6/1999	83.63	79.50
1/7/1999	83.56	81.75
1/8/1999	86.63	82.06

figure 4.16

43

1. We need two pieces of information when beginning to construct a Point & Figure chart:

   a) Are we starting in an O or X column?

   b) What box was the last O or X recorded in?

   As you will recall, we always check if the price can continue in the direction it is already headed. As a result, if the chart is in an O column, we first look at the daily low; if the chart is in an X column, we first look at the daily high. (If necessary, refer to *figure 4.6* as a refresher on the order.) Looking at *figure 4.15*, we can see that the last entry was an O at $61. Since O's mean the price is declining, we know the initial direction of the price is down. We also know to look at the lowest box in the column of O's since O means we are heading down and since the most recent recording would be the lowest price level for the column.

2. We are going to start updating the chart with November 16. We first look at the low for the day to see if the price continued down to the next box, which would require the low to reach $60 or lower. The low on November 16 was $60.13. That price is not low enough to record another O in the column. (Remember, we do not round numbers for Point & Figure charts.) Since the price does not continue to move down, we then look at the high to see if the price rose enough to reverse up into an X column. A reversal would require a high of $64 or higher (three boxes up from the last O recorded at $61). The high on November 16 is $62.13. The high is not enough to reverse the chart. If the low is not low enough to add an O in the current column and the high is not high enough to reverse to an X column, there is no recording made for the day. The two price levels that will result in a recording for this chart are a low of $60 or lower and a high of $64 or higher. Given that neither of these prices was reached on November 16, we move on to the next day.

   Thinking about the high and low prices needed helps with reviewing daily high and low data. By doing so, you mentally create the two critical price levels needed to make a recording. In our example, you now know to look for a minimum low of $60 or a minimum high of $64. We will refer to these two levels as *recording prices*.

3. Neither recording price is reached until November 23 when the high reaches $64. You can see that all the lows up to that date are above $60, so there is not another O recorded in the column. In addition, all the highs up to that date remain below $64, so the chart does not reverse up. As a result, there are no recordings on the chart until November 23. On November 23, the daily high is an even $64; therefore, you can record a reversal up into an X column. To make this recording, move to the next column to the right and up one square (in a diagonal direction) and record X's in the $62, $63, and $64 boxes. The chart would now look like *figure 4.17*.

	1	2	3	4	5	6	7	8	9	10	11	12
70.0												
69.0												
68.0												
67.0												
66.0												
65.0	X							X				
64.0	X	O						X	O	X		X
63.0	X	O						X	O	X	O	X
62.0	6	O						X	11	X	O	X
61.0	X	O	X					X	O	X	O	
60.0	X	O	X	O			X		X	O	X	
59.0	X	O	X	O		X	O	X	O			
58.0	X	O	X	O	X		X	O	X			
57.0		O	X	8	X	O	X	10				
56.0		O	X	O	X	O	X					
55.0		7		O		O	X					
54.0				O			X					
53.0				O			X					
52.0				O			X					
51.0				O			X					
50.0				O			X					
49.0				9								
48.0												
47.0												
46.0												
45.0												

figure 4.17

4. Now the chart is in a column of X's. As a result, on November 24 we first look to the high to see if the price increase continues. This

increase would require a high of $65 or higher. (Remember, when the chart is in an X column, first look at the high to see if the column can continue up.) If the price does increase, then you record the X's for each box reached on the way up. If the price does not increase, then you look at the low to see if the chart reverses three boxes into an O column. The high on November 24 is $64.25. This price is *not* high enough to record another X in the current column. Since the price does not continue to move up, we then look at the low to see if the price falls enough to reverse down into an O column. This reversal would require a low of $61 or lower (three boxes down from the last X recorded at $64). The low on November 24 is $62.53. The low is *not* enough to reverse the chart. Thinking in terms of recording prices, we were looking for a minimum high of $65 or a minimum low of $61.

5. You can see by looking at the daily high and low data on *figure 4.16* that neither recording price is hit until December 8, when the high reaches $68.50. On December 8, you would continue to record X's in the current column in the $65, $66, $67, and $68 boxes. In addition, since this is the first entry made in December, rather than record an X in the $65 box, you replace the X with a "12" to note the first entry in December. After recording the December 8 data, the chart would look like *figure 4.18*.

```
70.0 |
69.0 |
68.0 |                     X
67.0 |                     X
66.0 |                     X
65.0 | X          X       12
64.0 | X O         X O X   X
63.0 | X O         X O X O X
62.0 | 6 O         X 11X O X
61.0 | X O X       X O X O
60.0 | X O X O   X X O X
59.0 | X O X O   X O X O
58.0 | X O X O X   X O X
57.0 |   O X 8 X O X 10
56.0 |   O X O X O X
55.0 |   7   O   O X
54.0 |           O X
53.0 |           O X
52.0 |           O X
51.0 |           O X
50.0 |           O X
49.0 |           9
48.0 |
47.0 |
46.0 |
45.0 |
```

figure 4.18

This is a good time to point out one of the main benefits of using Point & Figure charts over other methods of charting, such as the commonly used bar chart. From November 24 through December 7, there were no recordings made on the chart because the price movement during that time frame was minor and insignificant. A bar chart would have recorded the high and low every day. When a price movement is recorded on a chart, an investor thinks he or she should analyze the significance of the price movement. If the price movement is meaningless, why try to analyze its significance? In fact, why bother making a recording? Point & Figure charts help you avoid going through mental exercises that will not help you make money. The charts reduce the noise by removing the minor and irrelevant price movements, allowing you to focus only on important price movements.

6. Since the chart is still in a column of X's, on December 9 we first look at the high to see if the price increase continues. The next recording price for the high would be $69 or higher. If this price level does not occur, the recording price for the reversal down would be $65 or lower. On December 9, the high reaches $71.25. This increase is enough to add three more X's in the current column. You can see the appropriate recording in *figure 4.19*.

75.0													
74.0													
73.0													
72.0													
71.0													X
70.0													X
69.0													X
68.0													X
67.0													X
66.0													X
65.0	X								X				12
64.0	X	O							X	O	X		X
63.0	X	O							X	O	X	O	X
62.0	6	O							X	11	X	O	X
61.0	X	O	X						X	O	X	O	
60.0	X	O	X	O			X		X	O	X		
59.0	X	O	X	O			X	O	X	O			
58.0	X	O	X	O	X		X	O	X				
57.0		O	X	8	X	O	X	10					
56.0		O	X	O	X	O	X						
55.0		7		O		O	X						
54.0						O	X						
53.0						O	X						
52.0						O	X						
51.0						O	X						
50.0						O	X						
49.0						9							
48.0													
47.0													
46.0													
45.0													

figure 4.19

7. We continue to be in an X column, so again we first look at the daily high. On December 10, the high is $72.25. The high is enough to advance this X column one more box and to record the X in the $72 box. The chart now looks like *figure 4.20*. At this point, you do not need to look at the low for the day since we know the chart will continue to advance in the column of X's. Remember, a Point & Figure chart does not go in both directions in the same day.

75.0												
74.0												
73.0												
72.0												X
71.0												X
70.0												X
69.0												X
68.0												X
67.0												X
66.0												X
65.0	X							X				12
64.0	X	O						X	O	X		X
63.0	X	O						X	O	X	O	X
62.0	6	O						X	11	X	O	X
61.0	X	O	X					X	O	X	O	
60.0	X	O	X	O			X	X	O	X		
59.0	X	O	X	O			X	O	X	O		
58.0	X	O	X	O	X		X	O	X			
57.0		O	X	8	X	O	X	10				
56.0		O	X	O	X	O	X					
55.0		7		O		O	X					
54.0						O	X					
53.0						O	X					
52.0						O	X					
51.0						O	X					
50.0						O	X					
49.0						9						
48.0												
47.0												
46.0												
45.0												

figure 4.20

8. At this point, in order to continue the X column, we need to see a high of $73 or higher, or a low of $69 or lower, to reverse columns down into O's. Looking at the high-low data, neither occurs until December 14. On December 14, the low hits $68.25, and the chart reverses down into a column of O's. To record this reversal, we move into the next column to the right and record O's in the boxes at $71, $70, and $69. The chart will look like *figure 4.21*.

	1	2	3	4	5	6	7	8	9	10	11	12	13
75.0													
74.0													
73.0													
72.0												X	
71.0												X	O
70.0												X	O
69.0												X	O
68.0												X	
67.0												X	
66.0												X	
65.0	X								X			12	
64.0	X	O					X	O	X		X		
63.0	X	O					X	O	X	O	X		
62.0	6	O					X	11	X	O	X		
61.0	X	O	X				X	O	X	O			
60.0	X	O	X	O			X		X	O	X		
59.0	X	O	X	O			X	O	X	O			
58.0	X	O	X	O	X		X	O	X				
57.0		O	X	8	X	O	X	10					
56.0		O	X	O	X	O	X						
55.0		7		O	X								
54.0				O	X								
53.0				O	X								
52.0				O	X								
51.0				O	X								
50.0				O	X								
49.0				9									
48.0													
47.0													
46.0													
45.0													

figure 4.21

9. The chart is now in an O column, so we first look at the next day's low to see if the price decreased and reached the next lower box. If the price did not continue down, we then look at the high to see if the chart can reverse up three boxes. If neither of the recording prices is

hit, there are no recordings on the chart for the day, and we go on to the next day.

10. The next day with a recording is December 17 when the daily high reaches $72. After a few days with no recordings, this date is the first time the daily high and low data reach a recording price, either a minimum low of $68 or a minimum high of $72. In this case, we have a high that is three boxes up from the last O recorded. As a result, the chart reverses up into an X column. As noted in *figure 4.22*, we make a recording to the next column to the right by placing X's at $70, $71, and $72.

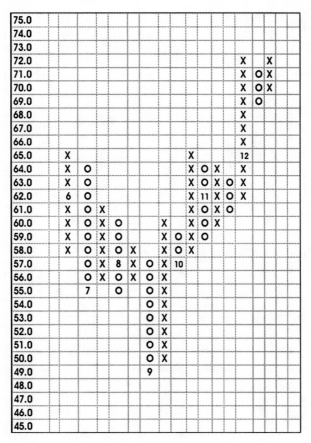

figure 4.22

11. The chart is again in an X column. On December 18, the high reaches $73, and an X is placed in the $73 box in the current column. On December 21, the high reaches $76.50, and X's are recorded in the $74, $75, and $76 boxes. The chart would then look like *figure 4.23*.

Price													
80.0													
79.0													
78.0													
77.0													
76.0													X
75.0													X
74.0													X
73.0													X
72.0											X		X
71.0											X	O	X
70.0											X	O	X
69.0											X	O	
68.0											X		
67.0											X		
66.0											X		
65.0	X							X			12		
64.0	X	O						X	O	X	X		
63.0	X	O						X	O	X	O	X	
62.0	6	O						X	11	X	O	X	
61.0	X	O	X					X	O	X	O		
60.0	X	O	X	O			X	X	O	X			
59.0	X	O	X	O			X	O	X	O			
58.0	X	O	X	O	X			X	O	X			
57.0		O	X	8	X	O	X	10					
56.0		O	X	O	X	O	X						
55.0		7		O		O	X						
54.0						O	X						
53.0						O	X						
52.0						O	X						
51.0						O	X						
50.0						O	X						
49.0						9							
48.0													
47.0													
46.0													
45.0													

figure 4.23

This is a good time to step back from the daily recordings and look at what is happening on the chart. Look at *figure 4.18*. Do you see a buy signal on the chart? As the chart advanced into the $66 box, there was a **spread triple top** broken. Remember from the previous chapter that when a price stops increasing at a particular level three times, you have a triple top. In this AT&T example, there are two X columns that stopped at the $65 level. This occurrence indicates that supply was strong and that demand was unable to push the stock any higher than $65 for several months. The third time the price reached $65, the demand was strong enough to push AT&T's shares through the $65 price level. On December 8, the stock broke the spread-triple-top pattern when the column of X's hit $66. In fact, the price went all the way up to $68 that day.

When a stock price breaks a triple top, it's a good time to buy the stock. For AT&T, the chart was able to advance up to the $72 level before supply again met the demand. On December 14, supply temporarily was stronger than demand, and the chart reversed down three boxes to $69. The supply didn't last very long, and demand snapped the shares up quickly, causing the chart to reverse back up on December 17 into an X column. It is a good sign when the O columns are brief and shallow, indicating that supply is weak and that demand is in control of a stock price. Do you see how all of the O columns coming off the bottom of the chart stop at a higher level than the previous O column? Higher lows indicate that demand is in control. Similarly, on December 18, the next column of X's had extended higher than the previous X column, indicating that demand is continuing to gain strength.

12. Continuing with the AT&T example, after the price increase on December 21 and additional boxes in the X column, we have two new recording prices. The high must be $77 or higher, and the low must be $73 or lower. Notice that the high on December 22 is $74.19. This price is not high enough to continue the current column of X's. The low is $72.56, which is low enough to reverse the chart down into an O column. As a result, we again move over to the next column to the right and record O's in the $75, $74, and $73 box. With this reversal, the chart now looks like *figure 4.24*.

Price	1	2	3	4	5	6	7	8	9	10	11	12	13	14	15	16
80.0																
79.0																
78.0																
77.0																
76.0															X	
75.0															X	O
74.0															X	O
73.0															X	O
72.0													X		X	
71.0													X	O	X	
70.0													X	O	X	
69.0													X	O		
68.0													X			
67.0													X			
66.0													X			
65.0	X								X				12			
64.0	X								X	O	X		X			
63.0	X	O							X	O	X	O	X			
62.0	6	O							X	11	X	O	X			
61.0	X	O	X						X	O	X	O				
60.0	X	O	X	O			X		X	O	X					
59.0	X	O	X	O			X	O	X	O						
58.0	X	O	X	O	X		X	O	X							
57.0		O	X	8	X	O	X	10								
56.0		O	X	O	X	O	X									
55.0		7		O		O	X									
54.0						O	X									
53.0						O	X									
52.0						O	X									
51.0						O	X									
50.0						O	X									
49.0						9										
48.0																
47.0																
46.0																
45.0																

figure 4.24

13. As we continue to watch the daily highs and lows, we notice that the low is not able to reach the next box lower; at the same time, the high hits $76.44 on December 28. This high causes another reversal up into an X column on the chart. Again, we move to the next column to the right and record X's in the $74, $75, and $76 boxes. On December 29, the high is $79. X's are recorded in the $77, $78, and $79 boxes. Demand pushes this stock up to new highs on the chart, as seen in *figure 4.25.*

	1	2	3	4	5	6	7	8	9	10	11	12	13	14	15	16	17
80.0																	
79.0																	X
78.0																	X
77.0																	X
76.0																X	X
75.0															X	O	X
74.0															X	O	X
73.0															X	O	
72.0													X		X		
71.0													X	O	X		
70.0													X	O	X		
69.0													X	O			
68.0													X				
67.0													X				
66.0													X				
65.0	X							X					12				
64.0	X	O						X	O	X			X				
63.0	X	O						X	O	X	O	X					
62.0	6	O						X	11	X	O	X					
61.0	X	O	X					X	O	X	O						
60.0	X	O	X	O		X		X	O	X							
59.0	X	O	X	O		X	O	X	O								
58.0	X	O	X	O	X	X	O	X									
57.0		O	X	8	X	O	X	10									
56.0		O	X	O	X	O	X										
55.0	7			O		O	X										
54.0						O	X										
53.0						O	X										
52.0						O	X										
51.0						O	X										
50.0						O	X										
49.0						9											
48.0																	

figure 4.25

14. The high on December 30 is $79, yet we know that the high needs to reach $80 or higher to continue the current X column. Since we did not have a high of $80, we look at the low to see if the price will cause a reversal down three boxes to $76 or lower. On December 30, the low is $75.50, so we move to the next column to the right and record O's in the $78, $77, and $76 boxes. The low on December 31 is $74.38, and we place another O in the $75 box. *Figure 4.26* reflects the reversal and recording.

55

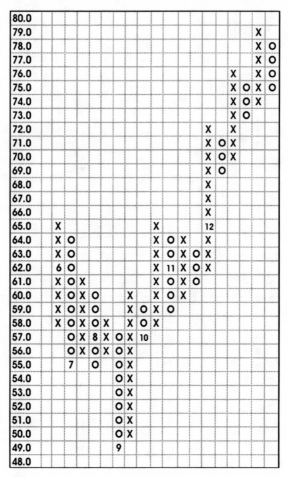

figure 4.26

15. On the next trading day, January 4, the low was $76.88. The high is $79.88, causing the chart to reverse up into an X column. In the next column to the right, X's are recorded in the $76, $77, $78, and $79 boxes. Since this recording is the first entry made in January, a "1" is placed in the third box. On January 5, the high is $80.38, allowing for another X to be recorded in this column. On January 6, the high is $83.63, allowing three more X's to be added in the $81, $82, and $83 boxes. No recordings occur on January 7 since neither a new high nor a three-box reversal occurs. The

high on January 8 is $86.63, and the X column moves up to $86. At this point, the chart looks like *figure 4.27*.

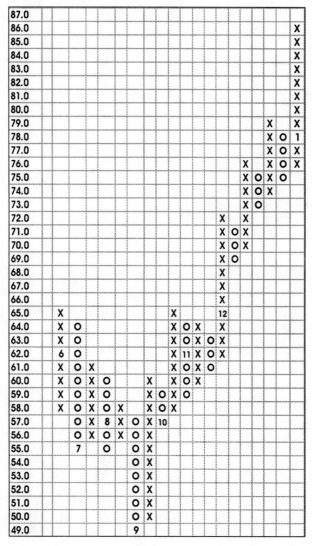

figure 4.27

Let's take a good look at *figure 4.27*. Through the period we were recording the chart, the stock moved from $61 to $86. Look closely at the pattern created on the chart. The pattern shows higher X and O columns as the price rose. We are seeing a classic pattern for a stock that is being accumulated (i.e., in demand) with very few shareholders willing to sell. The lowest point on this chart is $49. Every column of O's, after the column of O's that recorded the $49 low, has its lowest point at a higher level than the previous O column. The highest point of every column of X's exceeds the previous X column. (With one exception. In November there was a lower X column on the chart. This pattern formed a triangle shape on the chart. Triangles are common patterns on Point & Figure charts. I will cover triangles and other valuable price patterns in chapter 5.) Remember, the X's represent demand, and the O's represent supply on a Point & Figure chart. When the O columns stop declining at higher levels, we have an indication that supply in the stock is weak. When X's continually move up to higher levels, with each X column high exceeding the previous X column high, we have an indication that demand is strong. You want to own stocks that show this pattern. Clearly, demand is controlling the trend for AT&T during our sample period.

You now know the basics for constructing a Point & Figure chart. Though you may feel I have explained creating and recording the price movement at great length, this process is necessary to make sure you have a strong understanding of the basic concepts. The Point & Figure price-movement concept, driven by supply and demand, is the core of everything else I will cover in this book. You will need to understand Point & Figure concepts to comprehend the sector and market analyses I cover in the next two sections.

The best way to make sure Point & Figure information stays fresh in your mind is to record Point & Figure charts for the stocks you own. You probably look at the prices of your stocks regularly. Why not record a Point & Figure chart of them? Once you have the hang of charting, the process of going through a rather large number of a company's daily high-low information and making a recording for the day only takes a few minutes.

Computerized charts can provide historical information and a starting point for a particular stock. For example, if you want a chart of ExxonMobil, there are a number of charting programs and Web sites that will load historical high-low data and construct an initial Point & Figure chart for you.

The Investor Education Institute's Web site (http://www.institute4investors. com) offers a charting database on which you can access Point & Figure charts. This will help you get started. You can see the last chapter of this book for instructions to access this Web site. You can log in and print the historical charts of stocks you own. I strongly suggest you start looking at the daily high-low data and manually recording the charts. Yes, you could let a computer update the chart for you every night; however, you will not learn very much using this automated approach. As we all know, regular practice is the best way to learn and solidify understanding.

Logarithmic Scale Charts

The traditional Point & Figure charting method uses the price scale outlined in chapter 4; $.50 boxes for stocks priced between $5 and $20, $1 boxes for stocks priced between $20 and $100, etc. The Investor Education Institute has been conducting an extensive study, with excellent results, using a logarithmic scale to record Point & Figure price movements. A logarithmic scale records movement in a stock's price based on a fixed percentage, as opposed to a fixed dollar amount. A logarithmic scale will record, for example, every three percent price movement in a stock. The percentage scale can increase for more volatile stocks and can decrease for less volatile stocks. For the remainder of this book we will continue to use examples of the traditional scale, but you are likely to see and hear more about the benefits of using logarithmic charts in the future.

CHAPTER 5

BUY AND SELL SIGNALS IDENTIFIED WITH POINT & FIGURE CHARTS

Buy and Sell Signals

Buy Signals: Demand is stronger than supply; prices are likely to increase.

Sell Signals: Supply is stronger than demand; prices are likely to decrease.

In analyzing supply and demand relationships, we are not interested in the short-term edge. Our interest lies in the dominant trend in effect. In other words, we are interested in whether supply or demand has ultimate control, not the short-term, intermittent tugs-of-war. Again, Point & Figure charts have an edge over other charting methods because they do not track minor changes in pricing; they record important price movement.

In the stock market, overall trends—not day-to-day or week-to-week activity—have significance. If we were to focus on just the short run, we would continually react to random stock movement. Investors gain more value from waiting until prices move to a level that reflects demand or supply taking control and a trend beginning. Obviously, the challenge lies in knowing when these action levels occur. This challenge is where Point & Figure charting becomes invaluable; Point & Figure charts identify the appropriate price levels and times to buy or sell when significant price trends are beginning.

As I've said before, the Point & Figure methodology helps to reduce the market noise in the short run and helps to identify the important price changes. You will make significant sums of money if you can identify when a new trend is emerging in a stock and invest in the main trend. Buy and sell signals are the price points that indicate a new trend is emerging. When I went through the examples in chapters three and four, I highlighted a few of the most popular signals, such as the triple top and the triple bottom. As you may recall from those examples, a *buy* signal is one in which a column of X's exceeds previous columns of X's, indicating that the demand for the stock is gaining strength. A *sell* signal is one in which a column of O's exceeds previous columns of O's, indicating that the supply of a stock is increasing.

As I mentioned earlier, it's important to note that a buy or a sell signal in and of itself is not enough information with which to buy or sell a stock. Other considerations need to be made, such as the industry or sector condition, the overall market condition, the major trend for the stock, and the relative strength of the stock. In summary, if these other considerations are positive or negative, only then should you act on a buy or a sell signal on the Point & Figure chart. How to combine these other considerations will be covered in following chapters and summed up in the last section of the book. Right now, I want to focus on a basic understanding of buy and sell signals.

Before we look at specific buy and sell signals, we need to define two terms regularly used with Point & Figure charts, namely, support levels and resistance levels. These definitions will help with interpreting the buy and sell signals.

Support levels identify a price level at which there is sufficient demand for an investment, thereby causing a halt in any downward trend. Support levels can be identified by horizontal rows of O's that mark the bottom of respective columns (*figure 5.1*).

50						
49						
48					X	
47					X	O
46	X		X		X	O
45	X	O	X	O	X	O
44	X	O	X	O	X	O
43	X	O		O		O
42	X					
41	X					
40						

⇐ Support Level

figure 5.1

Resistance levels identify a price at which there is sufficient supply for an investment, thereby causing a halt in any upward trend. Similar to support levels, the resistance level can be identified by horizontal rows, in this case, rows of X's that mark the top of respective columns (*figure 5.2*).

50						
49						
48						
47			X		X	
46	X		X	O	X	O
45	X	O	X	O	X	O
44	X	O	X	O	X	O
43	X	O		O		O
42	X					
41	X					
40	X					

⟸ Resistance Level

figure 5.2

When a price breaks either the support level or resistance level, a balance between supply and demand has been broken. When a stock breaks through a support level, it indicates supply has the upper hand and that prices may continue to decline. Breaking through a resistance level indicates that demand has the upper hand and that prices may continue to increase.

I will discuss resistance and support levels at greater length in the next chapter.

Buy Signals

Many chart patterns can form a buy signal. The most common is the *double top*. All other buy-signal patterns are an extension of the double top. In this section, I am going to describe some of the more important buy-signal patterns. Note that you will want to refer back to this section frequently as I move forward in the book since buy signals play a significant role in interpreting market conditions, industry conditions, and timing of individual stock selection.

40					
39					X
38			X		X
37		O	X	O	X
36		O	X	O	X
35		O		O	
34					
33					

⇐ Double-Top Buy Signal

figure 5.3

The double top (*figure 5.3*) is the most common buy signal. This pattern typically occurs when a positive trend is already in progress. The double top means that demand continues to be stronger than supply and that the up trend is proceeding nicely. The double top rarely occurs at a turning point (i.e., when a trend changes from supply being in control to demand being in control). Changes in trends take time to develop, and simple double tops are not strong enough to suggest a major turning point in a stock. Because the double top is not a strong buy signal, one should not take large positions in a stock that breaks a simple double top solely because this pattern is broken. Other buy-signal patterns that take longer to develop are better indicators for taking large positions. The double top is primarily used to confirm continuation of a trend; therefore, the pattern is nice to see after you have taken a position and if you want verification that the trend continues to progress.

45					X
44	X		X		X
43	X	O	X	O	X
42	X	O	X	O	X
41	X	O		O	
40	X				
39					

⇐ Triple-Top Buy Signal

figure 5.4

The *triple top* (*figure 5.4*) is a stronger pattern than the double top in that the pattern takes a little longer to develop; this extended time usually means a balance in the supply and demand relationship exists prior to the pattern being broken. I like balancing patterns broken in favor of demand since this often is the time a stock will make its strongest move.

In the example in *figure 5.4*, we see the columns of X's stop at $44, indicating there is enough supply for the stock price to reverse down from that level two times. The columns of O's stop dropping at $41, meaning demand is strong enough at that level to keep the price from decreasing further. The balance pattern exists in the first four columns between $44 and $41. The third time that demand lifts the stock up to $44, the supply is not present to contain the price. As noted on the chart, an X is placed in the $45 box in the third column of X's, breaking the triple top. At this point, the price has broken the resistance level, and your conclusion is that demand is controlling the trading in these shares. The supply-demand balance is broken, and a new trend is beginning. When a stock breaks a triple top, the probabilities are high the stock will continue to advance. All the sellers willing to sell at $44 or lower have sold; removing that supply is like taking a lid off the stock's price.

37								X	
36	X				X				X
35	X	O			X	O	X		X
34	X	O	X		X	O	X	O	X
33	X	O	X	O	X	O	X	O	X
32	X	O	X	O	X	O		O	
31	X	O		O					
30	X								

⇐ Spread-Triple-Top Buy Signal

figure 5.5

A *spread triple top (figure 5.5)* occurs when the column of X's that form the triple top are separated by additional columns. The interpretation of this pattern should be the same as for the triple-top pattern. A spread triple top takes a little longer to develop than the triple top. Again, this extended time means the supply and demand balance that exists in the stock is more substantial. Remember, an extended balance pattern means a stronger resistance level. Once a stock breaks out of a strong balance pattern and a strong resistance level, the stock can have a strong advance.

	1	2	3	4	5
38					X
37	X		X		X
36	X	O	X	O	X
35	X	O	X	O	X
34	X	O	X	O	X
33	X	O		O	X
32	X			O	X
31	X			O	
30	X				
29	X				
28	X				

figure 5.6

The *bullish shakeout (figure 5.6)* is a form of a triple top. The first two columns of X's stop at the same level, which is $37 in the chart above. The two columns of O's on the chart during this pattern actually break a double bottom. Since there is no follow-through of the double bottom, the selling or supply is weak. In this scenario, the next three-box reversal can be used as an indicator to purchase the stock. At this time, the probability is high that the next column of X's will follow through and break a triple top. In order to use this pattern effectively, you want to make sure the major trend for the stock is up and that the Relative Strength chart for the stock is on a buy signal. I will address major trends and Relative Strength charts in later chapters.

	1	2	3	4	5	6	7
39							X
38					X		X
37					X	O	X
36	X		X		X	O	X
35	X	O	X	O	X	O	
34	X	O	X	O	X		
33	X	O	X	O	X		
32	X	O	X	O	x		
31	X	O		O			
30	X						

figure 5.7

A bullish catapult (figure 5.7) occurs when a double top follows a triple top. This pattern provides confirmation the triple top break is successful. In addition to the signals that demand is strong, the column of O's following the triple top needs to hold above the previous column of O's. In other words, there cannot be a sell signal between the triple top and the double top. The higher column of O's helps indicate weak supply. Prior to making a stock purchase, a conservative investor may want to wait for a catapult pattern rather than just a triple top. If you wait, you may buy at a little higher price than if you bought immediately after a triple top; however, the catapult indicates that the trend following the triple top is proceeding as expected. You can also use a strategy of easing into a full position using the catapult pattern. Buy a partial position following the triple top, then purchasing the remainder of your position following the catapult.

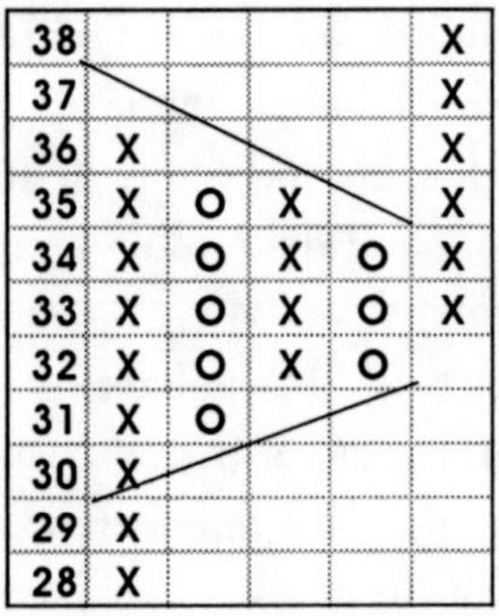

figure 5.8

The **bullish triangle** (**figure 5.8**) consists of a minimum of five columns, but the pattern can have more columns. The pattern begins with lower columns of X's and a higher column of O's, indicating there is a balance in the supply and demand relationship. The bullish-triangle pattern is broken when a column of X's exceeds a previous column of X's, indicating that the balance is broken and that a new trend is beginning for the stock. Usually, a bullish-triangle pattern will occur after a stock has already begun an advance. The triangle indicates supply is meeting demand on a short-term basis. The break of the triangle pattern means the short-term supply is exhausted, and demand is still strong. A new "leg" of the advance is likely to result.

38				
37	O			
36	O			
35	O			
34	O			X
33	O	X		X
32	O	X	O	X
31	O	X	O	X
30	O	X	O	
29	O	X		
28	O			

figure 5.9

The *bullish signal (figure 5.9)* will occur after a sizable drop in a stock price, indicated by a long column of O's. Eventually, the selling will subside, the demand will meet the supply, and the column of O's will end. In the example above, the long column of O's ends at $28. When the demand exceeds the supply, the chart will change to a column of X's. Above you will see the first column of X's up to $33. Rarely will a stock drop and then go straight up. More often, a bottom will form with some up-and-down action on the chart. As a result, after the initial move up, supply again takes over, and the chart changes to a column of O's. If this column of O's ends up higher than the previous column of O's, we can assume supply is losing strength. This assumption is confirmed when the stock reverses back up into a column of X's. A bullish-signal pattern is formed when the second column of X's rises above the previous column of X's, indicating a bottom is potentially in place for the stock.

The interpretation of a bullish signal will vary, based on the longer-term trend of the stock. If the stock is trading above the bullish support line (which I'll cover in the next chapter), a bullish signal indicates that a short-term correction in the stock is over and that the main trend is reemerging. If the bullish signal happens while the stock is trading below the bearish resistance line (addressed in the next chapter), the bullish signal suggests that the stock's advance will probably stop at the resistance line and, therefore, is more suitable for investors trading short term.

38							X
37	X						X
36	X	O	X				X
35	X	O	X	O	X		X
34	X	O	X	O	X	O	X
33	X	O		O	X	O	X
32	X			O		O	X
31	X					O	
30	X						
29	X						
28	X						

figure 5.10

The *bearish signal reversal (figure 5.10)* is a pattern that consists of at least seven columns. The first six columns show lower columns of X's and lower columns of O's, creating bearish signals on the chart. During the seventh column, or thereafter, the bearish pattern is broken when a column of X's exceeds the previous column of X's and reverses the bearish pattern. Similar to the bullish signal, you should treat this pattern differently, depending on the major, overall trend for the stock. If the stock is trading above the bullish support line, a bearish signal reversal indicates that a short-term correction in the stock is over and that the main trend is reemerging. If the pattern happens while the stock is trading below the bearish resistance line, the bearish signal reversal suggests, at least initially, that the stock's advance will be limited to the level of the resistance line and is, therefore, more suitable for investors trading short term. The bearish signal reversal is one of the rarest Point & Figure patterns, yet, when found, can be very profitable.

38							
37	X				X		
36	X	O	X		X	O	
35	X	O	X	O	X	O	X
34	X	O	X	O	X	O	X
33	X	O		O		O	X
32	X					O	
31	X						
30	X						

figure 5.11

The **bear trap** (*figure 5.11*) is a pattern formed when a balance pattern is broken by a triple bottom, giving the appearance that supply is taking over. The triple bottom being broken is normally a negative pattern; however, if there is no follow-through to the downside, this pattern sets up the potential for a bear trap. *In order for a bear trap to occur, the triple bottom should only be broken by one box.* In *figure 5.11*, the triple bottom was broken at $32, but there was no follow-through to the decline. If the supply is weak, the chart immediately reverses back up into a column of X's, and the triple bottom is considered a bear trap. The timing to buy takes place after the three-box reversal into a column of X's occurs. In *figure 5.11*, the time to buy takes place when the chart reverses up to $35 (in the last X column shown). A bear-trap pattern can occur during a consolidation phase of a stock trading in a strong upward trend or at the very bottom of a stock's chart.

38	O			
37	O	X		
36	O	X	O	
35	O	X	O	
34	O	X	O	
33	O		O	X
32			O	X
31			O	X
30			O	X
29			O	X
28			O	

figure 5.12

The **low pole reversal** (*figure 5.12*) is a pattern that begins with a long column of O's (called the low pole). A low pole is defined as a column of O's that drops more than three boxes below the previous column of O's. In *figure 5.12*, note that the second column of O's falls below the first column of O's by five boxes. When demand resurfaces, initial demand is considered substantial if the column of X's that follows the low pole retraces the low pole by more than 50%. To determine the 50% level, you add up the number of O's in the low-pole column. In *figure 5.12*, there are nine O's in the low pole. Therefore, the next column of X's needs to retrace the O's by more than 50%, or by at least five X's. In *figure 5.12*, the necessary reversal point is at $33. In order for the low-pole-reversal pattern to be used effectively, the stock's Relative Strength chart should be on a buy signal. I have found that if a stock price drops down toward the bullish support line during the low pole, buying on the reversal can often be very profitable.

Sell Signals

Just as there are buy signals, there are sell signals as well. A sell pattern is one in which a column of O's declines below a previous column of O's, indicating that the supply for a stock is gaining strength.

I can't stress this point enough—A sell signal in and of itself is not enough information to sell the stock. Other considerations need to be made, such as the industry or sector conditions, overall market conditions, the major trend for the stock, and the relative strength of the stock.

In the final analysis, if the weight of the evidence of all these considerations is negative, then you should act upon a sell signal on the Point & Figure chart.

Like buy signals, there are many different chart patterns that indicate a sell signal. The most basic and most common is the double bottom. Other sell signals are an extension of the double bottom. The following are some of the more important sell signal patterns. Note that you will want to frequently refer back to this section as we move forward in the book because sell signals play a significant role in interpreting market conditions and industry sector conditions.

40				
39				
38				
37	X		X	
36	X	O	X	O
35	X	O	X	O
34		O		O
33				O

⇐ Double-Bottom Sell Signal

figure 5.13

The **double bottom (figure 5.13)** is the most basic and common sell signal. This pattern typically occurs when the major decline trend is already in progress. A double bottom means that supply continues to be stronger than demand, and the downtrend is continuing. A double bottom rarely occurs at a major turning point (i.e., when a trend changes from demand being in control to supply being in control). Changes in trends take time to develop, and a double bottom is not strong enough to suggest a major turning point in a stock. Because this signal is not a strong sell signal, you should not sell all of your position in a stock that breaks a simple double bottom. Other patterns, which take longer to develop, are more significant sell signals.

38	O				
37	O	X			
36	O	X	O	X	
35	O	X	O	X	O
34	O	X	O	X	O
33	O			O		O
32					O
31					
30					

⇐ Triple-Bottom Sell Signal

figure 5.14

The *triple bottom (figure 5.14)* is a stronger pattern than the double bottom in that the pattern takes a little longer to develop. In other words, there is a stronger balance in the supply and demand relationship prior to the pattern being broken. As I mentioned before, when extended balancing patterns are broken, the stock will often make a strong move in the direction of the breakout. In the case of a triple bottom, the move will be down. *Figure 5.14* shows that the columns of O's stop at $33, indicating that demand is strong enough at this price level for the stock to turn up from the level two times. The columns of X's stop climbing at $37 for the first column and at $36 for the second. The balance pattern exists in the first four columns between $33 and the $36–$37 range. The third time supply brings the stock down to $33, the demand is not present to push the stock up. When you are able to place an O in the $32 box in the third column of O's, the triple bottom is broken, and the price has broken through an important support level. The conclusion is that supply has taken control, the balance is broken, and a new trend has begun. When a stock breaks a triple bottom, the probabilities are high that the stock price will continue to decline. All the buyers willing to spend $33 or higher have bought. Removing the demand from the equation is like taking the floor out from under the stock's price.

44	O								
43	O	X		X					
42	O	X	O	X	O	X		X	
41	O	X	O	X	O	X	O	X	O
40	O	X	O		O	X	O	X	O
39	O	X			O	X	O		O
38	O				O				O
37									O
36									

figure 5.15

A *spread triple bottom (figure 5.15)* occurs when the column of O's that forms the triple bottom is separated by additional columns. The interpretation of this pattern should be the same as for the triple-bottom pattern. A spread triple bottom takes a little longer to develop than the triple bottom (i.e., the extended time means that the supply and demand balance that exists in the stock is more substantial). Remember, the stronger the balance pattern being broken, the stronger the resulting decline can be.

44	O			X	
43	O			X	O
42	O	X		X	O
41	O	X	O	X	O
40	O	X	O	X	O
39	O	X	O	X	O
38	O		O		O
37					O
36					

figure 5.16

The *bearish shakeout (figure 5.16)* is a form of a triple bottom. The first two columns of O's stop declining at the same level, namely, $38 in *figure 5.16*. The two columns of X's on the chart during this pattern actually break a double top. Since there is no follow-through of the double top, the buying (demand) is weak. In this scenario, the next three-box reversal can be used as an indicator to sell the stock. At this point, the probability is that the next column of O's will follow through and break a triple bottom. In order for this pattern to be effectively used, you want to make sure that the major trend for the stock is down and that the Relative Strength chart for the stock is on a sell signal.

44	O						
43	O	X		X			
42	O	X	O	X	O		
41	O	X	O	X	O	X	
40	O	X	O	X	O	X	O
39	O	X	O		O	X	O
38					O		O
37							O
36							

figure 5.17

A *bearish catapult* (*figure 5.17*) occurs when a double bottom follows a triple bottom. This pattern provides confirmation that a downtrend is in place. In addition to the signals that supply is strong, the column of X's following the triple bottom needs to hold below the previous column of X's. In other words, there cannot be a buy signal between the triple bottom and the double bottom. The lower column of X's helps indicate weak demand.

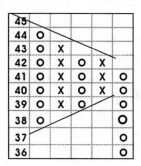

figure 5.18

The *bearish triangle* (*figure 5.18*) consists of a minimum of five columns, but the pattern can have more columns. The pattern begins with lower columns of X's and a higher column of O's, indicating a balance in the supply and demand relationship. The bearish-triangle pattern is broken when a column of O's exceeds a previous column of O's, indicating that the balance is broken and that a new trend is beginning for the stock. A bearish-triangle pattern will usually form after a stock has already begun a decline. The triangle indicates that demand is meeting supply on a short-term basis. The break of the triangle pattern means that the short-term demand is exhausted and that supply is still strong. A new "leg" of the decline is likely to result.

44	X			
43	X	O	X	
42	X	O	X	O
41	X	O	X	O
40	X	O	X	O
39	X	O		O
38	X			O
37	X			
36	X			
35	X			
34	X			

figure 5.19

The *bearish signal (figure 5.19)* will occur after a sizable advance in a stock, indicated by a long column of X's. Eventually, the buying will subside, the supply will meet the demand, and the column of X's will end. In the example above, the long column of X's ends at $44. When the supply exceeds the demand, the chart will change to a column of O's. Above you will see that the first column of O's is down to $39. Rarely will a stock advance and then drop straight down. More often, we see some back-and-forth price action as a top is formed. As a result, after the initial move down, demand begins to take over, and the chart reverses to a column of X's. If this column of X's stops advancing below the previous column of X's, we can assume demand is losing strength. This assumption is confirmed when the stock reverses back down into a column of O's. When this column of O's falls below the previous column of O's, a bearish-signal pattern is formed, indicating that a top is potentially in place. This pattern should be interpreted differently depending on the longer-term trend of the stock. If the stock is trading below the bearish resistance line, a bearish signal indicates that a short-term advance in the stock is over and that the main downward trend is reemerging. If this pattern happens while the stock is trading above the bullish support line, the bearish signal suggests that the stock's decline will probably stop at the support line.

	1	2	3	4	5	6	7
44	O						
43	O					X	
42	O			X		X	O
41	O	X		X	O	X	O
40	O	X	O	X	O	X	O
39	O	X	O	X	O		O
38	O	X	O				O
37	O						O
36							O
35							O
34							

figure 5.20

The *bullish signal reversal (figure 5.20)* is one of the rarest Point & Figure patterns. This pattern consists of at least seven columns. The first six columns show higher columns of X's and higher columns of O's, creating bullish signals on the chart. During the seventh column, or thereafter, the bullish pattern is broken when a column of O's drops below the previous column of O's and reverses the bullish pattern. Similar to the bearish signal, this pattern should be treated differently, depending on the major, overall trend for the stock. If the stock is trading below the bearish resistance line, a bullish signal reversal indicates that a short-term advance in the stock is over and that the main trend is reemerging. If the pattern happens while the stock is trading above the bullish support line, the bullish signal reversal suggests that the stock's decline should stop at the support line.

	1	2	3	4	5	6
44						
43					X	
42	X		X		X	O
41	X	O	X	O	X	O
40	X	O	X	O	X	O
39	X	O		O		O
38	X					O
37	X					O
36						O
35						O
34						

figure 5.21

The *bull trap (figure 5.21)* is formed when a balance pattern is broken by a triple top, indicating that demand is taking over. A triple top that is broken is normally a positive pattern; however, if there is no follow-through to the upside, this pattern sets up the potential for a bull trap. *In order for a bull trap to occur, the triple top should only be broken by one box.* In the chart seen in *figure 5.21*, the triple top was broken at $43, but there was no follow-through. If the demand is weak, the chart immediately reverses back down into a column of O's, and the triple top is considered a bull trap. The timing to sell takes place when the next three-box reversal down into a column of O's occurs. In the chart seen in *figure 5.21*, that time would occur at $40. A bull-trap pattern can occur during a consolidation phase of a stock trading in a strong downward trend or at the very top of a stock's chart.

44			X	
43			X	O
42			X	O
41			X	O
40			X	O
39			X	O
38	X		X	O
37	X	O	X	
36	X	O	X	
35	X	O	X	
34	X	O		
33	X			

figure 5.22

The *high pole reversal (figure 5.22)* begins with a long column of X's up, which is considered the high pole. A high pole is defined as a column of X's that exceeds a previous column of X's by at least three boxes. In the chart in *figure 5.22*, you can see that the second column of X's exceeds the first column of X's by six boxes. When supply resurfaces, the initial supply is considered substantial if the column of O's that follows the high pole retraces the high pole by more than 50%. To determine the 50% level, you would count the number of X's in the high-pole column. In the chart in *figure 5.22*, there are ten X's in the high pole; therefore, the next column of O's needs to be retraced by more than 50%, or by at least six O's. In the chart in *figure 5.22*, the necessary reversal occurs at $38. In order for the high pole reversal to be used effectively, the stock should be on a sell signal on its Relative Strength chart.

The buy and sell signals I have described tell you when to buy and sell specific stocks. Prior to acting upon a Point & Figure signal, however, a number of other conditions should be preexisting. For example, prior to buying, you would want the major trend in the stock to indicate that demand is in control. When selling, supply should be controlling the major trend. A stock's Relative Strength chart should be positive when you are buying and negative when you are selling.

The most significant preexisting condition is the status of the industry or sector the stock is in. It is highly desirable to buy stocks in sectors that are market leaders and to sell in underperforming sectors. Additionally, indicators for the overall market should be bullish before you buy and bearish before you sell. Do not make the mistake of using only Point & Figure buy and sell signals to make all of your decisions. Most of the remaining chapters in the book will help you identify the desirable preexisting conditions before you act on a buy or sell signal.

CHAPTER 6

MAJOR TRENDS IDENTIFIED
WITH POINT & FIGURE CHARTS

Three Long-Term Trends:

DEMAND in Control
SUPPLY in Control
Supply and Demand in BALANCE

Often, investors new to Point & Figure charting miss the forest for the trees; it's easy to get caught up in trying to interpret the latest buy or sell signal on the chart and not pay enough attention to the major trend in force for the stock. Keep in mind that the major trend plays a *significant* role in making decisions about your investments. The buy and sell signals are treated differently, depending on the major trend.

For example, a buy signal when demand is controlling the major trend in a stock (i.e., when overall prices are increasing) should be acted upon differently than when supply is controlling the major trend in a stock. We are more likely to act upon a buy signal when demand is in control and usually avoid buy signals when supply is in control. The reason is that most buy signals that occur when supply is in control of the main trend are weak and lack any follow-through. Similarly, buy signals given while the main trend is a balance pattern are also treated differently than those when demand is in control. This treatment is due to not knowing during balance patterns if demand or supply will have ultimate control.

To better understand how to combine overall trends with buy or sell signals and how to respond to buy and sell signals, I want to explain the three major trends:

1. Demand in Control
2. Supply in Control
3. Supply and Demand in Balance

Demand in Control

In order to understand the overall trend of demand in control, you also need to understand the bullish support line. The bullish support line is the primary trend line on a Point & Figure chart when the major trend is demand in control.

Using the chart in *figure 6.1*, note the recording of the bullish support line. First, find the lowest column of O's on the chart. Second, in the box immediately below the lowest O, begin marking the bullish support line. On the chart in *figure 6.1*, the lowest column of O's is at $37, so the bullish support line starts just below that level, at $36. As the chart progresses and alternating columns of X's and O's are recorded, the bullish support line continues to advance on a 45-degree angle. When the chart records the next column of X's, the bullish support line would be recorded by moving up one price level and over one column (on a 45-degree angle), and the support line would be recorded at $37. When the Point & Figure chart reverses from the column of X's to the next column of O's, the bullish support line would go up to $38, that is, up one price level and over one column to the right. Every time there is a reversal from a column of O's to X's or from a column of X's to O's, the bullish support line is recorded by moving up one price level and over one column to the right.

	c1	c2	c3	c4	c5	c6	c7	c8
51								X
50								X
49						X		X
48						X	O	X
47		X		X		X	O	X
46		X	O	X	O	X	O	X
45		X	O	X	O	X	O	X
44		X	O		O	X	O	
43	O	X			O			*
42	O	X					*	
41	O	X				*		
40	O	X			*			
39	O	X		*				
38	O	X	*					
37	O	*						
36	*							
35								
34								
33								
32								
31								
30								

figure 6.1

As long as the chart is able to stay above the bullish support line, the major trend for the stock is considered to be increasing, meaning demand is in control. When stocks are strongly trending up, the price will often rise substantially above the bullish support line. The bullish support line also tends to provide support during times of temporary weakness for stocks with demand in control. When stocks in the midst of an overall advance encounter some supply and show some weak sell signals, the bullish support line tends to hold the sell signals within a particular price-level range. Often, stocks will bounce off the support line like a rubber ball and begin the next stage of their advance.

Challenges to demand exist when a stock penetrates, or falls below, the bullish support line. At that point, demand is no longer in control, and a downward trend is beginning.

Example of Point & Figure Chart with Demand in Control
Tenet Healthcare Corp (March 2000–October 2002)

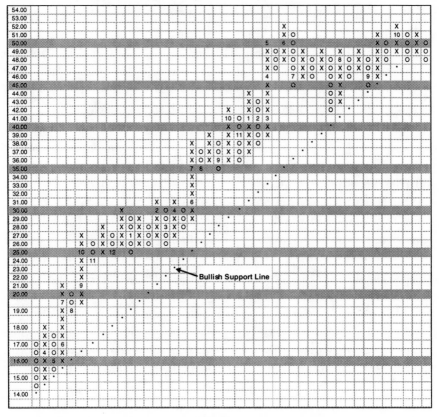

figure 6.2

Demand in Control is characterized by:

-Strong buy signals above the bullish support line
-Weak sell signals above the bullish support line
-Mostly higher columns of X's and O's
-Balancing patterns broken by demand

The chart in *figure 6.2* is an example of a Point & Figure chart that shows demand in control of the major trend. This chart is a recording of Tenet Healthcare's stock from March 2000 through October 2002. Note that generally higher columns of O's and higher columns of X's characterize this chart (i.e., the overall trend is upward). The higher columns of both X's and O's indicate that demand continues to control trading and that supply continues to be weak. A long-term trend with higher columns of both X's and O's is only in force when the stock is trading above the bullish support line.

Stocks in which demand is controlling the major trend will often make strong advances, consolidate the advance, and then make another strong advance. The cycle can repeat itself several times before the trend is finally over. A strong advance is characterized by significantly higher columns of X's and O's; there will also be multiple double-top buy signals during the advance. In *figure 6.2*, you can see the multiple double-top buy signals as the stock moves from $15 up to the $30 level. Notice how the columns of X's all exceed the previous columns of X's and that the columns of O's are all higher than the previous columns of O's. There are four consecutive double tops during this phase, suggesting demand is much stronger than supply.

When the stock hits $30, notice how the chart pattern in *figure 6.2* changes. The columns of X's do not exceed the previous X columns for a period, as they tend to stop near the same price level for a while. When we see this change on the chart, our conclusion is that more shareholders want to sell at this level, increasing the supply. This change is considered a balance pattern between the stock's supply and demand. At this time, the chart tends to move sideways. Think of the balance pattern as the stock catching its breath after a run and gearing up for the next run. Notice, also, that during balancing patterns, the bullish support line tends to catch up to the price level where the stock is trading.

Once a stock enters a balancing pattern, one of two events will eventually happen. One scenario is that all of the demand that pushed the stock higher is exhausted, and supply will take control. In this case, as demand fades, it is like pulling the floor out from under the stock, and supply is able to push the price lower. If this scenario occurs, you will see a column of O's decline below the previous columns of O's in the balancing pattern. You will also see the O's penetrating the bullish support line. When the bullish support line is penetrated, the main trend will be downward, with supply controlling the action. Remember, the balance pattern is a battle between supply and demand. If the balance pattern gets broken on the downside, supply would have won the battle, and it would be time to sell.

The other potential scenario is that demand is not exhausted and is able to meet the supply until all the sellers in the $30 range have sold. Once all the sellers have sold, and if demand persists, you will see the balance pattern broken by a higher column of X's. The chart in *figure 6.2* reflects this scenario. When the stock price is finally able to break through $30 level, the balance pattern is broken, and the price rises significantly. The break allows the stock to make another strong advance. As I mentioned earlier, if a stock breaks a balance pattern, the stock will often have a strong advance, especially if the balance pattern was a strong one, with several tops or bottoms. Removing the supply near $30 is similar to taking the lid off the price. See how the chart then goes into another string of higher columns of X's and O's with demand once again in control.

After the break out at $32 (*figure 6.2*), the demand was strong enough to push the stock up to the $50 price level before enough supply was present to halt the advance. At this point, another balancing pattern surfaces on the chart. Note that there are some weak sell signals during this balancing pattern. By weak, I mean there is no follow-through after a sell signal is given. When you see these signals in a chart that remains above the bullish support line, you should not consider them strong sell signals. It is too early to make such a call since the overall major trend is still indicating that demand is in control.

Commonly, investors believe they should sell a stock after it has made some predetermined profit. This approach can prove disappointing. Stocks tend to move to extremes both as they rise and as they fall. As you can see in *figure 6.2*, if you had sold after a 20% or 30% profit, you would have missed a substantial gain. In the next chapter, I will show you how to determine price objectives based on the Point & Figure chart pattern. Nevertheless, the price objective is not a price at which you should sell all of your shares. Rather than having a preexisting price target in mind, let the chart tell you when the trend is over.

Note in *figure 6.2* that the bullish support line moves closer to the columns of O's and X's as the price ranges between $45 and $50. This proximity indicates that the chart has entered into another balance pattern as the stock is consolidating its price increase from $30 to $50. If this balance pattern experiences a positive breakout, it would be an indication that demand is taking over again and that the price should make another run. If the balance pattern experiences a negative breakdown, it would indicate that supply is taking over and that you should sell.

Let me make this point—*actively using the chart patterns, as well as understanding the overall trends, will help you maintain investment discipline to make confident decisions.* The chart indicates the appropriate time to sell. If, during a balancing pattern, supply is strong enough to break the pattern and change the major trend to the downside, the bullish support line will be penetrated. This penetration is an indicator that the time has arrived to sell. Many investors sell their winners too soon and hold their losers too long. To be consistently successful in the stock market, you need to learn to turn the table around. In other words, hold on tightly to the winners while they are experiencing an upward and positive major trend. If the trend does not continue and begins to turn downward, that is your indication to sell. By following these guidelines for managing your portfolio, you will eventually own a number of stocks that are in major upward trends, and you will be free of stocks that are in major declining trends.

Supply in Control

In order to understand the overall trend of supply in control, you also need to understand the bearish resistance line. The bearish resistance line is the primary trend line on a Point & Figure chart when the major trend indicates that supply is in control.

Consider the bearish resistance line as the exact opposite of the bullish support line. To record the bearish resistance line, simply look for the highest column of X's on the chart. In the price level immediately above the highest X, begin recording the bearish resistance line. On the chart in *figure 6.3*, the price level with the first asterisk is $48. Every time the chart changes columns from X's to O's or from O's to X's, the bearish resistance line would move down one price level and over one column to the right. On the chart in *figure 6.3*, the second asterisk would be at $47. As the chart reverses into the next column of X's, the bearish resistance line would come down another price level and over one column to the right, and so on.

	1	2	3	4	5	6	7	8
51								
50								
49								
48	*							
47	X	*						
46	X	O	*					
45	X	O		*				
44	X	O			*			
43	X	O				*		
42	X	O	X		X		*	
41	X	O	X	O	X	O		*
40		O	X	O	X	O		
39		O	X	O	X	O	X	
38		O		O	X	O	X	O
37				O		O	X	O
36						O		O
35								O
34								O
33								
32								
31								
30								

figure 6.3

As long as the chart remains below the bearish resistance line, you should consider the major trend of the stock to be down, that is, that supply is in control of trading. When the supply is strong, the stock price will fall to price levels considerably below the bearish resistance line. Stocks with a strong pattern of supply in control may see demand lift the shares on a short-term basis. During these times, the stock tends to advance up or near the bearish resistance line but does not penetrate the line. When a stock is in a strong decline and temporarily rises to the resistance line, a weak advance often will end near the line.

Challenges to supply exist when a stock penetrates, or rises above, the bearish resistance line. At that point, supply is no longer in control, and a new upward trend is beginning.

Example of Point & Figure Chart with Supply in Control
Sun Microsystems (May 2001–October 2002)

Price	1	2	3	4	5	6	7	8	9	10	11	12	13	14	15	16	17	18	19	20	21	22	23	24
25.00																								
24.00	*																							
23.00	X	*																						
22.00	X	O	*																					
21.00	X	O		*																				
20.00	X	O			*																			
19.50	X	O				*																		
19.00	X	O	X				*																	
18.50	X	O	X	O		*	*																	
18.00	X	O	X	O			X	*																
17.50	X	O	6	O			X	O	*															
17.00		O	X	O			8	O	*															
16.50		O	X	O	X		X	O		*														
16.00		O		O	X	O	X	O			*													
15.50			O	X	O	X	O	X	O			*												
15.00			O	X	7	X	O	X	O	X				*	*									
14.50			O	X	O	X	O	X	O	X	O				12	*	*							
14.00			O		O		O		O	X	O		X		X	O	X	*						
13.50							O		O				X	O	X	O	1	O	*					
13.00							O						X	O	X	O	X	O	*					
12.50							O						X	O		O	X	O		*				
12.00							O						X			O		O		*				
11.50							O						X			O			*					
11.00							O	X	11							O			*					
10.50							O	X	O	X					2	X		*						
10.00							9	X	O	X					O	3	O		*					
9.50							O	10	O						O	X	O	X		*				
9.00							O	X							O	X	O	X	O	*				
8.50							O	X							O	X	O	X	O		*			
8.00							O									O		4	O					
7.50																		5	X					
7.00																		O	X	O				
6.50																		O	X	O	X			
6.00																		O	6	X	O			
5.50																				O	X	O		
5.00																				O	X	O		
4.75																				O	X	O		
4.50																				7		O	X	
4.25																						O	8	O
4.00																						O	X	O
3.75																						O	X	9
3.50																						O		O
3.00																								O
2.50																								O
2.00																								10

figure 6.4

Supply in Control is characterized by:

-Strong sell signals beneath the bearish resistance line
-Weak buy signals beneath the bearish resistance line
-Mostly lower columns of X's and O's
-Balance patterns broken by supply winning the battle

The chart in *figure 6.4* is an example of a Point & Figure chart, showing supply in control of the major trend. This is a price recording of Sun Microsystems from May 2001 through October 2002. Generally, lower columns of X's and lower columns of O's characterize the chart pattern when supply is controlling the major trend. The lower columns of both X's and O's indicate that supply is strong and that demand continues to be weak. A long-term trend of supply in control is only in force when the stock is trading below the bearish resistance line.

Stocks in which supply controls the major trend will often make strong declines, consolidate the decline, and then make another strong decline. The cycle could repeat itself several times before the trend is finally over. The strong declines are characterized by significantly lower columns of X's and O's. Usually, there will also be multiple double-bottom sell signals during the declining patterns. On the chart in *figure 6.4*, you can see this pattern on two different occasions—first, when the stock declines from the low $20s down to $8, and again when the stock declines from $14.50 down to $2.00. (Remember, when a stock price is below $20, we use $.50-increments for recording price movement.) Notice how, with a few, short exceptions, that the columns of O's decline below the previous columns and that the columns of X's are mostly lower than the previous columns of X's. This pattern means that supply is much stronger than demand.

The chart in *figure 6.4* shows that there are a couple of brief periods in which the general decline appears to stop temporarily. When the stock first drops to $14, the O columns stop declining. In fact, three O columns stop right at $14. This temporary halt in the decline indicates that the demand for the stock at $14 is now a little stronger and that more investors are buying as the price declines from $23. The Point & Figure chart indicates that the stock has entered a balance pattern. Now, supply and demand have equal strength.

Once a stock enters a balancing pattern, one of two events will eventually happen. One scenario is that all the supply that pushed the stock lower has been exhausted and that demand will take control. In this case, as supply fades, it is like taking the lid off the stock, with demand pushing the stock higher. If supply fades and demand increases, you will see a column of X's exceed the previous columns of X's in the balancing pattern. You will also see the X's penetrate the bearish resistance line. When the line is penetrated, the main trend will be upward, and demand will control the action. As I noted earlier, the balance pattern is a battle between supply and demand. In this scenario, demand has won the battle. Note on the chart in *figure 6.4* that we do see a few columns of X's exceeding a previous column of X's. For example, the first occurrence is when an X column advances to $18. Note, however, that the bearish resistance line contains this advance and that the shares begin declining again. When supply is controlling the major trend, buy signals are often weak and will be contained at the bearish resistance line. When supply is in control, it is important to wait until the bearish resistance line has been penetrated before concluding that the trend has changed.

The other potential scenario is that supply is not exhausted and is able to meet demand. If supply persists, you will see the balance pattern broken by a lower column of O's. This scenario is reflected in *figure 6.4*. When the stock price is finally able to decline to the $13.50 level, the stock breaks out of the balance pattern. This action indicates that the stock is likely to make another strong decline; removing the demand near $14 is similar to taking the floor out from under the price. See how the chart then goes into another strong decline down to $8.

Demand surfaces again when the stock reaches $8. Again, for a period, demand is meeting the supply. In fact, at this point, the stock price begins to rise back up toward the bearish resistance line, and a couple of weak double-top buy signals occur. Interestingly, in this case, there wasn't even a balancing pattern. The stock price went pretty much straight down to $8 and straight up to $14.50. It is common to see weak buy signals while the major trend is moving lower. By "weak," I mean there is no follow-through after a buy signal occurs, the stock price does not penetrate the bearish resistance line, and supply maintains overall control.

Many investors try to buy stocks at their lows. This approach can be a dangerous strategy. First, how do you know the stock has really bottomed? Second, stocks tend to go to extremes, both on their way up and on their way down. I would like to have a dollar for every investor who thought Lucent Technologies was a good buy just because it dropped from $80 down to $50. In hindsight, we know the price also dropped to $40, $30, $20, and even more. If a bottom is in place, you will see the reversal and the buying opportunity on the Point & Figure chart; this opportunity will be identified by the balance pattern being broken with a column of X's exceeding the other X's followed by a sure break through the bearish resistance line. Sure, with this approach you won't buy the stock at its lowest price, but you also won't get caught buying while it is still in a major downtrend.

Here is another point I want to emphasize—*actively using the charts, as well as understanding the trends, will help you maintain investment discipline.* Unless you are a short-term trading investor, seeing a buy signal when the trend indicates that supply is the dominant force should not be considered an indication to buy stock. If you do buy stock at this point, you want to make sure you sell as it approaches the bearish resistance line. Longer-term investors should not attempt stock purchases based on buy signals that occur below the bearish resistance line. In order for the major trend to turn positive, you need to see a balancing pattern followed by a definitive break of the pattern on the upside and penetration of the bearish resistance line. At that time, the major trend will be controlled by demand, and your chances of being successful will greatly increase.

Supply and Demand in Balance

As I have said, there are often times when supply and demand are in balance and when the balance pattern covers an extended period. These are times when the buy and sell signals are weak and when the support and resistance levels are easily identifiable. As noted on the chart in *figure 6.5*, the price tends to go back and forth between set prices—in this example, between $30 and $22. During the balance pattern, the support is $22 since demand for the stock increases when it reaches this price. Conversely, the resistance is $30 since supply for the stock takes over when it reaches this price.

Supply and Demand in Balance

30.00	X				X				X				
29.00	X	O			X	O			X	O	X		X
28.00	X	O	X		X	O			X	O	X	O	X
27.00	X	O	X	O	X	O	X		X	O	X	O	X
26.00	X	O	X	O	X	O	X	O	X	O	X	O	X
25.00	X	O	X	O		O	X	O	X	O	X	O	
24.00	X	O				O	X	O		O	X		
23.00	X					O	X			O	X		
22.00	X					O				O			
21.00	X												
20.00	X												

figure 6.5

Supply and Demand in Balance is characterized by:

-No major buy or sell signals
-Weak buy signals followed by weak sell signals
-Easily identifiable or highly defined support and resistance levels
-Either major top or bottom formations or as consolidation during a strong trend
-A breakout usually results in a strong move in the same direction

---

Balancing patterns are best viewed as sideways movements across the chart. In essence, the balance means there is no real trend in place. During a balance pattern, neither demand nor supply are in control. Rather, supply and demand are balancing each other, preventing the stock from making a strong advance or decline. Think of the balance like a tug-of-war. As I mentioned before, in the chart in *figure 6.5*, you can see that a balance pattern exists between $22 and $30. Whenever demand pushes the stock up to $30, supply meets demand, and the price begins declining. Once the price gets back down to the low $20s, demand meets supply and pushes the price up toward $30. The cycle repeats itself several times.

Balancing patterns are important for investors to identify on a Point & Figure chart. When these patterns are broken, there is usually a strong move in the direction of the breakout. For example, a breakout in the upward direction usually results in the emergence of a strong upward price trend (i.e., demand in control). A breakout in the downward direction usually results in the emergence of a strong downward price trend (i.e., supply in control). As you may recall from the buy and sell signal chapter, the longer the balance period, the stronger the advance or decline following the balance period. The reason for the strong movement is that once a stock enters a balancing pattern, one of two events will eventually happen. I have already covered these two scenarios in the previous two sections about demand in control and supply in control. However, given the importance of your ability to recognize these two trends emerging, I want to quickly review.

In one scenario, using the chart in *figure 6.6* as an example, all the buyers who want to own the stock have bought it. If there are no buyers left, but supply persists, the balance pattern will get broken in favor of supply. As the demand fades, the floor is pulled out from under the stock, and supply pushes the price lower. In this scenario, you will see a column of O's decline below the previous columns of O's in the balancing pattern. Remember, the balance pattern is a tug-of-war between supply and demand; in this scenario, supply has won the tug-of-war. If you owned a stock that breaks a balance pattern, you would probably want to sell it because it has likely entered into a major trend with supply in control.

Supply Takes Over

30.00	X				X				X					
29.00	X	O			X	O			X	O	X		X	
28.00	X	O	X		X	O			X	O	X	O	X	O
27.00	X	O	X	O	X	O	X		X	O	X	O	X	O
26.00	X	O	X	O	X	O	X	O	X	O	X	O	X	O
25.00	X	O	X	O		O	X	O	X	O	X	O		O
24.00	X	O				O	X	O		O	X			O
23.00	X					O	X			O	X			O
22.00	X					O				O				O
21.00	X													O
20.00	X													O
19.50														O
19.00														O

figure 6.6

91

The other potential scenario, as reflected on the chart in *figure 6.7*, is that all the sellers in the $30 range have sold and that demand is still present. If there are no sellers left and if demand persists, you will see the balance pattern broken by a higher column of X's above the previous columns in the balance pattern. On the chart in *figure 6.7*, you can see this pattern break when the stock is finally able to get up to the $31 level. At this point, the stock price has broken out of the balance pattern. Demand has won the tug-of-war. This break indicates that the stock is likely to make a strong advance.

Demand Takes Over

33.00													X
32.00													X
31.00													X
30.00	X				X				X				X
29.00	X	O			X	O			X	O	X		X
28.00	X	O	X		X	O			X	O	X	O	X
27.00	X	O	X	O	X	O	X		X	O	X	O	X
26.00	X	O	X	O	X	O	X	O	X	O	X	O	X
25.00	X	O	X	O		O	X	O	X	O	X	O	
24.00	X	O				O	X	O		O	X		
23.00	X					O	X			O	X		
22.00	X					O				O			
21.00	X												
20.00													

figure 6.7

It is important to separate balance patterns that are significant breaks or reversals of trends from balance patterns that occur after a major growth or decline trend. For example, if a stock is in a demand trend and has a period of balanced supply and demand—but the balance is broken to the upside—the balance was just a consolidation of the recent advance. In this case, the break-out represents a continuation of an overall demand trend. If the same balance pattern is broken to the downside, there might be an indication of a change in trend, or of supply taking control. *To make this conclusion, we would also like to see the bullish support line penetrated.*

Conversely, a balance pattern that occurs after a major decline, broken to the downside, was just a consolidation of the prior decline. In this case, the breakout represents a continuation of an overall supply trend. If this same balance pattern is broken to the upside, there might be an indication of a change in trend, or of demand taking control. *To make this conclusion, we would also like to see the bearish resistance line penetrated.*

With practice, you will increase your understanding of these trends and patterns. The following grid may help you become more comfortable and may help you take the appropriate action when combining the major trends with buy or sell signals.

	Demand in Control	Supply in Control	Demand and Supply in Balance	Potential Action
Buy Signal	X			Invest in stock
Buy Signal		X		No action unless short-term investor
Buy Signal			X	No action unless breakout and demand takes control
Sell Signal	X			No action
Sell Signal		X		Sell investment
Sell Signal			X	No action unless breakout and supply takes control
Break Bullish Support Line	X			Sell investment
Break Bearish Resistance Line		X		Buy stock

figure 6.8

Major Trend Changes

As I mentioned earlier in this chapter, stocks commonly trend to extreme highs and extreme lows, but eventually, the major trend will change, and the time will come for you to take appropriate action. Using the chart in *figure 6.9* as an example let me show you a chart that experienced a major trend change.

To begin, notice that the chart starts with demand in control and that the stock is making a major advance from around $22 up to the mid-$60s. During that period, the main trend shows that demand is in control. There are two balance patterns during this major advance—the first between $45 and $51, and the second between approximately $56 and $64. The balance pattern exists when supply meets the demand for a period and when the chart moves sideways without a general advance or decline.

As I mentioned in the previous section, when demand is the main trend in control and when a stock enters a balancing pattern, one of two events will eventually happen. Supply temporarily contains the demand (i.e., consolidation occurs with supply being relatively short-lived and with demand reemerging as the major trend). In this scenario, demand regains control, and there is an upside breakout of the balance pattern. On the chart in *figure 6.9*, this breakout is noted by a higher column of X's that breaks above the resistance level of the balance pattern. On the chart, you can see this example when the shares first get up to the $45–$51 level. The price advance is contained temporarily at that price level. Demand eventually wins the battle when the column of X's is able to get above $51. This action indicates that the stock is likely to make another strong advance. Do you see how the stock in *figure 6.9* engages on another strong advance after the balance pattern is broken at $52? Demand maintains control.

The other potential scenario during a balance pattern is that all the demand that pushed the stock higher is exhausted and that the supply increases. This change is noted by a column of O's declining below the lowest O columns in the balance pattern. You will also see the bullish support line penetrated, causing supply to take control of the main trend.

You can see an example of this scenario, in which the trend changes from demand to supply controlling the trading activity, near the top of the chart in *figure 6.9*. The chart enters a balance pattern between $57 and $64. As supply and demand battle, also notice how the bullish support line eventually catches up to the price level where the stock is trading. Eventually, demand fades away, and the supply is able to take over when the balance pattern experiences a downside breakout. Also notice how the long-standing bullish support line is penetrated around the same price. Once this pattern is broken, you can see how quickly the stock begins to decline. The major trend has changed from demand to supply being in control. You should use the break in the balance formation as your indication to sell. This is also a good time for aggressive investors to sell short (i.e., a strategy that will profit when a stock drops).

Example of Point & Figure Chart with Major Trend Change from Demand to Supply Controlling the Action

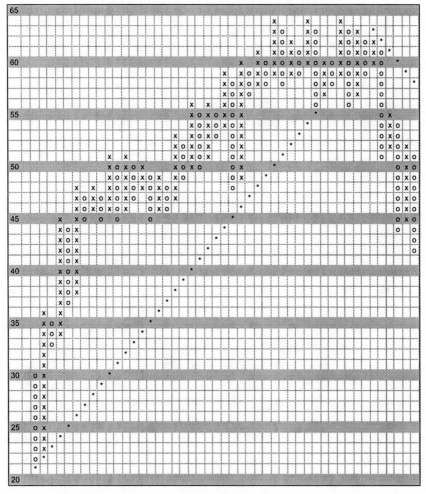

figure 6.9

You will see just the opposite action when a stock is forming a major bottom and when the trend is changing from supply to demand taking control. Eventually, a balance pattern will take shape, following a long period of supply that controls a stock's price action. The balance pattern indicates that demand is finally strong enough to meet the supply. When a balance pattern near the bottom of a chart experiences an upside breakout and when the trend line changes from a downward, *bearish* resistance line to an upward, *bullish* support line, you have a very strong signal that the price trend will move higher. This is an ideal buy signal for a stock because it begins a new trend of demand in control.

The chart in *figure 6.10* shows an example of such a trend change. On this chart, you can see that the stock price drops from around $60 to $35. The bearish resistance line remains the main trend line in effect. Every attempt to penetrate the resistance line fails. Supply is in control during this trend. Finally, when the price falls to the mid $30s, demand is strong enough to meet the supply, and a solid balance pattern forms.

At the very bottom of the chart, a bear-trap pattern forms. Review this pattern in chapter 5 (Buy and Sell Signals Identified with Point & Figure Charts) in *figure 5.11*. Just when it appears that the balance pattern at the bottom is experiencing a downside breakout, the price begins to reverse up. You can see a quadruple-bottom pattern broken when the price drops to $35. However, it immediately reverses up. When the quadruple-bottom pattern was broken but the price was unable to continue lower, that is a sign that supply is not strong enough to continue being the dominant force. As the price reverses up from the low and penetrates the bearish resistance line, the major trend is changing from supply to demand controlling the price action.

Look for similar patterns when you are making new investments. Stocks that are engaging on a new trend will deliver your best results. If you can limit your purchases to stocks that are just beginning a trend change from supply to demand in control, you will position your investment portfolio into issues that could potentially trend significantly higher. In some cases, the new trend will continue higher for years. Hold these issues until the Point & Figure chart indicates that the trend is over.

Certainly, not every new trend change will develop into a significant price increase, but many of them will. If the new trend does not follow through and if the newly established bullish support line gets broken use that as your signal to sell. The bullish support line is an excellent risk-management tool and gives you a solid sell discipline. Most investors desperately need sell discipline.

Buy stocks that are beginning to change their trend from supply to demand. Hold the positions that experience a long-term trend of demand in control. Sell the positions that do not. Using this strategy will help you hold on to significant winners while keeping losses to a minimum. Eventually, the issues that provide substantial profits will also have to be sold. That indication will occur once the trend changes from demand back to supply in control. When you see such patterns, you know it will be time to let go of winners and lock in the profit.

Example of Point & Figure Chart with Major Trend Change from Supply to Demand Controlling the Action

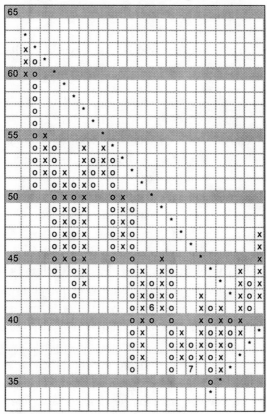

figure 6.10

CHAPTER 7

PRICE TARGETS: HOW TO DETERMINE TARGET-PRICE OBJECTIVES USING POINT & FIGURE CHART PATTERNS

> **Two methods for establishing price objectives:**
> **Vertical Count**
> **Horizontal Count**
>
> **Price targets help determine risk/reward tradeoffs.**

When considering the purchase of a particular stock, it is helpful to determine a target-price objective, which is an estimate of the potential price movement. Wall Street analysts use a variety of methods to determine price targets, most of which are based on fundamental analysis, using price/earnings, price/sales, and price/growth rate ratios. For the most part, these methods are dependant upon the ability of an analyst to project earnings, sales, and growth rates of a company accurately. If this analysis is not accurate, the price objective will be of little use to you.

Point & Figure charts create price objectives based on the supply and demand relationship. I think you will find this approach to be a more reliable method of determining the extent to which a stock might advance or decline. Since the market prices a stock based on its supply and demand relationship, not on its fundamentals, the most reliable method to determine a price objective is to quantify the supply and demand relationship when a new trend emerges for a stock. The more significant the initial amount of demand that moves a stock out of a balance pattern into a new trend of *demand in control*, the higher the target-price objective for the expected advance. Conversely, the more significant the initial amount of supply that moves a stock out of a bal-

98

ance pattern into a new trend of *supply in control*, the lower the target-price objective for the expected decline.

The main purpose of a price objective is to help you determine whether the current price provides a reasonable entry point. You wouldn't want to buy a stock that has already increased to a price close to its target. You want to make sure your expected profit is substantial relative to the amount of risk you are taking.

You can use two basic methods with Point & Figure charts to determine a target-price objective: the *vertical count* and the *horizontal count*. Both methods are effective. The vertical count measures the initial advance on the chart following a bottom and projects a price target based on the strength of that advance. I suggest using the vertical count in most situations. Certain situations, however, merit using the horizontal count.

The Vertical Count

The more demand present when a stock begins to move out of a balance pattern and into a new trend of *demand in control*, the higher the target-price objective will be for the stock. As you already know, a column of X's defines demand on a Point & Figure chart. The vertical count uses the first column of X's that produces a buy signal when a stock begins to move up from a low on its Point & Figure chart.

Vertical Count Calculation of Price Objective

1. Count the number of X's in the column producing the buy signal.
2. Multiply the number by three (because we use a three-box reversal method).
3. Multiply again by the scale used on the chart.
4. Add the result to the bottom of the chart; the bottom is usually the lowest O in the column immediately to the left of the X column.

Let's use the chart in *figure 7.1* to create a price objective. You can see that the low on this chart is $50. After the low, look for the first buy signal, defined as a higher column of X's. You can see that the double top was broken at $57 (see the arrow on the chart). Count the number of X's in this column; there are fourteen X's. Multiply the number by three ($14 \times 3 = 42$). Multiply again by the $1-scale used on the chart. (Remember, the scale is $1 for stocks that trade between $20 and $100.) Add the result to the lowest O on the chart: $42 + $50 (the low) = $92. The target-price objective for this stock is $92, based on the vertical count.

```
75 |   |   |   |   |   |   |   |   |   |   |   |   |   |   |   |   |
74 |   |   |   |   |   |   |   |   |   |   |   |   |   | X |   |   |
73 |   |   |   |   |   |   |   |   |   |   |   |   |   | X | O |   |
72 |   |   |   |   |   |   |   |   |   |   |   |   |   | X | O |   |
71 |   |   |   |   |   |   |   |   |   |   |   |   |   | X | O |   |
70 |   |   |   |   |   |   |   |   |   |   |   |   |   | X |   |   |
69 | • |   |   |   |   |   |   |   |   |   |   |   |   | X |   |   |
68 | O | • |   |   |   |   |   |   |   |   |   |   |   | X |   |   |
67 | O |   | • |   |   |   |   |   |10 |   | X |   |   |12 |   |   |
66 | O |   |   | • |   |   |   |   | X | O | X | O | X | X |   |   |
65 | O |   |   |   | • |   |   |   | X | O | X | O | X | O | X |   |
64 | O |   |   |   |   | • |   |   | X | O | X |11 | X | O | X |   |
63 | O |   |   |   |   |   | • |   | X | O |   | O |   | O |   |   |
62 | 5 | X |   |   |   |   |   | • | X |   |   |   |   |   |   |   |
61 | O | X | O |   |   |   |   |   | 9 |   |   |   |   |   |   |   |
60 | O | X | O |   |   |   |   |   | X |   |   |   |   |   |   |   |
59 | O | X | O |   |   |   |   |   | X |   |   |   |   |   |   | • |
58 | O | X | O |   |   |   |   |   | X |   |   |   |   |   |   |   |
57 | O |   | O |   | X |   | X |   | X | ← First Buy Signal
56 |   |   | O |   | X | O | X | O | 8 | X |   After The Low is
55 |   |   | O | X | X | O | X | O | X | O | X |   Established
54 |   |   | O | X | O | X | 7 | X | O | X | O | X |   |   |   | • |
53 |   |   | O | X | O | X | O |   | O | X | O |   | • |
52 |   |   | O | 6 |   | X |   |   | O | X |   | • |
51 |   |   |   |   |   |   |   |   | O | X | • |
50 |   |   |   |   |   |   |   |   | O | • |
49 |   |   |   |   |   |   |   | • |
48 |   |   |   |   |   |   |   |   |   |   |   |   |   |   |   |   |
```

figure 7.1

You can also use target-price objectives to help determine the extent to which a stock may decline when supply is in control. The more supply present when a stock begins to move out of a balance pattern and into a new trend of *supply in control,* the lower the target price objective will be for the stock. Again, as we already know, a column of O's defines supply on a Point & Figure chart. The vertical count uses the first column of O's that produces a sell signal as the stock begins to move down from the high on its chart. In this case, the calculation would be to count the number of O's producing the sell signal and multiply the number by three. Multiply again by the scale used on the chart. Subtract the result from the highest X on the chart.

The Horizontal Count

The horizontal count uses the number of columns it takes to form a balance pattern on a Point & Figure chart. This approach is based on the theory that the longer the time for a stock to break out of a balance pattern, the more significant the breakout will be. In other words, when a balance pattern is broken with a buy signal, indicating demand is beginning to take control of the stock price, the higher the number columns within the balance pattern, the higher the stock is projected to advance. Conversely, when a balance pattern is broken with a sell signal, indicating supply is beginning to take control of a stock, the more columns within the balance pattern, the lower the stock is projected to decline.

Horizontal Count Calculation of Price Objective

1. Count the number of columns in a balance pattern prior to the breakout.
2. Multiply the number by three (because we use a three-box reversal method).
3. Multiply again by the scale used on the chart.
4. Add the result to the bottom of the balance pattern; the bottom is the lowest O in the balance pattern.

Using the chart in *figure 7.2* as an example, let's calculation a price objective, using the horizontal count. You can see that a balance pattern takes shape between \$47 and \$38. The balance pattern consists of nine X and O columns. To determine the price objective after the balance pattern is broken, multiply $9 \times 3 \times \$1 = \$27$. Add the result to the low: $\$27 + \$38 = \$65$. The target-price objective for this stock is \$65.

	C1	C2	C3	C4	C5	C6	C7	C8	C9	C10	C11	C12	C13	C14
62														
61														4
60												X		X
59												X	O	X
58								X		X		X	O	X
57								X	O	X	O	X	O	
56								X	O	X	O	X		
55								X	O		O	X		
54								X			O	X		
53								X			O			
52								X						
51								X						
50								X						
49								X						
48								X						
47	X							X						
46	X	O				X		X						
45	X	O	Balance Pattern		3	O		X						
44	X	O				X	O	X						
43	2	O		X		X	O	X						
42	X	O		X	O	X	O	X						
41	X	O	X	X	O	X	O							
40	X	O	X	O	X	O	X							
39	X	O	X	O	X	O								
38	X	O		O										
37	X													
36	X													
35	X													
34	X													
33														

Balance Pattern Broken (arrow pointing to the X at row 48)

figure 7.2

When a balance pattern is broken with a sell signal, subtract the count from the highest X in the balance pattern to determine how far a stock may decline. To determine this price objective, count the number of columns in the balance pattern and multiply the number by three (because we are using a three-box reversal method). Multiply again by the chart scale. Subtract the result from the top of the balance pattern. The top is the highest X in the balance pattern.

When to Use the Vertical and Horizontal Counts

There are times when you may want to use the vertical count over the horizontal and vice versa. I want to review some situations you may encounter and help you decide which method is more appropriate.

The vertical count is the preferred method when a stock is beginning to move up from a low or down from a high. When supply is in control of a stock, the stock price will experience a downtrend. Eventually, demand will begin to meet supply, and the decline will end. After the low is in place, a buy signal will form on the Point & Figure chart if enough demand emerges. A vertical count, using the first X column that generates the buy signal, should be used in these situations.

On the chart in *figure 7.3*, you can see that the low on the chart occurs at $12. The first column of X's that produces the buy signal has fourteen X's in it. Determine the initial price objective by multiplying the number of X's by three, then multiply that number by $.50. (Remember, for stocks under $20 we use a $.50-scale.) The calculation is as follows: $14 \times 3 \times \$.50 = \$21$. Add $21 to the $12 low. The price objective is $33. Here's something to keep in mind: when the price crosses over a scale change, count the number of X's in the $.50-scale and the number in the $1-scale. Perform separate calculations for each number and add them together. For example, if there were five X's in the $.50-scale and five in the $1-scale, the vertical count would add $22.50 to the lowest O on the chart. The calculation would be $(5 \times 3 \times \$.50) + (5 \times 3 \times \$1)$, or $\$7.50 + \$15 = \$22.50$.

The horizontal count is more appropriate when a stock breaks a significant balance pattern while it is already experiencing a strong trend. When a balance pattern occurs in the midst of a demand or supply trend, it signals a consolidation of the trend. If the balance pattern breaks in the direction of the trend, a horizontal count can establish the next price objective. For example, let's assume demand is in control of a stock, and supply meets the demand to develop a balance pattern. After a brief balance pattern, demand regains control, and the chart experiences a positive breakout. A horizontal count can determine how high the price is expected to climb after the breakout.

The vertical count is the preferred method for determining an initial target-price objective as a stock begins a new trend of demand in control. Once demand takes control of the stock, the Point & Figure chart should show a series of higher X and O columns. Demand is in firm control of the stock price during this stage. As the stock price moves higher, buyers become less aggressive and more shareholders want to sell (or some combination thereof). When this occurs, there is a balance in the supply and demand relationship, and a balance pattern will form on the chart. Often you will see the balance pattern occur near the level of the initial price objective.

On the chart in *figure 7.3*, notice how the initial advance carries the stock up to $35, very close to the initial price objective of $33. At this point, supply meets the demand, and a balance pattern occurs on the chart. For approximately four months, this stock is unable to advance above the balance pattern, a sure sign that supply and demand are in balance.

If demand remains in control for the stock, the balance pattern will ultimately be broken with a buy signal, and the stock will begin the next "leg" of its advance. In this case, the horizontal count is the more appropriate way to determine the price objective after the balance pattern is broken. On the chart in *figure 7.3*, this type of balance pattern takes place between $35 and $27 and consists of nine columns. When the balance pattern is broken, we need to calculate a new price objective. Again, using the information on the chart in *figure 7.3*, the calculation is $9 \times 3 \times \$1 = \$27$. Add $27 to the low in the balance pattern ($27 + $27 = $54). The new price objective is $54.

The same scenario could occur as a stock goes through a period in which supply is in control. Again, the vertical count is the more appropriate way to determine the initial price objective as a stock begins to decline from a top. Once the supply trend is established, a balance pattern will form when demand meets the supply. If supply remains in control for the stock, the balance pattern will ultimately be broken with another sell signal, and the next "leg" of the decline will commence. In this case, the horizontal count is the more appropriate way to determine the next price objective after the stock breaks down from the balance pattern.

As you start to use Point & Figure charts and price objectives, I think you will be surprised at how many times a stock will tend to stop advancing or declining near its price objective. However, I have to warn you that the use of price objectives is not a perfect science. Don't take it to the bank. Do not consider price objectives etched in stone; rather, use them to estimate the extent to which a stock may advance or decline while in a trend.

A stock will often advance well beyond the initial price objective. Do not use the price objective as a price level for selling all of your position in the stock. However, when a stock approaches the target, you may want to sell a portion of your position because the odds of the price continuing to advance without some sort of consolidation are low. You should consider many other variables before deciding to sell, such as the sector's technical position, general market indicators, and the stock's Relative Strength chart. I'll cover all of these variables later in this book.

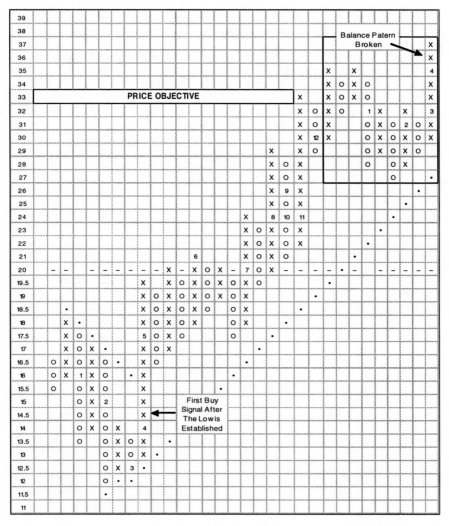

figure 7.3

Sometimes, demand does not follow through after a Point & Figure buy signal. In these cases, the stock will not reach the initial objective before a significant sell signal occurs. When this occurs, there are usually other influences holding the stock back. For example, the sector may have lost its support, or cash may be flowing out of the overall market. As you will read later in the book, market and sector activity will be key considerations for almost every investment decision. Whatever the reason may be, you have to recognize when a particular investment is not providing the desired result, and you must have the discipline to take action and minimize risk.

CHAPTER 8

RELATIVE STRENGTH CHARTS

> Relative Strength charts record stock-price movement relative to market-price movement.
>
> The charts are based on percentage movement, not dollar movement.
>
> The charts are a long-term indicator.

This chapter covers a very important tool for making good investment decisions: Relative Strength charts. As the title implies, Relative Strength charts record the price movement of a stock relative to the price movement of the general market or of another index. Use Relative Strength charts together with Point & Figure charts to make confident decisions and to implement proactive investment strategies.

Later in the book, I will show you other forms of Relative Strength charting. I will show you how sector Relative Strength charts can help you decide which industries are leading the market. Sector Relative Strength charts will help you with industry selection for your investment decisions.

In this chapter, I am going to focus on the Relative Strength chart of an individual company compared to the strength of the broad market. Although there are several different relative-strength charting methodologies, I will focus on a method I think is most effective.

Relative Strength charts are an important part of an investment discipline for several reasons:

> ➤ The charts help narrow your investment-selection process from a huge universe of stocks down to those stocks trading the strongest relative to the overall market.

➢ The charts help you focus your research efforts on the stocks with the best opportunities.

➢ The charts are an additional aid in helping you know when to sell. This benefit will help you manage risk and further define your sell discipline, something most investors desperately need.

Relative Strength charts are important because they help you avoid buying stocks that are underperforming the overall market. When considering a stock for purchase, you want to narrow your selection to the stocks likely to provide returns better than a broad market index; otherwise, you might as well just buy an index fund and go on vacation.

The most successful investors I know maintain a well-defined sell discipline. A sell discipline is a set of rules an investor establishes that helps him or her decide when to sell a stock. Disciplined investors adhere to this set of rules. Relative Strength charts will alert you when one of your positions is beginning to perform worse than the overall market. This alert will help you manage risk and is an important part of a solid sell discipline.

Individual stocks that have good patterns in their Relative Strength chart provide meaningful contribution to above-average investment returns. The correct use of Relative Strength charts in a well-rounded investment discipline is a key determinant to consistently good results.

Relative-Strength Calculations

A Relative Strength chart directly compares the price movement of a stock to the price movement of a broad market index. Most Relative Strength charts use popular indexes such as the Dow Industrials or S&P 500 Index. Although such indexes can be used effectively, I prefer to use an index that covers a broader variety of equities. The Dow Industrials and the S&P 500 only include the largest companies. If large companies are going through a period of exceptionally strong performance, such as they did during the second half of the 1990s, Relative Strength charts of smaller companies will always look poor. If the large companies go through a period of bad performance, such as they have in the first half of the 2000s, Relative Strength charts of smaller companies will always look better than they should.

I will use the S&P 1500 Index in this book. The S&P 1500 is an index of 1,500 stocks with representation in large, mid-sized, and small companies.

The calculation of a stock's relative-strength number is a simple two-step process.

Relative-Strength Calculation

1. Divide the stock's closing price by the index's closing price. For most issues, this calculation will result in a small decimal.
2. Multiply the result in step one by one hundred.

Let's work through an example using Apple Computer (AAPL). On May 17, 2006, AAPL closed at $65.25; the S&P 1500 Index closed at 288.69. The relative-strength calculation is as follows: $65.25/288.69 x 100 = 22.6021

The relative-strength number for AAPL on May 17, 2006, is 22.6021. If the number is moving *higher*, the chart tells us the price movement in AAPL shares is stronger than the movement in the S&P 1500 Index or in the market in general. If the relative-strength number is moving *lower*, the chart tells us the price movement in AAPL shares is weaker than the movement in the S&P 1500 Index or in the market in general.

Obviously, the relative-strength number for every stock will change from day to day. Don't be concerned with the daily changes in the relative-strength number. More important is the general trend of the relative-strength number. You want to know if a stock is performing stronger than the overall market on an intermediate to longer-term basis. This level of performance is where the real opportunity for profit lies in the equity market.

The next step in the process of creating a Relative Strength chart is to construct a chart using the relative-strength number. The recording of a Relative Strength chart is very similar to the Point & Figure chart. The traditional Point & Figure chart records the daily price movement of a stock. The Relative Strength chart records the daily movement in the relative-strength number. The Point & Figure chart records a stock's price movement in *absolute* terms; the Relative Strength chart records a stock's price movement in terms *relative* to the movement in the broad market.

Figure 8.1 shows a Relative Strength chart for Apple Computer. Similar to a Point & Figure chart, the Relative Strength chart is recorded using X's when the relative-strength number is rising and O's when the number is declining.

You can also see the numbers on the chart representing the first entry made in a month in place of the X or O. The chart forms patterns similar to those on a Point & Figure chart. For example, in *figure 8.1* you can see two triple tops broken in the early stages of its advance.

Apple Computer: Relative Strength Chart

Price												
33.8557												
31.9394										X		
30.1315										1	O	
28.4259										12	O	
26.8169										X	2	4
23.8670										X	3	X
22.5160										X	O	X
21.2415										11	O	
20.0392										10		
18.9049										X		
17.8348										9		
16.8253										X		
15.8729								X		8		
14.9744								2	O	X		
14.1268								X	O	X		
13.3272								1	5			
12.5728								X				
11.8611								X				
11.1898								X				
10.5564								11				
9.9588								X				
9.3951								X				
8.8633	O							X				
8.3616	O							X				
7.8883	9							10				
7.4418	O							9				
7.0206	O							8				
6.6232	O							X				
6.2483	O		Triple Tops					X				
5.8946	O		Broken					6				
5.5610	O							X				
5.2462	O				2		10	X				
4.9492	O				X	O	8	O	3			
4.6691	O	X		7	1	O	7	O	X			
4.4048	O	X	O	6	O	12	6	X	11	X		
4.1555	10	X	O	X	O	11	O	5	12			
3.9203	O	X	5	X	O	X	O	X				
3.6984	O	3	O		O	X	8	X				
3.4890	O	X		9	X	4						
3.2915	O	X		10								
3.1052	11	1										
2.9294	12	X										
2.7636	O	X										
2.6072	O											
2.4596												
2.3204												
	2			2	2		0	2				
	0			0	0		4	0				
	0			0	0		/	0				
	1			2	3		0	6				
							5					

figure 8.1

The Difference between Relative Strength and Point & Figure Charts

Relative Strength charts have similarities to a Point & Figure chart, yet there are a few significant differences:

1. The box size on the Relative Strength chart is on an increasing scale (logarithmic scale); the box size on a Point & Figure chart is a set scale based on the stock's price.

2. Fewer recordings are needed on a Relative Strength chart than on a Point & Figure chart.

3. Trend lines are not as effective on Relative Strength charts as they are on Point & Figure charts.

4. A change of columns is a more significant event on a Relative Strength chart.

The most significant difference between a Relative Strength chart and a Point & Figure chart is the scale used to record movement on the chart. The Point & Figure chart uses a fixed scale based on the price of the stock. The Relative Strength chart uses an increasing scale in which the box size increases at a fixed percentage (this is also called a logarithmic scale).

On a Point & Figure chart, if a stock is in an X column and trading at $95, the stock needs to move $1, to $96, to record another X on its chart. This recording represents a price movement of 1.05%. In contrast, if a stock is trading at $25 and moves up $1, this stock will also record another X. This $1 price movement, however, represents a 4% increase. The $25 stock has to increase approximately four times as much as a $95 stock to add another X on its chart. Therefore, on Point & Figure charts, most $95 stocks will usually have many more recordings than $25 stocks. The $95 stock will record more price movement and will generate more patterns and buy or sell signals than the $25 stocks. In a sense, Point & Figure charts discriminate against lower-priced stocks, requiring a greater percentage move to make new recordings and patterns.

The Relative Strength chart eliminates percentage inconsistencies. Relative Strength charts use a logarithmic scale to make the movement between boxes an equal percentage, regardless of the price of a stock. In other words, each box size represents an equal percentage movement in the relative-strength number, regardless of the price of the stock. Shares priced at $5 are treated equally with shares priced at $120.

The Investor Education Institute has found the best scale to use for most Relative Strength charts increases at a 6% rate. I will use a 6% increasing scale in this book, meaning the box size will increase at a rate of 6% as the scale moves higher. Referring to the chart in *figure 8.1*, the scale for the Relative Strength chart is the column farthest to the left. Each box size is 6% higher than the box directly below. For example, the lowest number shown in the scale in *figure 8.1* is 2.3204. The next higher box is 2.4596. The difference between these boxes is 0.1392, which represents 6% of the lowest box size. As you move higher on the scale, the next box is 2.6072, which represents another 6% increase. The scale continues to increase at a 6% rate. Each box size is carried out four decimals.

Looking at the highest scale number in *figure 8.1*, you will see 33.8557. This number is 1.9163 higher than the box below it, yet the number is still only 6% higher than the box directly below.

A Relative Strength chart contains fewer recordings than a Point & Figure chart. The Relative Strength chart records a stock's price movement relative to the overall market's movement. The Point & Figure chart is a recording of absolute-price movement. When a stock moves higher or lower, a price movement is recorded on the Point & Figure chart. Many times, a stock will move higher due to an advance in the general market, or the stock will move lower due to a decline in the general market. In such cases, when a stock is moving in line with the market, there will not be any recording made to the Relative Strength chart. As a result, the relative-price recording will result in fewer entries made on the chart.

The scale on the Relative Strength chart places a 6% spread from one box size to the next. In other words, the relative-price number must move 6% to add an X or O to an existing column. On most Point & Figure charts, the spread from one box to the next is much smaller than 6%. For example, an issue priced at $60 only has to move $1, or 1.67%, to add another X or O to an existing column. The increasing percentage scale on Relative Strength charts results in fewer recordings than a Point & Figure chart. Note that the Relative Strength chart for Apple Computer shown in *figure 8.1* covers nearly six years.

Since the Relative Strength chart has fewer recordings, there are some differences in its interpretation compared to that of a Point & Figure chart. First, simple buy and sell signals generated on the Relative Strength chart are significant events. A basic double top or a double bottom is an important signal on a

Relative Strength chart. Point & Figure charts require more complex patterns—such as triple tops or bottoms, bullish or bearish triangles, bullish or bearish signal reversals, etc.—before significant buy signals are generated. Although triple tops and other patterns also can form Relative Strength charts, the slower moving action on these charts will result in fewer complex chart patterns.

Trend lines are of little use on a Relative Strength chart but are an integral part of the interpretation of a Point & Figure chart. The slower development on the Relative Strength chart causes trend lines to lag behind the stock recordings. By the time most trend lines are broken, a substantial move in the Relative Strength chart has already occurred. As a result, we take the trend line out of the Relative Strength chart and base decisions more heavily on the new buy or sell signals.

A change of columns is a more significant event on the Relative Strength chart than on a Point & Figure chart. Column changes occur frequently on Point & Figure charts. Again, due to the slower movement on the Relative Strength chart, a change of columns takes longer to develop. The Relative Strength charts require a larger percentage movement to record a column change. Do you see in *figure 8.1* that the chart only had fourteen column changes in six years? Given the infrequency of column changes, you want to take special note when a stock reverses columns on its Relative Strength chart.

For the above reasons, the Relative Strength chart is a longer-term technical indicator for a stock than a Point & Figure chart. Often, buy signals will last for a number of years before a new sell signal develops and vice versa. This signal gives an investor a huge edge. When a stock gives a buy signal on its Relative Strength chart, you know the stock will perform better than the S&P 1500 Index over a significant period of time. This performance might last only three months, but it could possibly be five years or longer.

When to Buy

Relative Strength charts will help narrow your investment selection process from a huge universe of stocks down to those issues trading the strongest relative to the overall market. More than 9,300 common stocks trade on the NYSE, NASDAQ, and AMEX. Narrowing your focus within this huge universe can be extremely difficult. The investment selection process can often seem overwhelming.

For most investors, the amount of time allocated to investment research and portfolio management is limited. Relative Strength charts help focus your research efforts on the stocks with the best opportunities for superior results. By default, you will avoid wasting time on the weaker issues.

The strongest indication to buy is when a Relative Strength chart generates a new buy signal. Similar to a buy signal on a Point & Figure chart, the buy signal occurs when an X column exceeds a previous X column. As I mentioned earlier, a new relative-strength buy signal will endure for an extended length of time. As a result, stock purchases shortly after a buy signal are likely to be a strong performer for a considerable length of time. Of course, the Relative Strength chart is just one tool. In addition to the Relative Strength chart, you will also want to use the Point & Figure chart and sector-analysis tools. The combined use of all of these indicators forms a disciplined method of making confident investment decisions.

The chart in *figure 8.2* shows the relative-strength buy signal generated for Apple Computer (which I will also refer to simply as Apple) in January 2002. Prior to the buy signal, the relative-strength number was declining on this chart, falling from 9.3951 down to a low of 2.6072. At the same time, Apple's shares declined from a high of $37.59 earlier in 2000. Similar to a Point & Figure chart, when the Relative Strength chart is in a declining pattern, you do not want to consider purchasing shares.

The low on Apple's chart occurred in December 2000. After the low, you can see the first reversal up into an X column in January 2001. The reversal was the first sign that Apple's relative-strength number had stopped declining. Throughout the rest of 2001, Apple traded in a narrow range from the low up to 4.6691. There were not any new buy signals generated in 2001.

In January 2002, the chart gave a new buy signal when the column of X's advanced to 4.9492. The actual date for the buy signal was January 30, 2002, when Apple's shares closed at $12.05. This buy signal was a significant development for Apple's Relative Strength chart.

Over the next four and one-half years, Apple's Relative Strength chart moved higher (refer back to *figure 8.1*), and its shares traded up as high as $86.40. The closing price on May 17, 2006, was $65.26. This price movement represents a 441% increase, following the buy signal on Apple's Relative Strength chart.

Relative-Strength Buy Signal for Apple Computer

9.9588					|			|	
9.3951		X		|				|	
8.8633		X	O	|				|	
8.3616	O	X	O	|				|	
7.8883	O	X	9	|				|	
7.4418	8		O	|				|	
7.0206			O	|				|	
6.6232			O	|				|	
6.2483			O	|				|	
5.8946			O	|				|	
5.561			O	|				|	
5.2462			O	|				|	
4.9492			O	|				x	← Relative Strength Buy Signal
4.6691			O	X			7		1	
4.4048			O	X	O		6	O	12	
4.1555			10	X	O	X		O	11	
3.9203			O	X	5	X	O	X		
3.6984			O	3	O		O	X		
3.489			O	X			9	X		
3.2915			O	X			10	|		
3.1052			11	1				|		
2.9294			12	X				|		
2.7636			O	X				|		
2.6072			O	|				|		
2.4596				|				|		
2.3204				|				|		
				|				|		
				2				2		
				0				0		
				0				0		
				1				2		

figure 8.2

In the case of Apple Computer, the Relative Strength chart helped identify when to buy, following a substantial decline in stock price. At other times, Relative Strength charts will help identify buying opportunities in stocks that have already begun trending higher.

The chart in *figure 8.3* shows the Relative Strength chart for Cisco Systems. The chart starts in June 1995 when the chart was at its lowest level.

Here's an important point I want to share—investors rarely are fortunate enough to be following a stock at the exact time a new relative-strength buy signal is established. In the real world, there will be times when you begin to follow a new stock that has already been on a relative-strength buy or sell signal for some time. If so, you need to focus on the main trend in place on the Relative Strength chart.

Cisco Systems: Relative Strength Chart

Price	1	2	3	4	5	6	7	8	9
26.8169									
25.299									
23.867								X	
22.516								X	O
21.2415								X	O
20.0392								2	4
18.9049								X	5
17.8348								1	O
16.8253								X	
15.8729								12	
14.9744								X	
14.1268								X	
13.3272								11	
12.5728								9	
11.8611								8	
11.1898								7	
10.5564								2	
9.9588								X	
9.3951								1	
8.8633								X	
8.3616								12	
7.8883								X	
7.4418						X		X	
7.0206						8	O	11	
6.6232						7	O	X	
6.2483						X	10	X	
5.8946						6	O	X	
5.561						X	O		
5.2462						5			
4.9492				1		1			
4.6691				9	O	11			
4.4048				7	O	7			
4.1555				5	2	X			
3.9203				X	O	5			
3.6984		11		X	O	4			
3.489		X	O	2	3	X			
3.2915		10	O	X	O	X			
3.1052		9	12	X	O				
2.9294		X	1	X					
2.7636		8	O						
2.6072		7							
2.4596		X							
2.3204		X							
2.1891	O								
2.0651									
		1		1		1		9	
		9		9		9		9	
		9		9		9		/	
		6		7		8		0	
								0	

figure 8.3

Cisco Systems (which I will also refer to as Cisco) became a very popular issue in the mid-1990s. Prior to the mid-1990s, most investors had not heard of Cisco. Let's assume you began following Cisco in August 1995. At that time, Cisco's shares were trading near $3 on a split-adjusted basis. In August 1995, the Relative Strength chart was in the midst of a strong advance. All the columns of O's were higher than previous columns of O's. Cisco's shares moved from the $3 range in August 1995 to an ultimate high of $82 in March 2000.

In such a scenario, the Relative Strength chart gives you the confidence to hold on to stocks that are going through extended periods in which they are trending higher. Although you may have missed the initial buy signal earlier in the year on Cisco's Relative Strength chart, your conclusion should be that the stock is performing very strong relative to the broad market.

Cisco's Relative Strength chart progressed to form a series of higher X and O columns, generally advancing until the high reached in February 2000.

As you can see, there weren't any sell signals in Cisco's Relative Strength chart for the five-year period, from 1995 to 2000. That was a wonderful time to own Cisco's shares. Investors using Relative Strength charts for assessing the progress of the stock had a valuable tool for making better-informed decisions.

When to Sell

Although the decision on when to buy is important, for most investors, the decision on when to sell is even more important. Most investors will admit they have a hard time deciding when they should sell a stock. At the center of the problem are human emotions and psychological influences.

When faced with the difficult decision of when to sell a stock, any number of factors can get in the way of making a clear decision. When faced with the decision of when to sell a stock you have held for a long period, the decision can be especially difficult. Your long-term investment has probably treated you well over the years; otherwise, you would have already sold. Psychologically, investors have difficulty parting with stock that has held a positive emotional attachment; obviously, previous, strong stock performance is definitely a positive emotion. The Relative Strength chart is an invaluable tool to help get you through such difficult decisions.

Using the example for Cisco Systems, a strong sell signal occurred in October 2000 on its Relative Strength chart. You can see this sell signal in *figure 8.4*. As I mentioned earlier, the Relative Strength chart peaked in February 2000. The first sell signal on the chart was generated when the first lower O column occurred at 16.8253. The actual date of the sell signal was October 30, 2000, when Cisco's shares closed the day at $48.06. The price continued declining for the next two years. Cisco's price eventually dropped below $10.

Most long-term shareholders were unwilling to sell Cisco. The stock had made a considerable sum of money for those lucky enough to hold the stock for the five years prior to the relative-strength sell signal. Psychologically, cognitive bias began to control investors' minds, and they believed the upward trends from the past would perpetuate into the future.

In addition to cognitive bias, the feeling that one had **missed the optimal time to sell** also prevented many investors from selling Cisco at the $48 level. Knowing the shares had traded $34 higher eight months ago caused the investor to want to **wait until the price gets back to the high** before selling. Unfortunately, some stocks do not get back to their highs.

There are a number of other emotions and psychological characteristics that affect the decision to sell—one of the biggest is tax liability. Do yourself a favor and never let the fact that you have to pay taxes on a profitable investment prevent you from selling the investment. In my career, I have seen many poor decisions made solely on tax considerations. Taxes should be *a* consideration, not *the* consideration. Although there are strategies to control and minimize tax liabilities, paying a tax on your realized gains is a cost of successful investing. The alternative is not very desirable. Remember, if you have a $45 per share profit in a stock, at no time should you consider all $45 yours; your profit is the $45 minus any capital-gain taxes. Just think of the people who didn't sell their Enron, WorldCom, Cisco, Lucent, or Microsoft stock because they were unwilling to pay capital-gains taxes. In hindsight, I'm sure they would gladly trade a tax liability for their realized losses.

New Relative-Strength Sell Signal for Cisco Systems

Price	1	2	3	4	5	6	7	8	9	10	11
26.8169											
25.299											
23.867							X				
22.516							X	O			
21.2415							X	O	6		
20.0392							2	4	X	O	
18.9049							X	5	X	O	
17.8348							1	O		10	
16.8253							X			O	← Relative Strength Chart Sell Signal
15.8729							12			12	
14.9744							X			O	
14.1268							X			O	
13.3272							11			1	
12.5728							9			O	
11.8611							8			2	
11.1898							7			O	
10.5564							2			O	
9.9588							X			O	
9.3951							1			O	
8.8633							X			O	
8.3616							12			3	
7.8883							X			O	
7.4418						X	X			O	
7.0206					8	O	11			O	X
6.6232					7	O	X			O	X
6.2483					X	10	X			O	X
5.8946					6	O	X			4	
5.561					X	O					
5.2462					5						
4.9492				1	1						
4.6691				9	O	11					
4.4048				7	O	7					
4.1555				5	2	X					
3.9203				X	O	5					
3.6984			11	X	O	4					
3.489			X	O	2	3	X				
3.2915			10	O	X	O	X				
3.1052			9	12	X	O					
2.9294			X	1	X						
2.7636			8	O							
2.6072			7								
2.4596			X								
2.3204			X								
2.1891		O									
2.0651											
			1	1	1		9			2	
			9	9	9		9			0	
			9	9	9		/			0	
			6	7	8		0			1	
							0				

figure 8.4

The sell signal on Cisco's Relative Strength chart on October 30, 2000, was a clear indication the issue had peaked. Following the sell signal, statistics show Cisco is likely to perform worse than the market for a considerable length of time. Using Relative Strength charts to help decide when to sell will provide a logical basis for the answer. I do not suggest using Relative Strength charts alone to make all your sell decisions. When used in combination with Point & Figure charts, as well as with sector and market indicators, Relative Strength charts will reduce the emotional and psychological influences on your sell decisions.

Relative Strength charts provide another important benefit: they will help you avoid buying stocks that are beginning an extended period in which they will underperform the market. Relative Strength charts help you avoid the temptation of buying stocks that appear cheap but, in reality, are in the midst of a strong downtrend and headed lower.

The Cisco case study is a good example. After the shares dropped from their high of \$82 in March 2000 to \$48 in October 2000, many investors thought the time was right to buy Cisco low, expecting the price to eventually advance back toward its high. In reality, October 2000 was a poor time to buy Cisco, as the shares proceeded to decline for the next two years.

Another good example is Lucent Technologies (which I will also refer to as Lucent). The Relative Strength chart played a key role in helping investors avoid buying after what appeared to be a "correction" in Lucent's shares. *Figure 8.5* shows the Relative Strength chart for Lucent. This stock started trading as a public company in May 1996 at a price near \$7. The first recording on its Relative Strength chart was an X column, showing that Lucent's shares were performing better than the broad market. The Relative Strength chart continued moving higher until peaking at 26.8169 in November 1999. Those first three years that Lucent traded was an ideal time to own these shares. The price moved from \$7 to \$64.47, staging a nine-fold increase. In January 2000, Lucent suffered a sizable correction in price. The price dropped below \$40 at that time, down 40% from the high reached the prior month. To many investors, this drop in price appeared to be the opportunity to buy Lucent.

Lucent Technologies: Relative Strength Chart

Price										
28.4259	I		I		I		I			
26.8169	I		I			X				
25.299	I		I	X		11	O			
23.867	I		I	7	O	X	O	X		
22.516	I		I	4	O	X	1	X	O	
21.2415	I		I	X	10		O	3	O	
20.0392	I		X		X		O	2	O	← Relative Strength Sell Signal
18.9049	I		X	O	12		O	X	4	
17.8348	I		7	O	11		O	X	O	
16.8253	I		6	9	X		O		7	
15.8729	I		X	10	X	I		O		
14.9744	I		X	O	X	I		O		
14.1268	I		4	O	I	I		8		
13.3272	I		X		I	I		O		
12.5728	I		3		I	I		9		
11.8611	I		X		I	I		O		
11.1898	I		2		I	I		O		
10.5564	X		1		I	I		O		
9.9588	7	O	X		I	I		O		
9.3951	6	O	X		I	I		10		
8.8633	5	12	I		I	I		O		
8.3616	1		I		I	I		O		
7.8883	10		I		I	I		O		
7.4418	X		I		I	I		O		
7.0206	9		I		I	I		O		
6.6232	5		I		I	I		11	X	
6.2483	X		I		I	I		O	X	O
5.8946	X		I		I	I		O	X	O
5.561	X		I		I	I		O	X	O
5.2462	I		I		I		I	12		O
4.9492	I		I		I		I			O
4.6691	I		I		I		I			O
4.4048	I		I		I		I			
	1		1		1		2			
	9		9		9		0			
	9		9		9		0			
	7		8		9		0			

figure 8.5

In reality, Lucent's Relative Strength chart gave its first sell signal during the January 2000 "price correction." By following this chart, you know Lucent's price decline was not the result of a correction but the beginning of a major decline that would endure for the foreseeable future. Following the Relative Strength chart would have told you Lucent's $40 price was not the low. The chart would have indicated that these shares were expected to decline further. In the case of Lucent, the decline lasted nearly three years; Lucent ultimately bottomed below $1 in October 2002.

Start Using Relative Strength Charts Now

I strongly suggest you begin tracking the Relative Strength chart for any stock you own or are considering to acquire. The Investor Education Institute's Web site (http://www.institute4investors.com) lists the Relative Strength chart for virtually any stock. You can also view the Point & Figure chart of any stock at this Web site. I think you will find these two tools invaluable in your effort to make good investment decisions.

The site also posts daily reports, showing new, important signals on the Point & Figure and Relative Strength charts in an extensive research database.

Another excellent tool on this Web site allows you to create your own portfolio or list of stocks, and the charting system will automatically create a daily report on any important activity on the Point & Figure and Relative Strength charts for your stocks. Multiple lists are allowed. For example, you can create separate lists for your IRA account and any other accounts and get a report on any new developments to the holdings in each account. This feature allows you to monitor important changes to your holdings, making it easier for you to manage your investments.

CHAPTER 9

COMBINED USE OF POINT & FIGURE AND RELATIVE STRENGTH CHARTS: A STRATEGY FOR CONFIDENT DECISIONS

> Using Relative Strength + Point & Figure charts = profitable investments.
>
> A buy signal on both charts is the optimal technical position.
>
> A sell signal on both charts is the weakest technical position.

You now know the basics of both Point & Figure and Relative Strength charts. This chapter will help you tie both forms of charting into a strategy for profitable investment decisions.

First, a quick review: Point & Figure charts record the absolute-price movement in a stock. They measure the supply and demand relationship in any stock, helping you understand if demand or supply is in control, where balance patterns exist, and the main trend line in force.

Relative Strength charts record the price movement of a stock relative to a market index. They do not necessarily indicate if a stock is trending higher or lower at any particular point in time. They indicate if a stock is performing better or worse than the overall market.

When the broad market is declining, some stocks will decline more than others. In this case, stocks declining at a greater rate than the broad market will have a *weak* Relative Strength chart; those declining at a slower rate than the broad market will have a *strong* Relative Strength chart. A strong Relative Strength chart does not necessarily indicate that a stock is rising during times when the overall market is declining. Using Relative Strength charts in isolation will help you buy stocks that are stronger than the broad market, but those issues may not necessarily be advancing in absolute-price terms. Determining if a stock is advancing in absolute price is where the Point & Figure chart comes into the equation. Before you decide to buy, you want to know if an issue is advancing in absolute terms *and* in relative terms.

Using Point & Figure charts in isolation is also not desirable. During times when the broad market is rising, many Point & Figure charts will look strong. Even weaker stocks will sometimes have good patterns on their Point & Figure chart simply because demand is strong for the general market. When this occurs, it can be hard for an investor to focus on the best stocks to purchase. An investor could become like a "kid in a candy store" when all issues are advancing. At these times, you want to be able to focus on the issues with the highest profit potential. Relative Strength charts comes into play when you need to narrow down the universe of stocks and find the highest performers. Relative Strength charts help draw your attention to the top performers and avoid wasting time looking at the weaker issues. Combining the use of Point & Figure and Relative Strength charts will give you a competitive edge.

Entering Positions

In a perfect world, both the Point & Figure and Relative Strength charts for a stock will give a strong buy signal at the same time. In the real world, both buy signals rarely happen simultaneously. Usually, one chart will lead the other. The Point & Figure chart may have developed a strong buy signal well before the Relative Strength chart develops one of its own. At other times, the Relative Strength chart will be the first to develop the buy signal, and the Point & Figure chart will follow. In some cases, there could be months in between each chart's signal. Whichever chart gives the first signal is immaterial. The ideal strategy is to have *both* charts on a buy signal before buying. While this strategy takes patience, the results are well worth the time and effort.

For a case study, let's revisit the Apple Computer example used in the chapter on Relative Strength charts (chapter 8). The chart in *figure 9.1* shows the Relative Strength chart for Apple. Again, this chart gave the first buy signal in January 2002. This buy signal indicated Apple's shares had begun a period of performing better than the S&P 1500 Index. At the time of the relative-strength buy signal, Apple's shares closed at $12.05.

Relative-Strength Buy Signal: Apple Computer

9.9588				I			I	
9.3951		X		I			I	
8.8633		X	O	I			I	
8.3616	O	X	O	I			I	
7.8883	O	X	9	I			I	
7.4418	8		O	I			I	
7.0206			O	I			I	
6.6232			O	I			I	
6.2483			O	I			I	
5.8946			O	I			I	
5.561			O	I			I	
5.2462			O	I			I	
4.9492			O	I		X		← Relative Strength Buy Signal
4.6691			O	X		7	1	
4.4048			O	X	O	6	O	12
4.1555			10	X	O	X	O	11
3.9203			O	X	5	X	O	X
3.6984			O	3	O		O	X
3.489			O	X		9	X	
3.2915			O	X		10	I	
3.1052			11	1			I	
2.9294			12	X			I	
2.7636			O	X			I	
2.6072			O	I			I	
2.4596				I			I	
2.3204				I			I	
				I			I	
				2			2	
				0			0	
				0			0	
				1			2	

figure 9.1

Figure 9.2 shows Apple's Point & Figure chart. You can see the big decline in Apple's shares from the high in September 2000 at $32 all the way down to $7. By the end of 2000, the entire decline in Apple's shares had already occurred. Through most of 2001, Apple's shares never declined below the 2000 low. Apple's stock reflected a classic balance pattern on the Point & Figure chart and indicated that supply and demand were in balance. During this period the stock was unable to trend higher or lower on a sustained basis.

Apple's shares held their own in 2001 and early 2002. During the same period, the market was trending lower, and the S&P 1500 Index was declining. This market decline caused Apple's Relative Strength chart to begin an advance (see *figure 9.1*). In January 2002, the Relative Strength chart gave the buy signal due to the broad market declining while Apple's shares were holding stable. If you were using the Relative Strength chart in isolation, you might have taken the buy signal as a time to buy Apple.

Apple Computer: Point & Figure Chart

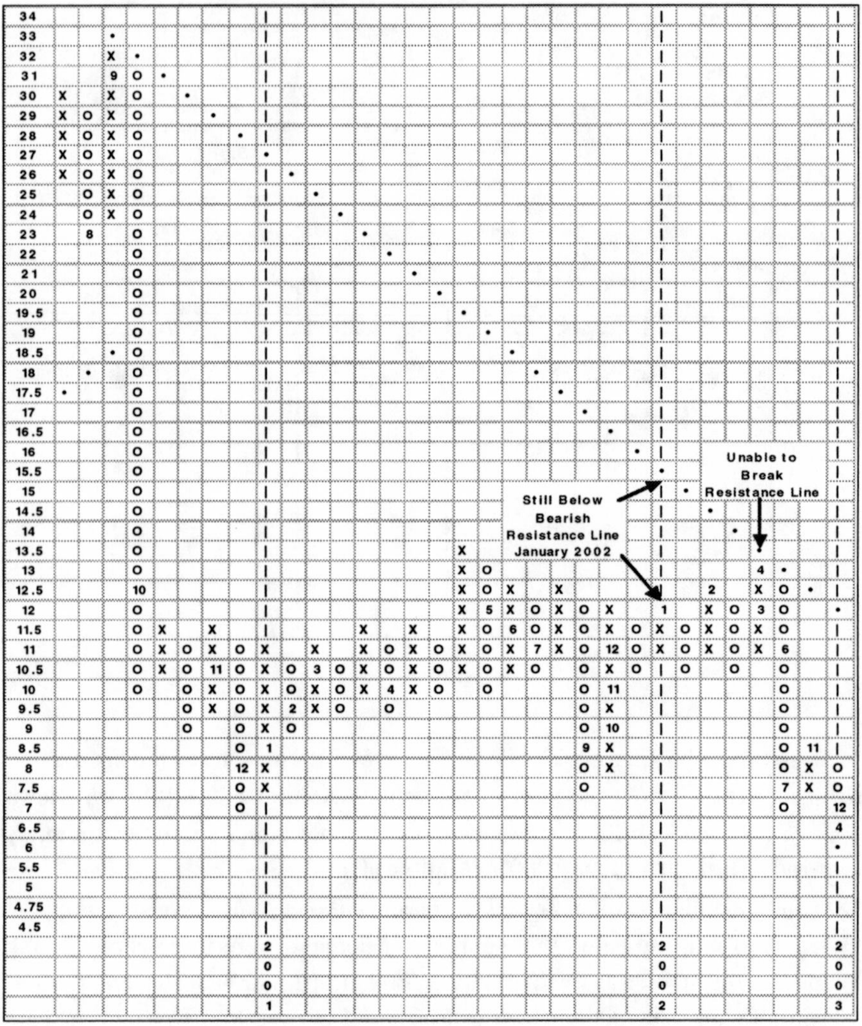

Annotations on chart:
- **Unable to Break Resistance Line**
- **Still Below Bearish Resistance Line January 2002**

figure 9.2

The Point & Figure chart told a different story. In January 2002, you can see Apple was still below the bearish resistance line, indicating that the main trend was still negative (*figure 9.2*). (Remember, supply is still in control until the bearish resistance line is penetrated; you want to avoid buying stocks that are trading below this trend line.) A stock will not be able to trend higher on a long-term basis until the resistance line is broken, and a bullish support line has begun. Therefore, because Apple was below the bearish resistance line, the Point & Figure chart did not give the same buy signal as the Relative Strength chart in January 2002.

In April 2002, Apple approached the bearish resistance line on the Point & Figure chart but was unable to break through the line (*figure 9.2*). The stock then proceeded to fall back near its low by the end of 2002.

Combining the use of the Relative Strength chart and the Point & Figure chart would have helped you avoid taking a position in Apple in January 2002 and would have protected you from owning a stock about to decline to a new low.

While Apple's shares made a new low in early 2003, the Relative Strength chart maintained a buy signal (see *figure 9.3*). Notice how each new column of X's and O's was higher than the previous columns of X's and O's. This trend was encouraging and indicated that Apple did not decline as much as the S&P 1500 Index. Although Apple was declining in absolute terms, in relative terms, the stock was holding up quite well.

Meanwhile, after Apple's shares made a low in April 2003, the Point & Figure chart began to reflect Apple's price moving up throughout 2003. Finally, in October 2003, the stock penetrated the bearish resistance line at $12 (see *figure 9.4*). (When the resistance line is broken, a bullish support line begins.) The main trend on the Point & Figure chart changed from down to up.

As demand continued to lift Apple's shares higher, the stock broke out of its long-standing balance pattern when the price reached $14 in March 2004. This breakout was a strong buy signal on the Point & Figure chart, indicating that demand was beginning to take control of Apple's shares.

At this point, both the Relative Strength *and* Point & Figure charts were on strong buy signals. (When both charts are on buy signals, you have the ideal situation to enter a position for a long- to intermediate-term basis.) Since both of these charts were positive, all indications pointed to the fact that Apple was moving higher on a relative- *and* absolute-price basis; the indication meant you had a strong chance of making a profitable investment.

Apple Computer: Relative Strength Chart

5.5610	O									
5.2462	O			2		#				
4.9492	O			X	O	8				
4.6691	O	X	7	1	O	7				
4.4048	O	X	O	6	O	12	6	X		
4.1555	10	X	O	X	O	11	O	5		
3.9203	O	X	5	X	O	X	O	X		
3.6984	O	3	O		O	X	8	X		
3.489	O	X			9	X	4			
3.2915	O	X			10					
3.1052	11	1								
2.9294	12	X								
2.7636	O	X								
2.6072	O									
2.4596										

Apple Maintained Relative Strength Buy, No Sell Signal Shown

Date columns:
2 0 0 1 — 2 2 0 0 — 0 4 / 0 5

figure 9.3

New Point & Figure Buy Signal for Apple Computer

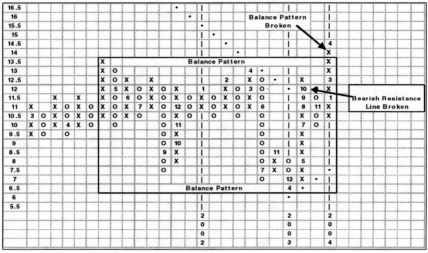

Balance Pattern Broken

Bearish Resistance Line Broken

Balance Pattern

figure 9.4

Figures 9.5 and *9.6* show the progression of the Relative Strength and Point & Figure charts for Apple Computer through March 31, 2005. From March 2004, when both the Point & Figure and Relative Strength charts were clearly trending higher, Apple continued to perform well on a relative *and* an absolute basis. (Remember, when both the Relative Strength and Point & Figure charts maintain strong patterns, they give you the confidence to hold your positions as they trend upward.)

Shortly after Apple broke the bearish resistance line and balance pattern on its Point & Figure chart (*figure 9.6*), the stock traded up to $17. At this point, supply met demand, and the price consolidated in a range from $17 to $14.50. As the chart indicates, a triangle pattern was formed during the consolidation. (Recall that the triangle pattern develops when the chart records *lower* X's and *higher* O's.) For Apple, the consolidation occurred between June and August 2004; during this time, neither demand nor supply was dominant.

Eventually, a triangle pattern has to be broken. Most of the time, a triangle pattern will be broken in the direction of the trend already in place. In the case of Apple, the trend was advancing. In August 2004, the triangle pattern was broken, and we saw another strong buy signal for Apple's shares on its Point & Figure chart. (Before acting on such a buy signal, you should review the Relative Strength chart to make sure the relative trend is still progressing upward.) *Figure 9.5* shows that the Relative Strength chart rose from 5.8946 in June to 7.0206 in August. While Apple's price movement was flat for those two months, the relative movement was advancing. In August, both charts were still on buy signals and trending higher. The positive breakout of the triangle pattern and the combined buy signals gave a green light to take action. If you had not bought Apple in March 2004, now was a good time to take a position. If you already owned Apple, now was a good time to add to your position. Looking at the chart in *figure 9.6*, you can see that the price of the stock exploded to $34 in three months, following the breakout from the triangle pattern.

The buy signals on both the Relative Strength and Point & Figure charts indicated Apple's shares were beginning to trend higher. (As an investor, you want to position yourself in stocks that are beginning such trends. The idea is to attempt to participate in trends as they are emerging and to stay with those trends as long as the stock's Relative Strength and Point & Figure charts show a positive pattern.) In the case of Apple Computer, following this strategy would have led you into buying Apple's stock near $14 and into owning the stock as it surged for the next two years.

Apple Computer: Relative Strength Chart

16.8253		I			I	I				I
15.8729		I			I	I				X
14.9744		I			I	I				2
14.1268		I			I	I				X
13.3272		I			I	I				1
12.5726		I			I	I				X
11.8611		I			I	I				X
11.1898		I			I	I				X
10.5564		I			I	I				11
9.9588		I			I	I				X
9.3951		I			I	I				X
8.8633	O	I			I	I				X
8.3616	O	I			I	I				X
7.8883	9	I			I	I				10
7.4418	O	I			I	I				9
7.0206	O	I			I	I				8
6.6232	O	I			I	I				X
6.2483	O	I								X
5.8946	O	I	Another Buy Signal							6
5.561	O	I			I	I			➘	X
5.2462	O	I			2	I	10			X
4.9492	O	I			X	O	8	O		3
4.6691	O	X	7		1	O	7	O		X
4.4048	O	X	O	6	O	12	6	X	11	X
4.1555	10	X	O	X	O	11	O	5	12	I
3.9203	O	X	5	X	O	X	O	X		I
3.6984	O	3	O		O	X	8	X		I
3.489	O	X			9	X	4			I
3.2915	O	X			10	I	I			I
3.1052	11	1				I	I			I
2.9294	12	X			I	I				I
2.7636	O	X			I	I				I
2.6072	O	I			I	I				I
2.4596		I			I	I				I
		2			2	2				0
		0			0	0				4
		0			0	0				/
		1			2	3				0
										5

figure 9.5

Apple Breaks Bullish Triangle Pattern

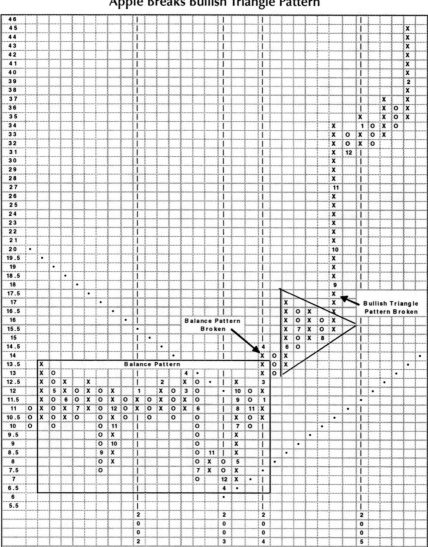

figure 9.6

Exiting Positions

For most investors, making sell decisions is more difficult than making buy decisions. Combining the use of Point & Figure and Relative Strength charts will help you make better-informed and well-timed decisions when exiting your positions. When both the absolute- and relative-price movements are negative, there is no reason to stay with a position.

Figure 9.7 shows a Point & Figure chart for Bristol-Myers Squibb (BMY), covering the period from March 2001 to January 2002. A massive balance pattern developed between the prices of $60 on the high end and $51 on the low end. The price hit $51 in March and September but was unable to break through this price level. The lows in May and June also approached this level but held at $52. (As you know, when you see a balance pattern developing, your conclusion should be that neither demand nor supply is in control of trading.) In December 2001, the balance pattern was broken with a strong sell signal. This break indicated that supply was in control of trading for BMY and that the absolute-price movement should continue lower. The chart in *figure 9.7* shows the price dropping to $45 in January 2002.

Bristol-Myers Squibb: Point & Figure Chart

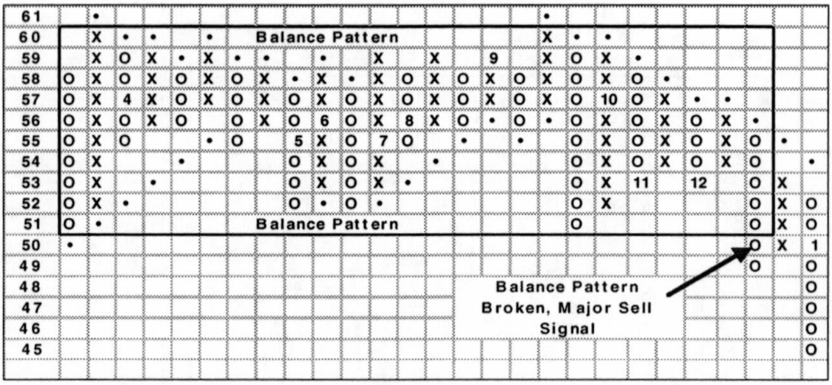

figure 9.7

Figure 9.8 shows the Relative Strength chart for BMY. You can see that the Relative Strength chart also gave a sell signal in January 2002 when the number fell to 18.9049. The sell signal indicated the relative performance for

BMY had moved lower and was likely to do so for a significant amount of time. Note that the relative-strength sell signal developed just one month following the sell signal on BMY's Point & Figure chart. As a result, in January 2002, *both* the Point & Figure *and* Relative Strength charts had developed strong sell signals for BMY. A BMY shareholder should have viewed the double sell signals as an indication to exit his or her position.

Bristol-Myers Squibb: Relative Strength Chart

Price								
28.4259			|		|		|	
26.8169			|		|		|	
25.299		12	|	X	|		|	
23.867		X	O	9	O		|	
22.516		11	O	X	O		|	
21.2415		X	1	X	12		|	
20.0392	O	X	5		1 ←		|	Relative Strength Sell Signal
18.9049	O	10		O			|	
17.8348	O	X	|	3			|	
16.8253	O	X	|	O			|	
15.8729	7		|	O			|	
14.9744			|	4			|	
14.1268			|	O			|	
13.3272			|	O	9		|	
12.5728			|	O	X	O		
11.8611			|	5	X	O		
11.1898			|	7		3		
10.5564			|		|	3		
9.9588			|		|	O		
9.3951			|		|	7		
8.8633			|		|	11		
8.3616			|		|	O		
			|		|	1		
			2		2	2		
			0		0	0		
			0		0	0		
			1		2	6		

figure 9.8

Every successful investor needs a *sell discipline* to avoid holding through devastating declines. An investor who is not following a sell discipline may find that any number of emotional and psychological influences will cause them to hold on to a stock. (You may want to refer back to the "When to Sell" section in the chapter on Relative Strength charts (chapter 8) when I cover some of the emotional and psychological influences.) Yet, when both the Point & Figure and Relative Strength charts are negative, the charts are clearly indicating that a stock is moving lower on a relative *and* an absolute basis. When both sell signals occur, there is no reason to hold a position.

Figure 9.9 shows BMY's Point & Figure chart through May 16, 2006. When the sell signals developed on BMY's Point & Figure and Relative Strength charts in December 2001 and January 2002, the time was ideal to sell these shares. The price declined from near $50 to $19.50 over the next seven or eight months.

Bristol-Myers Squibb: Point & Figure Chart

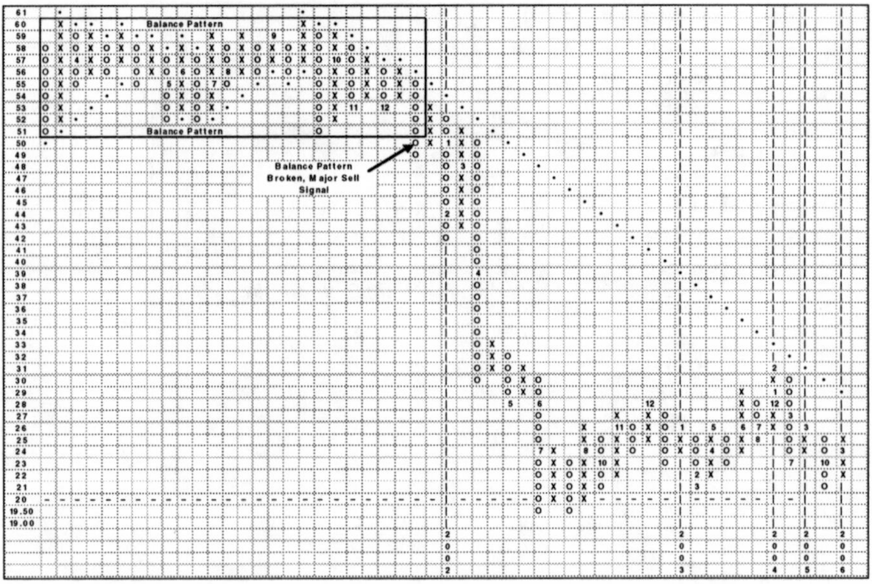

figure 9.9

BMY continued to be a poor performer on a relative and an absolute basis during 2002. (Again, when both the Relative Strength and Point & Figure charts maintain weak patterns, you have a clear indication to sell. Similarly, you have the necessary information to avoid the trap of buying a stock that is low with the hopes the price will return to an upward trend.)

Aggressive investors occasionally use the combined weakness in a stock's Point & Figure and Relative Strength charts to profit from declining shares. The strategy is called *selling short*. The optimal time to sell short is when both charts are *developing* sell signals. Unless you fully understand selling short, you should not attempt the strategy without professional help.

Decision Matrix for Combined Use of Charts

Keeping straight the best actions when combining Point & Figure charts with Relative Strength charts can be confusing. In total, there are sixteen different combinations when using Point & Figure and Relative Strength charts. To assist with drawing conclusions and making good decisions for these combinations, I have created a decision matrix (*figure 9.10*). Before looking at the matrix, let's review possible scenarios that occur when we combine the two charts:

➤ As we know, Point & Figure charts can have a buy or a sell signal. While certain buy and sell patterns are stronger indicators than others are, the basic signal is either buy or sell. Point & Figure charts can also show demand in control with a bullish support line or supply in control with a bearish resistance line. The best combination on a Point & Figure chart is a buy signal with demand in control; the worst is a sell signal with supply in control.

➤ When a Point & Figure chart shows a buy signal that is *below* the bearish resistance line, supply is in control on a long-term basis, and the price movement is only rising over the short term. A possibility does exist that the stock will create a new balance pattern and may ultimately form a bottom. If such a bottom occurs, the stock will still have to penetrate the resistance line prior to beginning a significant advance. In other words, as long as the stock stays below the bearish resistance line, there is no strong buy signal.

Point & Figure Chart		Relative Strength Chart		When Considering Purchase	Suggested Action
Trend	Signal	Signal	Column		When You Own
Up	Buy	Buy	X	Buy	Hold/Buy More
Up	Sell	Buy	X	Wait for P&F Buy or Bullish Pattern	Hold/Buy More if P&F Chart Develops Buy Signal or Bullish Pattern
Down	Buy	Buy	X	Wait for P&F Chart to Penetrate Resistance Line	Hold-Plan Exit Strategy
Down	Sell	Buy	X	Wait for Improvement in P&F Chart	Hold/Sell Partial Position/Risk Management Strategies/Plan Exit Strategy
Down	Sell	Sell	O	Avoid	Sell Immediately
Down	Buy	Sell	O	Avoid	Sell
Down	Sell	Sell	O	Avoid	Sell
Up	Buy	Sell	O	Wait for Improvement in Relative Strength	Hold/Sell Partial Position/Risk Management Strategies/Plan Exit Strategy
Down	Sell	Sell	X	Avoid	Sell
Down	Buy	Sell	X	Long-Term Investors Avoid/Possible Short-Term Trade	Long-Term Investors-Sell/Sell Partial Position/Risk-Management Strategies Short-Term Traders-Hold/Risk-Management Strategies/Plan Exit Strategy
Up	Sell	Sell	X	Wait for Buy Signals to Develop/Plan Strategy to Buy	Hold/Sell Partial Position/Risk-Management Strategies/Plan Exit Strategy Short-Term Traders-Wait for Buy Signal or Bullish Pattern on P&F Chart
Up	Buy	Sell	X	Buy/Buy Partial Position/Possible Short-Term Trade	Hold/Risk-Management Strategies
Down	Sell	Buy	O	Avoid	Sell/Sell Partial Position/Risk-Management Strategies/Plan Exit Strategy
Down	Buy	Buy	O	Wait for P&F Chart to Penetrate Resistance Line	Sell Partial Position/Risk-Management Strategies/Plan Exit Strategy
Up	Sell	Buy	O	Wait for P&F Buy or Relative Strength X Col	Risk-Management Strategies/Plan Exit Strategy
Up	Buy	Buy	O	Buy/Buy Partial Position	Hold/Buy More on Pullback/Risk-Management Strategies

figure 9.10

➢ When a Point & Figure chart reflects a sell signal that is *above* the bullish support line, demand is in control on a long-term basis, and the price is only falling over the short term. This stock may also be in the process of creating a new balance pattern and may ultimately form a top on the chart. If such a top occurs, the stock will still have to penetrate the support line prior to a significant decline. Therefore, as long as the stock is able to hold above the support line, there is no strong sell signal.

➢ The Relative Strength chart can also reflect a buy or sell signal, indicating that the long-term relative number is advancing or declining. The Relative Strength chart can also be in an X or O column, indicating that the relative number is rising or falling on a shorter-term basis. The best combination on a Relative Strength chart is a buy signal while in an X column. The worst combination is a sell signal while in an O column.

➢ When a stock has a relative-strength buy signal, but in a column of O's, the chart reflects that the relative strength is advancing on a long-term basis but falling on a short-term basis. When the chart reflects a sell signal but in an X column, the chart is indicating that the relative strength is declining on a long-term basis but rising in the short term. With either of these mixed scenarios, you could consider the relative-strength indicator neutral.

Prior to making a decision to buy a stock, you want to see positive patterns and trends in both the Point & Figure and Relative Strength charts for an individual stock. In terms of the decision matrix, your most profitable investment opportunities will have characteristics similar to those shown by Apple Computer's charts in late 2003 or early 2004 as its profitable trend was just beginning to emerge. The decision matrix for Apple computer looked like this:

Leading Issue

Symbol	Company Name	Point & Figure Signal	Trend	Relative Strength Signal	Column
AAPL	Apple Computer	BUY	Up	Buy	X

figure 9.11

137

The technical characteristics shown in *figure 9.11* are indicative of a leading stock in the market. I call stocks that sport these characteristics as a *leading issue* or a *relative-strength leader*. Owning stocks that exhibit these technical trends will help you participate in the strongest trends available in the market. The key to making profitable investment decisions is patience and discipline. Too many investors are impatient, feeling the need to put their money to work immediately. Successful investors are patient, letting the necessary indicators come together before investing their hard-earned money. Discipline is also required to achieve success. When entering into new positions, be disciplined. Don't try to force the charts to do what you want. Read what the charts are indicating and develop strategies based on those indications.

In the case of Bristol-Myers Squibb, as its Point & Figure and Relative Strength chart began to descend, the decision matrix for this issue looked like this:

Lagging Issue

		Point & Figure		Relative Strength	
Symbol	Company Name	Signal	Trend	Signal	Column
BMY	Bristol-Myers Squibb	SELL	Down	Sell	O

figure 9.12

The characteristics shown in *figure 9.12* indicate a weak or lagging issue in the market. I call stocks that sport these characteristics as *lagging issues*. Being disciplined means you should avoid buying issues with the characteristics in *figure 9.12*.

Equally, if not more important, is your sell discipline. You should always have a sell discipline for your investments. If you own a stock that shows the characteristics of a weak or lagging issue, take defensive action. Sometimes a sell discipline means making difficult decisions. Not every investment will work out as expected. Don't let your emotions get the best of you or get you in trouble. If the Point & Figure and Relative Strength charts develop bearish patterns and strong sell signals, have the discipline to sell.

Finally, if the charts are giving mixed signals or key information is missing from the equation, wait out the investment. Here is a philosophy I use—when in doubt, sit it out. If the charts do not look right or if you find yourself uncertain as to what to do, stay on the sidelines. You do not always have to be in the game. To coin a phrase, "There will be another boat leaving the dock," so don't feel that you must be on the boat in front of you. Yes, you might occasionally miss an opportunity, but more likely, you won't lose money on a "questionable" investment.

SECTION 3

SECTOR ANALYSIS

CHAPTER 10

SECTOR ANALYSIS: THE MOST IMPORTANT LEVEL OF ANALYSIS

> Sector analysis accounts for 75%–80%
> of an individual stock's movement.
>
> Sector analysis makes individual stock selection easier.

At this point, I want to delve into an exciting way to apply Point & Figure charting. This chapter covers what I consider to be the most important component of successful investing: sector analysis. Analyzing sectors is a critical step to disciplined investment selection and portfolio management.

When choosing investments, most individuals spend little to no time analyzing the overall market or sectors of the market. Instead, most people overwhelmingly pick a company and use fundamental analysis to evaluate it and its stock. Choosing an investment in this manner is known as the "bottom up" approach: an investor starts with the smallest part of the market—that is, a stock—and focuses his or her effort on understanding its performance. Ignoring market and sector trends leads to inconsistent results because an investor then focuses on only a small part of what causes a stock's price to move.

The popularity of the "bottom up" approach is not surprising, as most individual investors find the analysis of market and sector trends to be overwhelming. Most investors would prefer to read an article in a magazine or get a tip from a friend about the next hot stock. In this case, the investor is focusing on the "story" or appeal of a company. Everyone wants to try to hit it big by finding the next Microsoft or Dell Computer. Certainly, an investor can occasionally be successful in finding the next hot stock. However, considering there are more than ten thousand publicly traded companies in the United States alone, consistently finding the next hot stock is like trying to find a needle in a haystack. You can achieve consistent results easier by first identifying important market trends and by isolating sectors that are emerging as leaders prior to selecting individual stocks.

The directional price movement of an industry or sector plays a meaningful influence on the price movement of stocks in that sector. Unless the sector trends are favorable for the company under analysis, the fundamental position of a company translates into only a small part of stock-price movement. A company that offers good fundamentals but is a member of a sector with a declining trend will probably decline, too. Companies with good fundamentals that are a member of a rising sector will experience a rising stock price with a high degree of probability. Hence, researching sectors as a prelude to selecting stocks leads to both a greater understanding of the investment environment and—what we're all after—better returns.

Analyzing the market first, then sectors, and then individual stocks within the strongest sectors is considered a top-down approach. This method is thought to be more difficult, but using Point & Figure charting as the cornerstone of your analysis makes it a logical and straightforward process. In the next section of this book, I will cover broad market analysis. For now, we need to examine how sectors affect stock-price movement.

Simply put, the price movement in any sector has a large influence on the price movement of any stock within the sector. While different industry sectors will rise and fall for different reasons, the majority of stocks in a sector tend to move in the same direction. The best analogy I have heard describing sector trends came from Thomas J. Dorsey in his book *Point & Figure Charting*, where he wrote, "When I think of Sector Rotation ... I picture a herd of wildebeest romping across the African plains. They move in unison, first in one direction, then another. A few of the heard get out of synch, but the majority go together. Stocks operate the same way. Wall Street tends to follow the heard."[1] Most investors that have been in the market for a length of time realize this characteristic. However, few investors understand the total extent of the sector/stock relationship.

If you identify the correct sector, stock selection can often be quite easy. The challenge is selecting strong sectors. In 2004 and 2005, for example, the oil sector was strong, and nearly every issue gained ground. Fundamentals of the oil companies were a nonissue; institutional demand drove the sector higher and even the companies with weak fundamentals were able to go along for the ride. You will stand a much greater chance of making successful invest-ments if you focus on sectors that experience a high level of demand. Equally important is avoiding sectors that are out of favor.

Many investors make the mistake of concentrating on a familiar sector or one in which they have had investment success in the past. Investors tend to stay bullish on such sectors and do not have a way to understand when their conditions are changing. This is a dangerous approach to investing. Sectors that have produced better-than-average results in recent years will eventually experience an extended period of poor performance.

An example of this dilemma is the technology sector. From 1995 to 2000, the technology sector produced outsized returns. Chasing those strong returns caused many investors to focus their portfolio in technology stocks just in time to watch the sector go through an extended period of poor results. You need tools to be able to detect changes to sector trends so that you can proactively adjust your portfolio as conditions in the marketplace change. The financial markets are not static, and taking the same approach at all times does not work.

Having fixed opinions about market conditions is common among investors. Some investors are always positive and expect the market to rise, while others are always negative, expecting it to decline. No matter what happens, they do not change their minds. Yet, we all know we cannot make the markets conform to our way of thinking. We cannot make the market do what we want it to do. In contrast, the most successful professional investors are not rigid in their investment thought process; they adapt to market changes and manage their portfolios accordingly.

Successful investment management requires identifying sectors that are emerging as leaders and are generating institutional demand. These sectors provide the lowest-risk levels and best opportunities. During secular (long-term) bear markets, finding strong sectors is especially important.

A sector-rotation strategy provides you with a growth opportunity when the broad market languishes. Sector rotation makes it possible for you to partici-pate in sectors that are experiencing a cyclical advance and helps you avoid those in a cyclical decline. After the market peaked in 2000, for example, not every sector experienced a decline. The early phase of the market downturn was limited to technology- and telecom-related sectors; in contrast, the finan-cial, health-care, and energy sectors rotated higher over this period. Similarly, in 2004, investors in energy stocks were winners, while those focusing on the drug industry struggled.

Correct sector analysis in early 2000 could have helped investors identify the deteriorating conditions taking place within the technology sector, thereby alerting them to sell their technology holdings and realize some profits. Imagine if they then identified energy emerging as a new leader and bought energy stocks. In effect, they would have compounded their outsized technology-sector profits into lucrative profits that were generated in the energy sector during 2000 and afterward.

In the following chapters, I will take you through three sector-analysis tools: sector Bullish Percent charts, sector Relative Strength charts, and sector 10-Week charts. In the final chapters of this section, I will combine these three tools to develop powerful sector-analysis strategies.

CHAPTER 11

BULLISH PERCENT CHARTS

> **Reading Bullish Percent Charts**
> **Interpreting Bullish Percent Charts**
> **Understanding Bull and Bear Status Levels**

I've written at length about the importance that supply and demand play in forecasting a stock's price movement. Supply and demand relationships are equally important when forecasting a sector's price movement. Let's examine how this works.

The best buying opportunities in a sector will occur following a severe decline in stock prices in the industry. Usually, this situation occurs when there is a lot of bad news regarding the economic conditions of a sector, causing individuals to want to sell their holdings in this sector. Once investors have sold out, the amount of additional stock that is available for sale in the sector diminishes.

At some point, investors looking for good value will be attracted to this sector when prices are low. These investors are sometimes the industry insiders who know the true value of their stock. Once this initial demand begins to overtake the reduced amount of supply, the balance shifts, causing prices to start rising. The economic conditions in the industry will eventually improve, attracting more investors, who create more demand. As stocks in the sector move higher in price, sometimes momentum-investors will jump on board and want to participate in the positive trend. As long as the demand exceeds the supply in the sector, prices will continue to rise.

Eventually, the initial value-buyers realize that value in the sector is no longer attractive and begin selling to participate in newer sector opportunities. The selling increases supply, which balances out the demand, and prices stop advancing. Once the selling overwhelms the demand, the balance shifts in favor of supply, and the sector's trend is positioned to decline again.

The full cycle described above does not take place over days or weeks but will take months or years to complete.

How is this relevant to successful investing? Correct sector analysis allows you to buy when prices are low and beginning to appreciate (demand begins to take over supply) and to sell when prices are high and beginning to decline (supply takes over demand). You will also avoid buying into sectors that are positioned for a decline.

To do this consistently, you need a reliable indicator that determines the point when demand begins to take control in a sector, causing stock prices to rise, and when supply takes over, causing prices to decline. This reliable indicator is a Bullish Percent chart.

Bullish Percent charts are important for three reasons. They allow proactive investors to (1) participate early in a sector's advance, (2) take precaution to sell positions and protect profits in a sector that has advanced and may soon peak, and (3) avoid buying into high-risk sectors.

The following information is basic to understanding Bullish Percent charts:

> ➢ Bullish Percent charts are not new. A.W. Cohen first developed Bullish Percent charts in the 1950s. His company, Chartcraft, is still in business today, in large part due to the successful use of Bullish Percent charts. Bullish Percent charts are designed to help investors identify high- and low-risk levels in a sector. In essence, they help investors know when to make informed decisions.

> ➢ Bullish Percent charts tune out the media, Wall Street research, and emotions. The charts help you make objective investment decisions.

> ➢ You can use Bullish Percent charts for any universe of stocks. The more common uses are for industry sectors, such as drugs, banking, oil, software, etc., or for broad markets, such as the New York Stock Exchange and NASDAQ.

> ➢ Bullish Percent charts record the percent of individual stocks on a buy signal on their Point & Figure chart within the universe being recorded, which is, in effect, a snapshot picture of the number of issues being controlled by demand in that universe relative to those issues being controlled by supply.

How to Read a Bullish Percent Chart

In order to record and interpret a Bullish Percent chart, I first want to review the basic buy and sell signals generated on a Point & Figure chart. For a more detailed review, please refer to chapter 5 (Buy and Sell Signals Identified with Point & Figure Charts).

A buy signal develops when an X column surpasses a previous X column, indicating that demand is gaining strength in a stock. A double-top buy signal is the most basic buy signal on a Point & Figure chart. This signal is common; you will see many double tops on any Point & Figure chart. A double top is not a strong signal to buy in a particular security. One would prefer to see a more substantial chart pattern prior to buying (e.g., a triple top, a bullish triangle, breaking the bearish resistance line, etc.); however, a double-top pattern indicates that demand is gaining strength in the issue being charted.

A sell signal for a stock develops when an O column falls below a previous O column, indicating supply is strengthening in the stock. A double-bottom sell signal is the most basic sell signal on a Point & Figure chart. Again, this signal is common; you will see a double bottom multiple times on any Point & Figure chart. In and of itself, a double bottom is not a strong signal to sell all your shares of a particular security. One would prefer to see more substantial chart patterns prior to selling (e.g., a triple bottom, a bearish triangle, breaking the bullish support line, etc.); however, a double-bottom pattern indicates that supply is gaining strength in the issue being charted.

A sector's Bullish Percent chart records the percentage of stocks within the sector that show a basic buy signal versus those that show a basic sell signal on their individual Point & Figure charts. Essentially, every stock is placed into one of two "buckets": the buy-signal "bucket" or the sell-signal "bucket." Each stock gets placed in a bucket based on its last Point & Figure chart signal.

The Point & Figure chart in *figure 11.1* can help you grasp the relationship between Point & Figure charts and Bullish Percent charts. A buy signal for this stock occurred at $18.50 when the second X column surpassed the first X column. At that point, demand was gaining strength (i.e., a positive sign for the stock). Remember, the only way a stock advances on a sustained basis is if there is more demand than supply. At this point, the stock counts as one stock on a buy signal. It is placed into the buy-signal "bucket" for purposes of recording the sector's Bullish Percent chart of which the stock is one member. Buy and sell signals for all the stocks in that sector are tallied to determine the bullish-percent index for the sector.

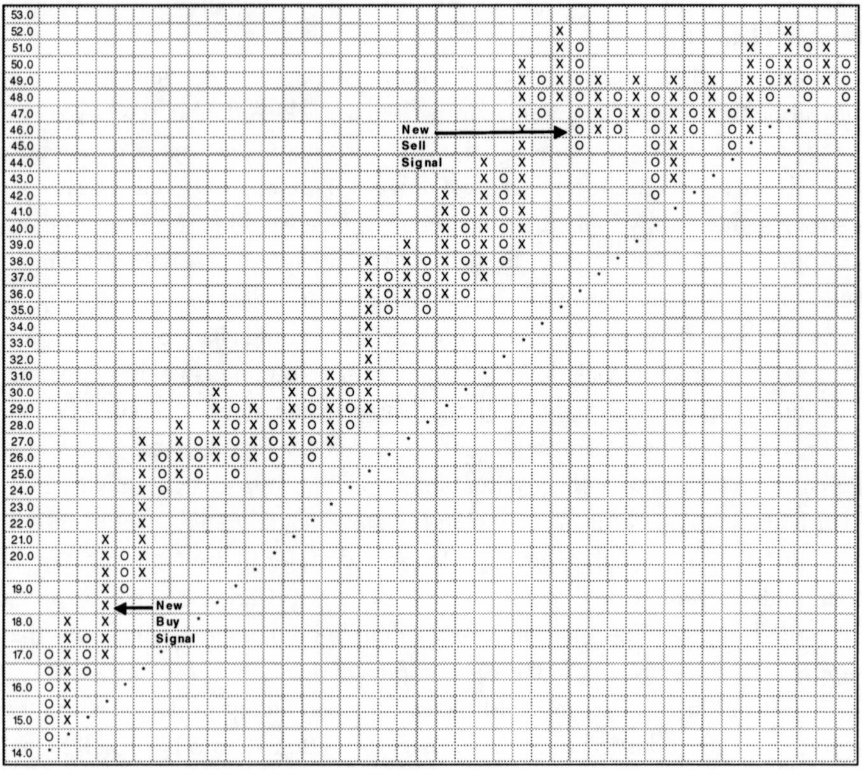

figure 11.1

The stock charted in *figure 11.1* will remain in the buy-signal "bucket" until an O column falls below a previous O column on its Point & Figure chart, at which point there is a new sell signal. On the chart in *figure 11.1*, you can see such a change at $46 when a double bottom occurred. At that point, the stock was taken out of the buy-signal "bucket" and placed into the sell-signal "bucket." When the chart generated the double-bottom sell signal, it was indicating that supply had begun to strengthen for the stock.

The significance of a Bullish Percent chart is not based on the movement of just one stock. A single stock shifting from a buy to a sell signal on its Point & Figure chart will not have much impact on a sector's Bullish Percent chart. However, the movement is significant if several issues give new buy or sell signals on or around the same time. This change tells us that supply or demand is gaining strength in a broad number of stocks in a particular sector. If the shift is toward buy signals, there is more demand in the sector. If the shift is toward sell signals, there is more supply in the sector.

NYSE Bullish Percent Chart: 1996–2005

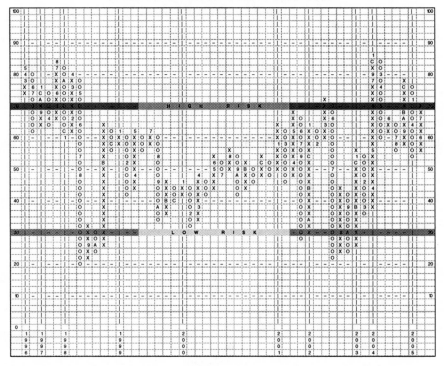

figure 11.2

Figure 11.2 is a copy of the NYSE Bullish Percent chart between 1996 and 2005. Although the NYSE is not an industry sector per se, its recording is the same as that of a sector, and it is one of the more popular Bullish Percent charts used for analyzing market conditions.

Recording a Bullish Percent chart is similar to recording a Point & Figure chart. Think of a Bullish Percent chart as graph paper. The vertical columns represent the bullish percentage, trending either higher (X columns) or lower (O columns). The horizontal columns reflect the overall percentage of stocks on buy signals on their Point & Figure charts. Again, similar to individual stock Point & Figure charts, X's are used to record an increasing percentage, and O's are used to record a declining percentage.

You will note that the percentages move in 2% increments. On the chart in *figure 11.2*, each box constitutes 2% of issues traded on the NYSE. Looking at the chart, notice that the left column shows the percentage at 10%, 20%, etc. Between each marking are four rows, or "boxes," that identify that the percentage of the NYSE members on a buy signal is at 12%, 14%, 16%, and 18%.

As with Point & Figure charts, a three-box reversal method is used to reverse columns from demand in control to supply in control and vice versa.

To practice creating a sector's Bullish Percent chart, let's hypothetically assume there are one hundred issues in a sector. Fifty of the issues are on a buy signal, which means that the sector's bullish-percent index (BPI) is 50%. Let's also assume the percentage is increasing, meaning we are in a column of X's. In this case, the beginning of the Bullish Percent chart would look like *figure 11.3*.

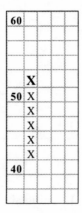

figure 11.3

The next day, eight stocks in the sector give new buy signals on their Point & Figure charts. On the same day, six stocks in the sector give new sell signals. The net change is two new stocks with buy signals. In other words, we now have fifty-two out of one hundred issues on buy signals, or 52%. At this point, as noted in *figure 11.4*, we would then put an X at the 52% level in the column of X's.

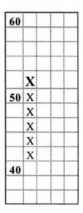

figure 11.4

On the third day, five stocks give new buys, while four give new sells. The net change is one new buy signal. In this case, the percentage moves up to 53%, but that is not enough to put another X in the column. Remember, a Bullish Percent chart records every 2% incremental movement. The percentage has to reach 54% prior to recording another X in the column.

On the fourth day, two stocks give new buy signals and none give new sells. The percentage is 55%. In this case, the percentage has moved from 53% to 55%. As noted in *figure 11.5*, we record another X in the 54% box in the current column. As long as the percentage of buy signals continues to increase, we will continue to record X's in the column.

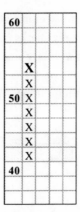

figure 11.5

If the percentage begins to decline, we would look for a 6% change (three-box reversal at 2% per box) to reverse to a column of O's. Anything less than a 6% decline is considered minor and irrelevant market fluctuations. A 6% decline is considered significant enough to indicate a change in the supply and demand relationship and, therefore, a change in our sector approach is needed. In our example, we would need to see the percentage of stocks on a buy signal in the sector drop to 48%. The reversal would look like *figure 11.6*.

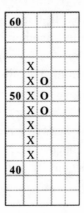

figure 11.6

In this hypothetical example of a Bullish Percent chart, we created recordings based on just a few days of activity. In reality, a similar pattern would most likely take place over a longer period of time. Depending on the sector being recorded, it could take weeks, even months. A Bullish Percent chart is not a short-term market indicator; the chart is used to help determine intermediate- to long-term trends.

As I've mentioned before, there are times in which the conditions for a sector are conducive for asset growth, and there are times when they are not. Since a Bullish Percent chart records the percent of individual stocks on a buy signal on their Point & Figure charts, a Bullish Percent chart helps guide an investor's overall approach toward the sector in question. The chart is a snapshot of the number of issues in a sector being controlled by demand relative to those being controlled by supply. As I've stated before, when supply is in control of a sector, you want to employ an overall defensive strategy. When demand is supporting higher stock prices, you should adopt an aggressive strategy.

A Bullish Percent chart identifies when a sector is at risk of stock prices being too high (demand near exhaustion) or if stock prices and risk are low (supply is limited). As a rule of thumb, for identifying when demand is exhausted and risk is too high, you should be cautious when a sector's Bullish Percent chart reaches 70% or higher (which means that 70% or more of stocks are on a buy signal). Similarly, to identify when supply is exhausted and sector risk is low, you should watch for when a sector's Bullish Percent chart reaches 30% or lower (which means that 30% or fewer stocks are on a buy signal). You will note on the NYSE Bullish Percent chart in *figure 11.2* that both the 30% and 70% levels are highlighted. This is common and is a reminder that stocks have reached extreme bullish-percent levels.

Interpretation of Bullish Percent Charts

There are two levels of analysis for interpreting Bullish Percent charts:

Direction: Is supply or demand controlling the market's trend?
Position: What is the market's level of risk?

When interpreting a Bullish Percent chart, two factors must be considered: *direction* (that is, whether supply or demand is controlling the sector being assessed), and *position* (that is, the risk level for the sector).

Direction

Similar to Point & Figure charts for individual stocks, direction has the following characteristics on a Bullish Percent chart:

1. A rising percentage of stocks with demand in control is recorded with X's. This demand is noted by a column of X's on the chart. X's indicate that demand is stronger than supply within the sector.

2. A declining percentage of stocks with demand in control is recorded with O's. This supply is noted by a column of O's on the chart. O's indicate that supply is taking control or is stronger than demand within the sector.

3. When demand is stronger than supply, the sector is providing an opportunity for growth; an aggressive approach toward the sector may be appropriate.

4. When supply is stronger than demand, growth opportunities are limited, and our approach toward a sector is defensive with a strategy of capital preservation. You want to manage risk carefully for any investment remaining in this sector.

Position

Position is interpreted differently on Bullish Percent charts than on stock Point & Figure charts. On an individual stock's Point & Figure chart, position is important when a stock is about to break through a support or resistance level (i.e., when the stock is breaking a balance pattern). Position on a Bullish Percent chart is most important when a market reaches certain percentage thresholds.

Before beginning, think of the positioning on a Bullish Percent chart as similar to a traditional bell curve. The indicators for high or low risk are 70% and 30%, respectively. The area between is the "comfort zone." Keeping this information in mind, position has the following characteristics on Bullish Percent charts:

1. A balance between demand and supply is noted by the market being at 50%, or in the middle. At this point, 50% of stocks have buy signals, and 50% of stocks have sell signals.

2. The extreme risk levels are at 70% and 30%. At 70%, too much of the available demand has already been exhausted in the sector; most investors have already purchased, capital is limited, and demand is not available for additional growth. At this level, risk is high, and you should not be aggressively buying in this sector. At 30%, most of the available supply has already been exhausted in the sector because most investors have already sold. At this level, risk is low and investors should consider buying in this sector.

3. A column reversal from the extreme levels indicates major turning points in direction. These reversals are strong buy and sell signals for the universe being charted.

4. *A reversal down from a position of 70% or higher is a major sell signal for the universe.* When the sector's chart has been at 70% or above and drops below 70%, the floor has been removed from the sector and prices can drop quickly.

5. Similarly, *a reversal up from a position below 30% is a major buy signal for the sector.* When the market has been at 30% or below and moves above 30%, the ceiling has been removed from the sector and prices are positioned to increase.

Bull and Bear Status Levels

Four main status levels are used on Bullish Percent charts. Understanding each status will help you identify trends in the market and make appropriate investment decisions.

Bull Alert status (*figure 11.7*) occurs when a Bullish Percent chart falls below 30% then advances by 6%, causing a reversal up into a column of X's. This status indicates that a potential bottom is in place for the sector as demand is beginning to take control away from supply. Usually the stronger stocks in the sector will be the first to give new buy signals. Although a bull alert does not confirm a bottom is in place, it at least indicates a trading (short-term) advance for the group. Note that the Bull Alert in the following chart occurs when the percentage of stocks reaches 26%.

Bull Confirmed status is stronger than Bull Alert status. This status occurs when a Bullish Percent chart records a column of X's that exceeds the previous column of X's. The status confirms that demand is in control of the sector being recorded. Bull Confirmed status indicates that the number of issues on buy signals within the sector is growing. The demand is broadening out to more stocks, and your chances of making successful investments are good. When you receive such an indication, you want to be more aggressive. Note in *figure 11.8* that Bull Confirmed status occurs when the percentage of stocks reaches 34%.

Bull Alert Status	Bull Confirmed Status
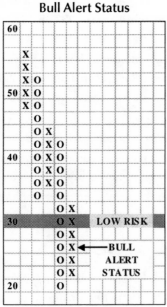	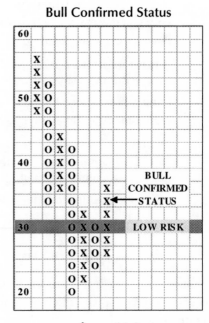
figure 11.7	figure 11.8

Bear Alert status occurs when a Bullish Percent chart rises above 70% then reverses down into a column of O's that drops back below the 70% level. This status indicates that a potential top is in place for the sector being charted as supply is beginning to take control. Usually, the weaker stocks in the sector will be the first to give new sell signals. Although a Bear Alert does not confirm a top is in place, it at least indicates a trading decline for the group. In *figure 11.9*, this alert occurs when the percentage moves down to 68%.

Bear Confirmed status is stronger than Bear Alert status. This status occurs when a Bullish Percent chart records a column of O's that falls below the previous column of O's. This status confirms supply is in control of the sector being recorded. Bear Confirmed status indicates that the number of issues on sell signals within the sector is growing. The supply is broadening out to more stocks, and your chances of making successful investments in this sector are low. When such an indication occurs, you want to take a defensive approach toward this sector. On the chart in *figure 11.10*, the status is noted when the percentage drops to 66%.

Bear Alert Status

figure 11.9

Bear Confirmed Status

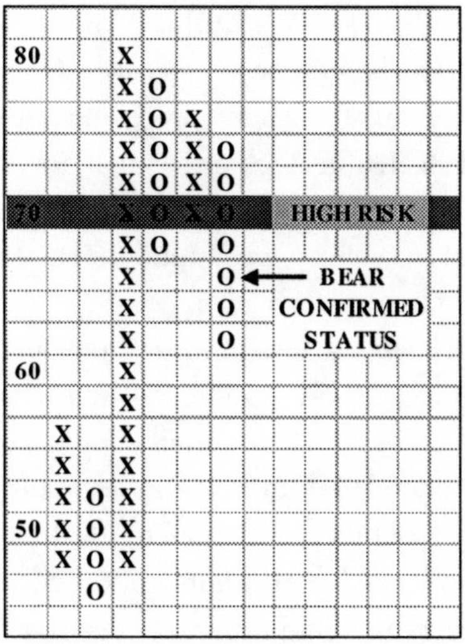

figure 11.10

In addition to the four main status levels explained above, there is also *Bull Correction* status and *Bear Correction* status. Bull Correction status occurs when a chart is in Bull Confirmed status (*figure 11.8*) and reverses down into an O column prior to reaching the high-risk zone at 70%. Bear Correction status occurs when a chart is in Bear Confirmed status (*figure 11.10*) and reverses up into an X column prior to reaching the low-risk zone at 30%. A change to Bull Correction or Bear Correction status indicates a short-term correction in the primary trend and not a change in trend from bull to bear or vice versa.

In summary, a sector's Bullish Percent chart is an intermediate- to long-term indicator that guides your overall approach to a sector. These charts are based on supply and demand in real time. Consequently, you could make objective decisions using Bullish Percent charts. This is vastly different than relying on the media for information that is too late to be of any real use. As I noted earlier, market extremes cause media reporting extremes, leading some investors to make emotional and reactive decisions. Because Bullish Percent charts yield timely and objective information, you are able to make informed and unemotional choices.

With a sector's Bullish Percent chart, you know when it is appropriate to buy stocks in a sector because (1) supply is reflected in stock prices that are likely near their lows, providing low-risk buying opportunities, and (2) demand is reflected in stock prices that are likely near their highs, which makes buying risky. Because when Bullish Percent charts show when positive imbalances exist in sectors' supply and demand relationships, they allow you to participate early in a sector's advance, even at a time when the news may appear negative. Purchasing stocks at these times may be emotionally difficult; this is a time of reduced supply—and risk—in the marketplace. Demand is likely to resurface, and prices will eventually increase. Sector Bullish Percent charts give you the confidence to make investments at these low-risk times when the media may be at its most negative. Bullish Percent charts likewise give investors the confidence to sell when market risk is elevated after a long advance—despite the media being extremely positive in reporting on the economy, on business, and on investment prospects.

CHAPTER 12

SECTOR BULLISH PERCENT CASE STUDIES

Understanding Demand and Supply on the Sector Level
Oil Sector Case Study
Drug Sector Case Study

To help bring home how to read a Bullish Percent chart and use sector analysis for making successful investments, I'll describe two sectors and their Bullish Percent charts.

Oil Sector Case Study

The last time the Bullish Percent chart for the oil sector gave a low-risk buy signal was during the period between August and November 2002. Crude oil was trading well below $30 per barrel at the time. The investing public had very little interest in energy stocks, and by late 2002, the sector was clearly out of favor. Reports on the oil sector issued by the media were negative, yet the sector's Bullish Percent chart was creating a bottom. The negative media coverage caused some additional selling to wash out supply. As we know from previous case studies about markets and individual stocks, such a scenario creates a low-risk buying opportunity.

Figure 12.1 shows the Bullish Percent chart for the oil sector. You can see that the bullish-percent indicator reached a low of 20% in July 2002—well into the low-risk zone. As is typical in such a scenario, after the July low, the sector reversed up into an X column, changing its status to Bull Alert. The status change indicated that a potential bottom was in place for the sector.

When a sector improves to Bull Alert status, an investor should begin putting together a "buy list" of stocks in the sector universe. Which issues should you include on your buy list? First, look for stocks in the sector with strong

Point & Figure chart patterns. Remember, these patterns indicate demand is in control, or, at least, beginning to take control of the stock. Ideally, the stock is in an uptrend, meaning the bullish support line is the main trend line on the Point & Figure chart.

The buy list should also include stocks with strong or improving Relative Strength charts. This strength indicates that the stock is trading stronger than the broad market. Ideally, the stock's Relative Strength chart would be on a buy signal and in an X column.

In addition to selecting stocks that are strong from a technical-analysis point of view, you may also want to include a fundamental analysis to determine your buy list. Essentially, you want to create a list of issues in the oil sector that are sound from both points of view.

Looking at the chart in *figure 12.1*, notice that following the initial advance from the bottom of the chart, the oil sector's Bullish Percent chart reversed down into an O column in September 2002. Once a sector's chart establishes Bull Alert status, we want to see the next O column reflect short-lived and weak activity. The O column in September 2002 created a higher low, declining to 26%, while the previous O column declined to 20%. This higher column of O's confirmed that supply was weaker and demand was gaining strength (fewer sellers, more buyers).

Again, looking at *figure 12.1*, notice that the oil sector's Bullish Percent chart reversed back up into an X column in October 2002. This time, demand was strong enough to push the column higher than the previous column of X's and changed the status to Bull Confirmed. At this time, you can conclude that a bottom is in place for the oil sector and that the time is ideal to accumulate oil stocks aggressively.

The low-risk buy signal that developed in the oil sector in late 2002 turned into a significant investment opportunity. Initially, oil stocks began to move up without much fanfare; however, as the price of crude oil began to advance, more and more investors became attracted to the sector's potential. The attraction fed further demand for oil stocks. When record-high oil prices eventually made the lead story on the evening news, investors who previously were unwilling to invest in the sector now believed the time had come to invest.

Oil Sector's Bullish Percent Chart

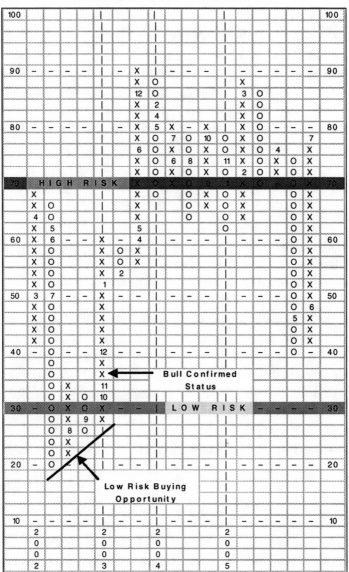

figure 12.1

When the sector cycle becomes mature and the media influences investors, the end of the advance is typically near. As you can see on the oil sector's chart, the last position was well above 70%, the high-risk zone. An objective analysis would conclude this to be a poor time to invest in the oil sector. Although the long-term prospects may have been bright for oil stocks, the risk/reward ratio at that time indicated that further investing in the sector was unattractive. As I stated in the previous chapter, when a sector bullish-percent indicator is above 70%, price corrections are most likely inevitable. A lower-risk opportunity awaits investors following such price corrections.

Drug Sector Case Study

Sectors may or may not move in tandem. The Bullish Percent chart for one sector may show that it's a good time to invest in stocks in that sector; the Bullish Percent chart for another sector may show it's a high-risk time to consider that sector's stocks. As noted in the Bullish Percent chart for the oil sector (*figure 12.1*), by late 2003 and most of 2004, the oil sector's Bullish Percent chart maintained a bullish status. During the same time, the drug sector's Bullish Percent chart experienced a significant decline (*figure 12.2*).

In June 2003, the Bullish Percent chart for the drug sector reached a high of 80%. By August 2004, it had dropped down to 28%. Most drug stocks experienced significant declines during this fourteen-month period. The chart in *figure 12.2* shows that a major sell signal was indicated prior to the slide in drug stocks.

These two sectors help outline the importance of analyzing and selecting the right sectors during a specific period. This ability, and resulting information, can make a significant difference in investment results during the same period.

While we could continue to go through many case studies of previous sector buy and sell opportunities, the object of this book is to provide you new tools to help you make profitable decisions. Although a historical review is a useful learning tool, access to current information is of more value to you. The current Bullish Percent chart for every sector is available on the Investor Education Institute's Web site (http://www.institute4investors.com). Once you are logged on to the Web site, go to the Sector Indicator section. Here you can select any sector from the dropdown menu to view its Bullish Percent chart.

Drug Sector's Bullish Percent Chart

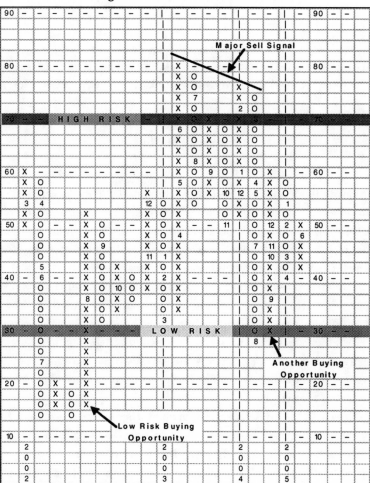

figure 12.2

CHAPTER 13

SECTOR RELATIVE STRENGTH CHARTS

> Recording and interpreting sector Relative Strength charts is similar to the process used for individual stock Relative Strength charts.
>
> Measures the strength of a sector's price movement compared to the overall market.

Your ability to identify sectors that are market leaders can very well determine the level of success you achieve with your investments. Portfolios that include the top-performing sectors can build wealth at a desirable clip. Equally important is your ability to identify sectors lagging the market. Obviously, you want to avoid buying the underperforming sectors.

Sector Relative Strength charts are a valuable tool for gauging a sector's price performance relative to the movement of the overall stock market. Whereas a sector's Bullish Percent chart measures the absolute movement in the sector (i.e., whether stocks in the sector are moving higher or lower in price), the Relative Strength chart measures the sector's price movement relative to a broad market index (i.e., are stocks in the sector performing better or worse than the rest of the market).

Recording a sector's Relative Strength chart is similar to recording a Bullish Percent chart. While a Bullish Percent chart calculates the percent of sector members on a buy signal on their individual Point & Figure charts, a sector's Relative Strength chart calculates the percent of sector members on a buy signal on their individual Relative Strength charts.

Let's quickly review the concept of Relative Strength charts for individual stocks. (For a complete review, refer to chapter 8.)

A stock's Relative Strength chart records the stock's price movement relative to the broad market as measured by the S&P 1500 Index. X's are used to record a rise in the relative-price movement, and O's are used to record a decline. The alternating columns of X's and O's create buy and sell signals on the chart. When a column of X's exceeds a previous X column, a buy signal occurs. An O column declining below a previous O column records a sell signal.

Relative-strength buy and sell signals are further illustrated in *figure 13.1*: a Relative Strength chart for Apple Computer, a member of the computer sector. In September 2000, Apple's Relative Strength chart gave a new relative-strength sell signal when the second O column shown on the chart fell below the first O column at 7.0206. This sell signal stayed in effect until January 2002—when the chart was able to record a higher X column at 4.9492.

Apple Computer: Relative Strength Chart

9.9588				|			|	
9.3951		X		|			|	
8.8633		X	O	|			|	
8.3616	O	X	O	|			|	
7.8883	O	X	9	|			|	
7.4418	8		O	|			|	
7.0206			O	← Relative Strength Sell Signal				
6.6232			O	|			|	
6.2483			O	|			|	
5.8946			O	|			|	
5.561			O	|			|	
5.2462			O	|			|	
4.9492			O	|			x	← Relative Strength Buy Signal
4.6691			O	X		7		1
4.4048			O	X	O	6	O	12
4.1555			10	X	O	X	O	11
3.9203			O	X	5	X	O	X
3.6984			O	3	O		O	X
3.489			O	X		9	X	
3.2915			O	X		10	|	
3.1052			11	1			|	
2.9294			12	X			|	
2.7636			O	X			|	
2.6072			O	|			|	
2.4596				|			|	
				|			|	
				2			2	
				O			O	
				O			O	
				1			2	

figure 13.1

167

Relative-strength signals typically stand for a long time before a new signal occurs. For Apple, the new buy signal came sixteen months after the sell signal. The buy signal remains in effect as of the writing of this book and has lasted for three and one-half years.

The duration of the individual stock's relative-strength signals make the sector's Relative Strength charts long-term indicators. There will generally be fewer recordings made on a sector's Relative Strength chart than on its Bullish Percent chart. On a Relative Strength chart, bullish and bearish status levels can endure for several years before succumbing to a reversal.

When the buy signal for a stock is generated, the action may affect the sector's Relative Strength chart. Apple is only one stock in the computer sector, and its action alone will not be able to influence the entire computer sector. However, if several other computer stocks simultaneously show new relative-strength signals, we have a good indication that the direction of computer stocks as a group is changing. The computer sector's Relative Strength chart will be rising (in an X column) when a statistically significant number of issues in the computer sector are giving buy signals on their individual Relative Strength charts. The chart will be declining (in an O column) when computer stocks are giving sell signals on their individual Relative Strength charts.

Figure 13.2 is the Relative Strength chart for the precious-metals sector. As the percentage of stocks that are on a buy signal rises and falls, the sector develops alternating columns of X's and O's. A column of X's records a rising percentage, while an O column records a declining percentage. Sectors that are in X columns are performing better than the broad market. Sectors in an O column are the weaker sectors. In addition to identifying the direction of the relative-price movement using X and O columns, sector Relative Strength charts also aid in identifying high- and low-risk levels and major changes in a sector's relative cycle.

Looking at *figure 13.2*, you can see that the high-risk level is marked at 70% and that the low-risk level is marked at 30%. As you will recall, the optimal time to buy is when the chart is advancing (in an X column) after first declining down into the low-risk zone. You can see that the chart for precious metals stayed in the low-risk zone for most of the period from 1997 through 1999. At the same time, the price of gold was trading at a secular low, near $250 per ounce. The weakness in the price of gold caused price weakness in precious-metals stocks. This weakness, in turn, caused the sector's Relative Strength chart to move down to its lowest level in the last ten years. At the bottom, only 6% of precious-metals stocks were performing better than the S&P 1500 Index.

Precious-Metals Sector's Relative Strength Chart

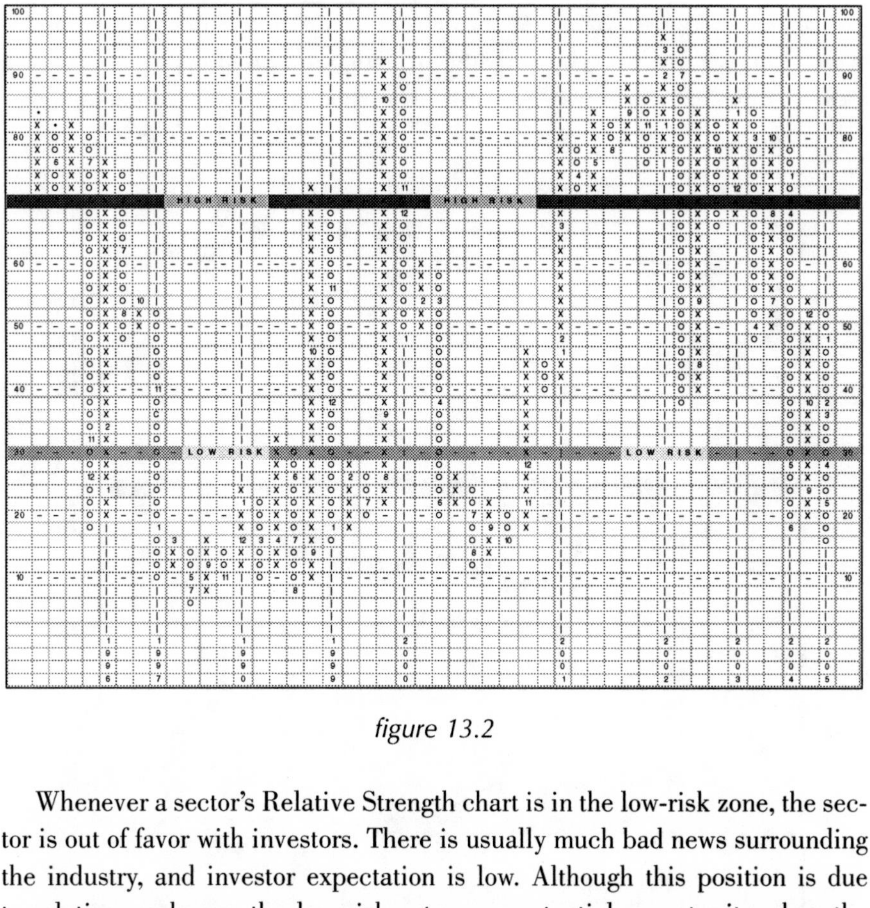

figure 13.2

Whenever a sector's Relative Strength chart is in the low-risk zone, the sector is out of favor with investors. There is usually much bad news surrounding the industry, and investor expectation is low. Although this position is due to relative weakness, the low risk sets up a potential opportunity when the Relative Strength chart begins to move higher.

For most sectors, one of the major differences between its Bullish Percent and Relative Strength charts is the time to create major tops and bottoms. In the case of the precious-metals sector, after first dipping below 30% in late 1996, nearly two years passed before the Relative Strength chart began to cycle higher. The Relative Strength chart is truly a long-term indicator.

Looking at the Relative Strength chart for the oil sector (*figure 13.3*), note that the lowest position on the chart occurred in 1998 at 8%. In 1998, crude oil was trading near $12 per barrel, and gasoline was less than $1 a gallon. In 1998, nobody wanted to own oil stocks, particularly since the technology and telecom sectors were soaring. As the oil sector's Relative Strength chart began to trend higher from its low, a significant, long-term profit opportunity was at hand. A buy signal occurred in April 1999 when the chart recorded a higher column of X's.

Oil Sector's Relative Strength Chart

(Point-and-figure chart showing relative strength of the oil sector, with a vertical scale from 10 to 100. The chart includes a "HIGH RISK" band near the 70–75 level and a "LOW RISK" band near the 30 level. An arrow labeled "BUY SIGNAL" points to a column of X's near the 20 level.)

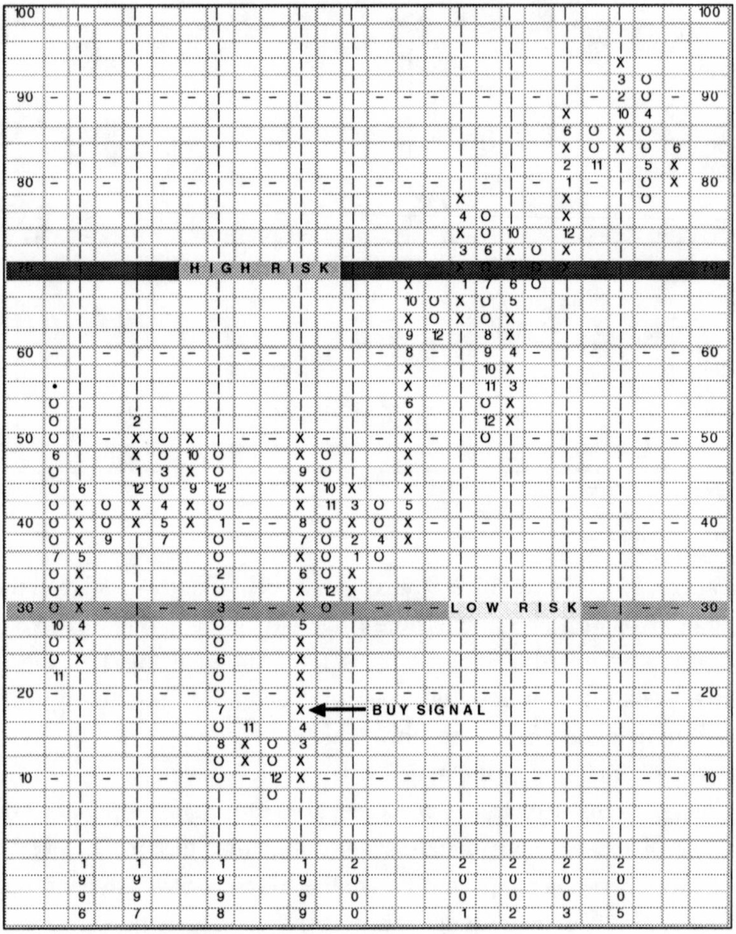

figure 13.3

Conversely, during the first half of 2005, you can see that the oil sector's Relative Strength chart was at the other extreme and well into the high-risk level above 80%. Investors who bought oil stocks in 2005 took on significantly more risk than those who bought earlier in the sector's trend. Buying at higher risk levels will not prevent you from making money if the sector continues to advance, but it does increase your risk and reduce your potential reward. Buying early in a sector's relative-strength cycle can generate outsized returns for your portfolio. For example, look at the list of oil stocks in *figure 13.4*, comparing their prices on April 1, 1999, to the prices on June 30, 2005. You can see the strong profit opportunity in these issues that followed the sector relative-strength buy signal in 1999.

Stock	Price		Gain
	1-Apr-99	30-Jun-05	
Murphy Oil	$ 10.37	$ 52.23	403.66%
XTO Energy	$ 1.40	$ 33.99	2327.86%
Sunoco	$ 36.06	$ 113.68	215.25%
Apache Corp	$ 11.28	$ 64.60	472.70%
Frontier Oil	$ 2.50	$ 29.35	1074.00%

figure 13.4

As I stated at the beginning of this chapter, your ability to identify sectors that are market leaders can very well determine the level of success you achieve with your investments. Equally important is your ability to identify sectors lagging the market. While investing in the leading sectors can build wealth, investing in the lagging sectors can destroy wealth. Sector Relative Strength charts can help you avoid buying or holding on to positions in a sector when its relative-strength cycle is negative.

Figure 13.5 shows strong sell signals in 2002 and 2003 on the drug sector's Relative Strength chart. You can see that the highest recording in the last ten years was at 80% in late 2001 and early 2002. Following these dates, the Relative Strength chart began to decline, indicating that the drug sector began to underperform the S&P 1500 Index. During this time, investors were wise to stay on the sidelines and avoid the drug sector. An investor was better off focusing on sectors in a stronger position. Similarly, an investor holding positions in drug stocks should have used the sell signals as a strong indication to sell.

Drug Sector's Relative Strength Chart

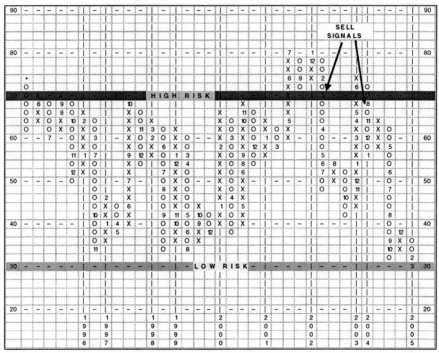

figure 13.5

Following the sell signals in 2002 and 2003, the drug sector's Relative Strength chart began to trend lower. The price of most drug stocks slid from the time of the first sell signal in March 2002 through 2004. *Figure 13.6* reflects this decline for several drug stocks.

Stock	Price		Loss
	1-Mar-02	31-Dec-04	
Merck & Co	$ 58.04	$ 32.14	-44.62%
Pfizer Inc.	$ 40.96	$ 26.89	-34.35%
Bristol-Myers Squibb	$ 47.00	$ 25.62	-45.49%
Schering Plough	$ 34.49	$ 20.88	-39.46%
Wyeth	$ 63.55	$ 42.59	-32.98%

figure 13.6

Sector Relative Strength charts are fabulous tools to help you stay out of trouble. Avoiding exposure to sectors in a declining trend will help you avoid making costly mistakes. A key to successful investment is not making critical mistakes.

At certain times, a group of sectors related to the same or similar industries will be flashing a similar warning. For example, the computer, electronics, Internet, semiconductor, and software sectors are all in the technology industry. In the early months of 2000, every one of these sectors, along with the telecom sector, began to reverse down on sector Relative Strength charts. Seeing a mass move in several related sectors indicates a major change is underway for an industry and gives you the confidence to avoid exposure.

Figures 13.7 through *13.12* show the Relative Strength charts for sectors within the technology industry. As you will note, between the months of January 2000 and April 2000, each of these Relative Strength charts began to reverse down from high-risk levels. This reversal was a clear indication that the prospects for technology stocks were turning negative and should have been sold. These charts were terrific aids in helping investors avoid exposure to the deflating telecom and technology bubble during that time.

Computer Sector's
Relative Strength Chart

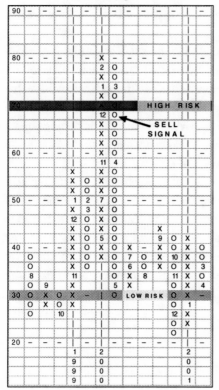

figure 13.7

Electronics Sector's
Relative Strength Chart

figure 13.8

Internet Sector's Relative Strength Chart

figure 13.9

Semiconductor Sector's Relative Strength Chart

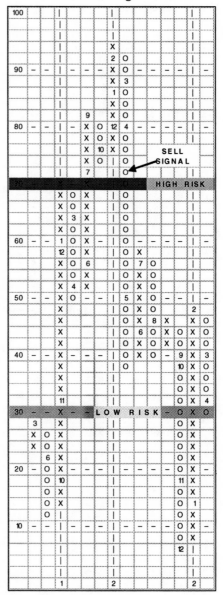

figure 13.10

175

Software Sector's Relative Strength Chart

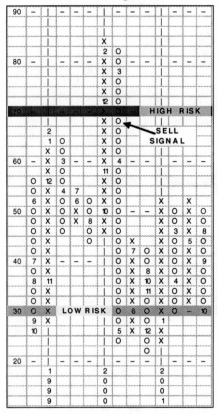

figure 13.11

Telecom Sector's Relative Strength Chart

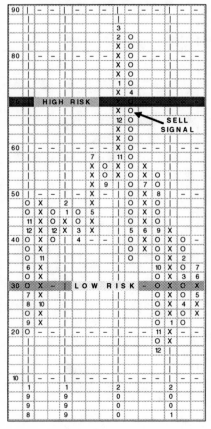

figure 13.12

CHAPTER 14

COMBINING SECTOR BULLISH PERCENT AND RELATIVE STRENGTH CHARTS

> Combining sector Bullish Percent charts and Relative Strength charts provides you with a sector strategy for confident investment decisions.
>
> Strongest indications are when *both* charts have a positive pattern.

In the section on selecting individual stocks, I combined the use of Point & Figure and Relative Strength charts to show you how to make confident decisions regarding stock selections. In this chapter, I'm going to show you how combining sector Bullish Percent charts and Relative Strength charts can help you optimize your sector selection.

Waiting for optimal sector opportunities requires patience. At times, both the Bullish Percent and Relative Strength charts will give a major buy or sell signal at or around the same time. Other times, one chart will show a major buy or sell signal prior to the other. The best opportunities occur when the Bullish Percent chart gives a good low-risk buy signal and when the Relative Strength chart for the same sector has shown a buy signal months, or even a couple of years, prior to that time. The positive relative-strength trend may already be well under way.

A sector's Bullish Percent chart will generally cycle faster than its Relative Strength chart. Therefore, a sector's Bullish Percent chart may provide more than one low-risk entry point at the time when the Relative Strength chart is trending upward on a long-term basis.

Figure 14.1 shows you another look at the oil sector's Relative Strength chart. The chart reached a low in December 1998 at 8%. It began to move higher in March 1999 and gave a buy signal in April 1999. Looking at the oil sector's Bullish Percent chart in *figure 14.2*, you will see that this chart gave a major buy signal near March 1999. In 1999, the oil sector had both its Bullish Percent and Relative Strength charts signaling a positive change in its trend. That was an ideal time to buy oil stocks.

The oil sector's Relative Strength chart continued to trend higher, and a second opportunity in the sector occurred in late 2002. This opportunity is illustrated in *figure 14.3*. I reviewed this opportunity in chapter 12 (Sector Bullish Percent Case Studies), but it's worth spending time to look at this chart again. The oil sector's Bullish Percent chart declined into the low-risk zone in the summer of 2002. As the chart began to reverse upward during the August–November 2002 time frame, another great, low-risk buying opportunity was presented in the oil sector.

Oil Sector Relative Strength Chart

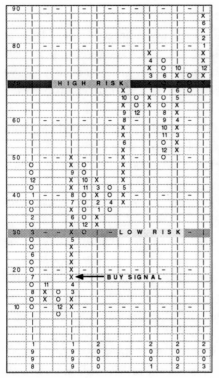

figure 14.1

Oil Sector Bullish Percent Chart
First Buying Opportunity

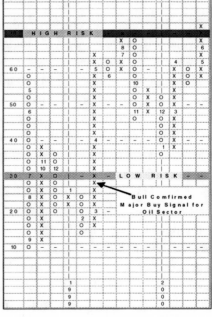

figure 14.2

As you can see by the dates, these opportunities were nearly four years apart. It's worth repeating: patience is required to put many technical-analysis strategies to work. The best profit opportunities are when both Bullish Percent and Relative Strength charts are in a favorable position. Most investors are too impatient and are not able to wait for everything to come together. If you can have the discipline to wait for these two charts to be in alignment before taking positions, you will be a consistently successful investor.

Oil Sector Bullish Percent Chart
Second Buying Opportunity

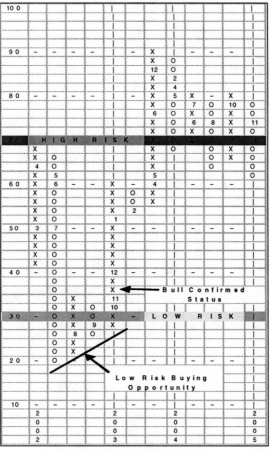

figure 14.3

179

Similar to buy signals, sell signals on Bullish Percent and Relative Strength charts often occur at different times. The Relative Strength chart can lead the Bullish Percent chart by several months, or vice versa. Let's look at the automobile sector as an example. The Relative Strength chart peaked in April 2002 at 82% (*figure 14.4*). This chart reversed down in August and gave a sell signal with a lower O column in October 2002. The reversal down and the sell signal indicated that the automobile sector was beginning a cycle that would perform worse than the broad market. However, at the same time, the Bullish Percent chart in the automobile sector had already declined into a low-risk position. In fact, the chart began to reverse up into a bullish status in October 2002 (*figure 14.5*).

When you see these conflicting signals, you have an indication that the relative-price trend is lower but that the absolute-price trend is higher. In other words, automobile stocks were rising, but the broad market was rising faster. The sell signal on the Relative Strength chart would have helped you realize this trend. Furthermore, although automobile stocks seemed well positioned to advance, other sectors that had a bullish Relative Strength chart were better alternatives for new investments.

As you can see on the automobile Bullish Percent chart, the automobile sector did experience an advance in late 2002. The advance carried the Bullish Percent chart up to a peak at 80% one year later. After some back and forth action in the following months, the chart gave a sell signal in March 2004. A look at the Relative Strength chart shows that this chart was still on a sell signal at that time and trending lower. With both charts negative in March 2004, this would have been an ideal time to sell automobile stocks. From the March 1, 2004, sell signal to the low in May 1, 2005, automobile stocks declined substantially. General Motors fell from $48.12 to $26.68, down 44%. One of the automobile-parts companies, Delphi Corp., fell from $10.20 to $3.30, down 67%.

Automobile Sector
Relative Strength Chart

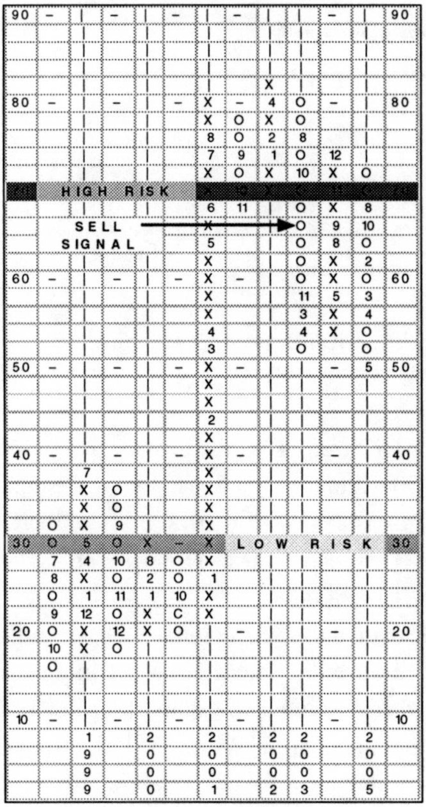

figure 14.4

Automobile Sector
Bullish Percent Chart

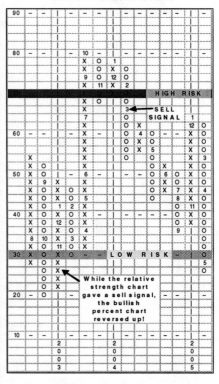

figure 14.5

CHAPTER 15

SECTOR 10-WEEK CHARTS

10-Week charts help you capitalize on short-term cycles
within longer-term trends.

10-Week charts help you determine entrance and exit points.

While sector Bullish Percent and Relative Strength charts provide you guidance for the intermediate- to long-term investment decisions, sector Percent Above 10-Week charts (usually referred to as 10-Week charts) help you with decisions on a shorter-term basis. Sector 10-Week charts are interpreted in the same basic way we interpret any Bullish Percent chart.

Sector 10-Week charts help us find the cycles within the longer-term trends. Depending on your trading strategy, you can use the Sector 10-Week Indicator in a number of different ways. For long-term-oriented investors, these charts will help fine-tune the entrance and exit points for your buy and sell decisions. You want to avoid buying into a sector when its 10-Week chart points to a heightened risk level for the sector or when the chart is declining in a bearish status. At such times, you will want to become a little less aggressive; the sector will most likely decline over coming weeks and provide you better prices to buy. You want to wait for the lower-risk entry point.

When exiting a position, you should try to sell when the sector's 10-Week chart is at a high-risk level or giving a new sell signal. Long-term investors should use sector Bullish Percent and Relative Strength charts as their main sector indicators but should always keep the status of the sector's 10-Week chart in mind.

For short-term or trading-oriented investors, the 10-week indicators show when there are opportunities to make investments that capitalize on the short-term cycles. Investors with a short-term trading style should use the 10-Week charts as their main sector indicator while keeping the status of the Bullish

Percent and Relative Strength charts in mind. For investors who have short-term objectives, the Sector 10-Week Indicators are extremely helpful in timing both buy and sell decisions. These charts also help with short-selling strategies.

Sector 10-Week charts measure the percent of sector members that are above their own 10-week average price. The 10-week average price for any issue is simply an average closing price for the last fifty trading days (ten weeks). If the latest closing price is higher than the 10-week average, then the stock is placed in the *above* bucket. If the last closing price is not above its own 10-week average, then the stock is placed in the *below* bucket.

What is the importance of knowing if a stock is above its 10-week average price? The answer is simple. If a stock is higher than its own 10-week average price, the short-term momentum for the particular issue is rising. Conversely, if a stock is below its 10-week average price, the short-term momentum is declining.

Similar to the bullish-percent concept, if only a few isolated issues in a sector are advancing above their 10-week average price, the advance is not important to the price momentum of the sector. However, when a significant percentage of sector members are rising above their 10-week average price, the advance is an important indication of the momentum of the sector. Since such an indication suggests that the momentum of the sector is advancing, from a short-term timing standpoint, the time is ideal to buy stocks in the sector.

Conversely, when a significant percentage of sector issues are falling below their 10-week average price, there is an indication that the price momentum of the sector is declining. During these times, it would be wise to take a step back from making new commitments in the sector. You should wait until the momentum bottoms and the sector risk level is reduced on a short-term basis.

The sector's 10-Week chart is recorded and interpreted the same way as sector Bullish Percent and Relative Strength charts.

Here is a brief summary of the interpretation. (For details, refer to the chapters that discuss recording those charts.) When interpreting a sector's 10-Week chart, there are two levels of analysis:

➢ Direction

➢ Position

We are concerned with the direction the chart is headed and the position of the chart. A higher percentage is recorded with a column of X's, meaning demand is in control on a short-term basis. A lower percentage is recorded with a column of O's, meaning supply has the upper hand on a short-term basis.

Any reading above 70% places the sector's 10-Week chart in a short-term, high-risk zone; readings below 30% mean the short-term risk is low.

Important buy signals develop on the sector's 10-Week chart when the percentage drops below 30% and then begins moving higher. This signal indicates that 70% of stocks in the sector have declined below their 10-week average (only 30% are left above the 10-week average) and are now beginning to advance, changing the momentum of the sector from down to up. At these times, short-term investors should take aggressive positions to profit from expected advance in the sector.

Important sell signals develop on a sector's 10-Week chart when the percentage above their 10-week average rises above 70% and then begins moving lower. This signal indicates that a large number of issues in a sector has advanced above their 10-week average and are now beginning to decline, changing the momentum of the sector from up to down. At these times, short-term investors should sell their positions.

Long-term investors should patiently wait for a lower-risk entry point and avoid buying at the high-risk points. However, if you are inclined to use a short-selling strategy, when the 10-week average rises above 70% then begins to decline, the time is ideal to implement short-selling strategies and profit from the expected short-term decline in the sector. It would be appropriate to sell short only in sectors that also have negative Bullish Percent and Relative Strength charts. We will cover short-selling strategies later in the book.

Figure 15.1 shows the oil sector's 10-Week chart. If you compare this chart to the oil sector's Bullish Percent or Relative Strength chart, you will easily notice that the 10-week indicator is a much faster moving indicator. The chart in *figure 15.1* covers about fifteen months (April 2004–July 2005) of activity. During those fifteen months, the chart reached a high-risk level on five separate occasions and a low-risk level four times. Even if the longer-term indicators for a sector are positive, an investor should avoid new commitments; in other words, avoid buying when the 10-Week chart is in a high-risk zone or declining. The best entry points occur when the 10-Week chart dips into the low-risk zone and then begins to reverse up into a bullish status. Remember, rising X columns indicate that more oil stocks are rising above their 10-week average price; declining O columns indicate that oil stocks are declining below their 10-week average price.

Looking at the oil sector's 10-Week chart (*figure 15.1*) in more depth, notice that there are four short-term sell signals. These signals occur in April, July, and October 2004 and March 2005. Although I am using the term "sell signal," for long-term investors, these are simply the times when the stocks are near a short-term high and when you want to avoid purchasing. You would be wise to wait for a price correction. There are also four short-term buying opportunities for the oil sector in *figure 15.1*. These signals occur in May and August 2004 and in January and May 2005. Although the oil sector was in a long-term advance, these were the best times to buy. When the 10-Week chart declined into the low-risk zone, oil stocks could have been purchased as they pulled back from their previous highs. (Purchasing on the pullback lowers your risk and increases your profit potential.)

Oil Sector's 10-Week Chart

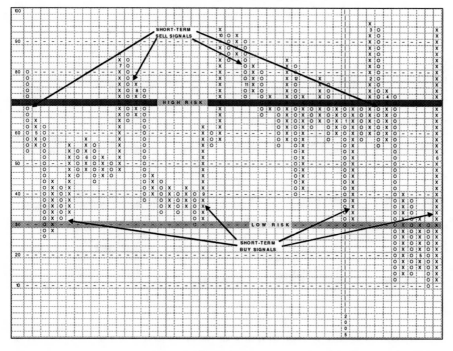

figure 15.1

The table in *figure 15.2* summarizes the high and low prices for five selected oil stocks. In every case, when the oil sector's 10-Week chart began to reverse down from the high-risk zone, these issues experienced price corrections. The average price correction for each of the five issues appears in the farthest column to the right on the table. For example, the average price correction for the April 2004 high to the May 2004 low was 16.17% for these five oil stocks. The largest correction occurred during the March–May 2005 cycle, resulting in an average price correction of 22.11%. During these periods investors were rewarded for being patient and for waiting for the oil sector to provide a better entry point.

The average price correction covering all four cycles appears at the bottom for each issue. Frontier Oil experienced the largest price corrections, averaging 21.09% for the four cycles. Investors in this stock were handsomely rewarded for patience. Sunoco produced the smallest price corrections, but the stock still declined 11.26% on average. The average price correction for all issues during the four cycles was 15.82%.

Oil Stock Table

Date	Murphy Oil	XTO Energy	Sunoco	Apache Corp	Frontier Oil	Cycle Avg
Apr-04	$ 35.95	$ 21.61	28.15	$ 45.99	$ 21.90	
May-04	$ 31.71	$ 18.68	23.2	$ 38.53	$ 17.15	
Price Correction	11.79%	13.56%	17.58%	16.22%	21.69%	16.17%
Jul-04	$ 39.82	$ 23.20	27.22	$ 47.20	$ 30.74	
Aug-04	$ 34.84	$ 19.05	27.01	$ 42.45	$ 26.46	
Price Correction	12.51%	17.89%	0.77%	10.06%	13.92%	11.03%
Oct-04	$ 43.69	$ 26.61	36.15	$ 54.35	$ 44.33	
Jan-05	$ 37.80	$ 23.86	31.96	$ 47.45	$ 34.70	
Price Correction	13.48%	10.33%	11.59%	12.70%	21.72%	13.97%
Mar-05	$ 52.70	$ 35.18	41.7	$ 65.90	$ 55.52	
May-05	$ 41.89	$ 26.00	35.4	$ 51.52	$ 40.52	
Price Correction	20.51%	26.09%	15.11%	21.82%	27.02%	22.11%
Avg Price Correction	14.57%	16.97%	11.26%	15.20%	21.09%	15.82%

figure 15.2

As you may recall, technical analysis does not give you the tools to buy at the absolute low. In fact, you will want to wait for the price movement to begin to advance, confirming that the momentum is turning positive. As a result, realizing the entire correction will be nearly impossible. However, the lion's share of the price correction is attainable if you follow this disciplined approach to investing. As noted with the oil sector, when you use the pullback strategy, you enter into positions that are well off their high price levels. Such a strategy reduces risk and increases profit potential.

Short-term investors can use the 10-Week chart as a timing tool, using the buy signals to enter positions and the sell signals to take profits. The gains can be impressive, particularly when you consider the compounding results. *Figure 15.3* reflects the semiconductor sector's 10-Week chart. Short-term buy signals occurred on this chart in September 2004 and May 2005. One sell signal occurred in December 2004. Using those dates to buy and sell semiconductor stocks yielded impressive short-term profits.

Semiconductor Sector's 10-Week Chart

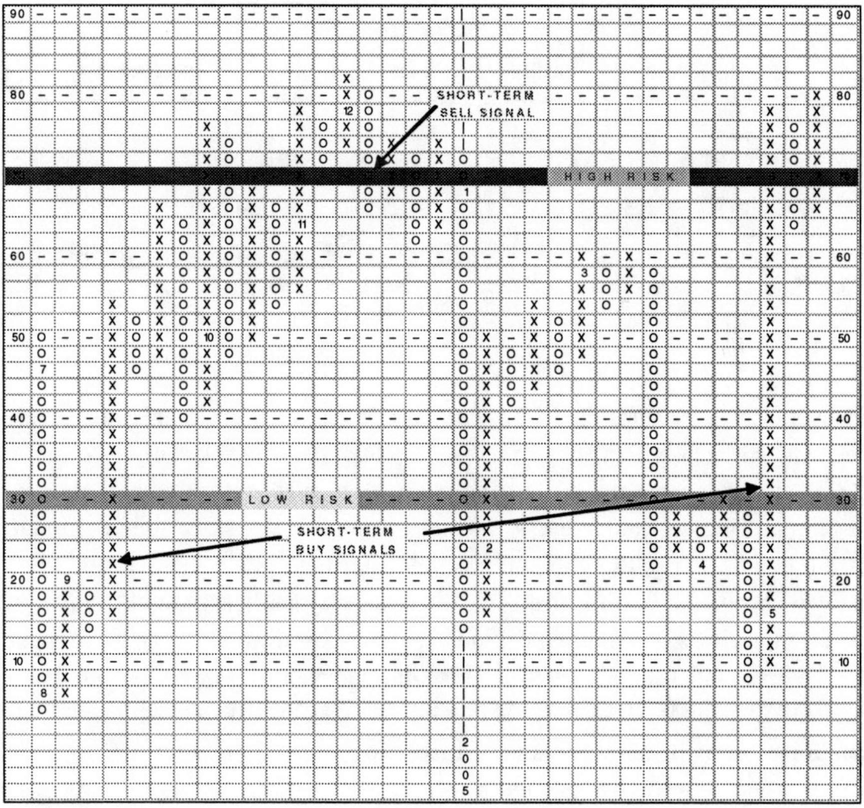

figure 15.3

187

Figure 15.4 is a select list of five semiconductor issues, including their high and low prices for the periods covered in the chart. Between September and December 2004, an average profit of 44.88% was realized for the five semiconductor issues. The May–July 2005 cycle provided a gain of 25.42%. Advanced Micro Devices was the best trading issue, advancing 86.35% between the two cycles. Analog Devices was the least profitable but still advanced 16.69%. The average advance for each issue covering both cycles was 35.15%. Again, you will not be able to buy at the absolute low and sell at the absolute high. You want to wait for the cycles to reverse and to indicate that the momentum is turning positive before buying. Conversely, you want to wait for the cycles to reverse and to turn negative before selling.

Semiconductor Stock Table

Date	Analog Devices	Applied Materials	Texas Instruments	Intel	Advanced Micro Devices	Cycle Avg
Sep-04	$ 35.59	$ 15.43	18.55	$ 19.69	$ 10.76	
Dec-04	$ 39.08	$ 18.33	25.88	$ 24.50	$ 24.95	
Short-Term Profit	9.81%	18.79%	39.51%	24.43%	131.88%	44.88%
May-05	$ 33.50	$ 14.90	24.93	$ 23.34	$ 14.21	
Jul-05	$ 41.40	$ 17.50	31.06	$ 28.16	$ 20.01	
Short-Term Profit	23.58%	17.45%	24.59%	20.65%	40.82%	25.42%
Avg Profit	16.69%	18.12%	32.05%	22.54%	86.35%	35.15%

figure 15.4

Looking back at *figure 15.3*, you can see that another abbreviated cycle began to emerge when the chart reversed up from the low-risk zone in February 2005. The advance only carried the chart up to 60% before reversing down in March. This particular cycle did not experience the same follow-through as the other two cycles. This lack of follow-through is a potential risk when using a short-term trading strategy. When such a risk occurs, make sure you manage the risk and sell any positions you purchased when the chart changes to a bearish status. In *figure 15.3*, this situation occurred when the O column reached 52% in March. A lower O column changes the 10-week status to Bear Confirmed even if the chart cannot reach 70% during the advance. At such a time, short-term investors should sell out on the negative status change in anticipation of another trading opportunity in the future (i.e., the next time the chart reverses up from the low-risk zone).

In summary, sector 10-Week charts give you an additional tool to make confident and proactive decisions. These charts help you avoid buying stocks in sectors that have already experienced a recent advance. At the same time, they help you know when corrections are likely over, allowing you to enter positions with lower risk and better profit potential.

CHAPTER 16

SECTOR STRATEGIES FOR CONFIDENT DECISIONS

Combining Bullish Percent charts, Relative Strength charts, and 10-Week charts allows you to create strategies for selecting sectors.

Once you select a strong sector, you can select strong stocks within the sector.

Three strategies used for sector selection:
Emerging Sector
Sector Momentum
Short-Selling

This chapter is designed to provide you with an ongoing routine for accurately assessing the overall market and easily pinpointing sector opportunities as they emerge. A complete sector analysis includes following Bullish Percent charts, Relative Strength charts, and 10-Week charts. However, regularly looking at all three indicators for every sector can be time consuming. Most investors do not have the time to create and maintain all these charts manually. Fortunately, technology exists to compile charts and indicators. Such technology allows you to focus your time and energy on making strong investment decisions. Access to this vast amount of information is essential in today's world.

The ability to identify sectors that are simultaneously advancing on both their Relative Strength and Bullish Percent charts, along with receiving timing signals from the 10-Week chart, is invaluable. A report that can show you each sector's bullish-percent, relative-strength, and 10-week position and status, along with the current column (X or O) for every sector, is referred to as a *sector snapshot*. This report allows you to gather and digest a large amount of information in little time. Such a report is readily available to you on the Investor Education Institute's Web site (http://www.institute4investors.com).

Figure 16.1 is an example of a sector snapshot for the banking sector. There is a lot of information in this snapshot. Using *figure 16.1* as a reference, note the definition of each column on a snapshot report.

Sector	Universe	BP %	BP COL	BP Status	RS %	RS Col	RS Status	10-WK %	10-WK COL	10-WK Status
Banking	Members	65.99%	O	Bear Con	74.32	O	Bear Alert	79.73%	X	Bull Con

figure 16.1

Heading	Description
Sector	The name of the sector analyzed.
Universe	Provides a link to a report that covers all of the members in the sector, including information on their Point & Figure and individual Relative Strength charts.
BP %	The actual bullish percentage of the sector. This column tells you the percent of sector members with a buy signal on their Point & Figure chart.
BP COL	The current column of the Bullish Percent chart. Is the chart rising in an X column or declining in an O column?
BP Status	The current status of the sector's Bullish Percent chart.
RS %	The actual relative-strength percentage of the sector. This column tells you the percent of sector members with a buy signal on their Relative Strength chart.
RS COL	The current column of the Relative Strength chart. Is the chart rising in an X column or declining in an O column?
RS Status	The current status of the sector's Relative Strength chart.
10-WK %	The actual percent of issues in the sector that are above their 10-week average price.
10-WK COL	The current column of the 10-Week chart. Is the chart rising in an X column or declining in an O column?
10-WK Status	The current status of the sector's 10-Week chart.

The example in *figure 16.1*, which is related to the banking sector, allows you to draw the following conclusions:

➢ The Bullish Percent chart is 65.99% and declining in a Bear Confirmed status. In other words, while 65.99% of stocks are on a buy signal, the stocks in the sector have been giving new sell signals on their Point & Figure charts, the supply/demand relationship in the banking sector is weak, and the absolute-price movement for the sector is declining.

➢ The Relative Strength chart is 74.32%, above the high-risk zone. The Relative Strength chart is in a declining O column and in a Bear Alert status.

➢ Both long-term indicators are negative for the banking sector. Both the absolute- and relative-price movements are bearish for the sector.

➢ The 10-Week chart is at 79.73% and moving higher in an X column. Its status is Bull Confirmed. The position of the 10-Week chart adds an additional negative to the banking sector analysis because the chart has moved into the high-risk zone.

➢ The snapshot of the banking sector is negative. Both long- and short-term indicators reflect that investors should focus on other sectors that are in a stronger position.

Let's look at another snapshot report: the biotechnology sector (*figure 16.2*). You can see that this sector is in a much better position.

Sector	Universe	BP %	BP COL	BP Status	RS %	RS Col	RS Status	10-WK %	10-WK COL	10-WK Status
Biotechnology	Members	39.57%	X	Bull Alert	34.45%	X	Bull Alert	61.71%	X	Bull Con

figure 16.2

➢ The Bullish Percent chart is relatively low—39.57%. Additionally, the chart is rising in an X column with a Bull Alert status. This position indicates that the sector is moving up after it declined into the low-risk zone.

➢ The Relative Strength chart is 34.45%, also rising in Bull Alert status.

➢ Both long-term indicators are positioned at relatively low-risk levels and are moving higher. The biotechnology sector is advancing in absolute *and* relative terms.

➢ The 10-Week chart is 61.71% and rising in an X column. The status is Bull Confirmed. Although it would be ideal to catch this 10-Week chart as it is reversing up from a lower level, it has not yet reached the high-risk level and is still advancing in a bullish status.

➢ All three indicators for the biotechnology sector are positive. You would want to take the next step with this sector. Drill down to the sector members to select the best individual issues to buy.

Figure 16.3 is a sample of a complete sector snapshot. When you access the Investor Education Institute's Web site and database, you will notice that you can sort snapshot reports by any of the columns, such as the B(ullish) P(ercent) % or R(elative) S(trength) %. Looking again at *figure 16.3*, notice that this version of the report is simply sorted alphabetically by sector name.

Figure 16.4 is an example of a report sorted by R(elative) S(trength) Col(umn). As a result, all sectors that are in a rising X column on their Relative Strength chart now appear at the top, followed by those in declining O columns. This sort allows you to see the leading sectors in the market easily because they will appear at the top of the list. Once the sort is completed, you can look at the other indicators to see if they are also well positioned. For example, the sector listed as "Food Beverage & Soap" shows the Bullish Percent chart in a declining column of O's; its Relative Strength chart is rising; the relative-price movement is higher, but the absolute-price movement is down. Based on what you have learned about combined Bullish Percent and Relative Strength charts, what would you do? That's right, you would most likely rule out this sector for investment.

In *figure 16.4*, the semiconductor sector shows both the Relative Strength and Bullish Percent charts rising in X columns. The 10-Week chart is 81.40%, meaning the short-term risk is high. For this sector, you would most likely wait for the 10-Week chart to decline before buying semiconductor stocks.

Figure 16.5 shows the snapshot report sorted by the R(elative) S(trength) % from highest to lowest. The oil sector is the highest, followed by oil-service, gas-utility, and electric-utility sectors. These are the strongest sectors in the market at the time of this snapshot report. Although their positions are at high-risk levels, these sectors have the highest percentage of members on buy signals on their individual Relative Strength charts. As long as the relative-strength column is rising, these are the leading sectors in the market.

Sector Snapshot

Sector	Unv	BP %	BP COL	RS %	RS Col	10-WK %	10-WK COL
AEROSPACE	Members	50.56%	X	52.81	O	64.04%	X
AUTOS	Members	50.00%	X	54.05	O	81.08%	X
BANKING	Members	65.99%	O	74.32	O	79.73%	X
BIOTECHNOLOGY	Members	39.57%	X	34.45	X	61.71%	X
BUILDINGS	Members	68.79%	X	68.79	O	80.14%	X
BUSINESS PROD & SERV	Members	58.70%	X	56.45	O	74.19%	X
CHEMICALS	Members	41.67%	O	67.06	O	58.82%	O
CHINA	Members	32.00%	X	56.00	O	56.00%	X
COMPUTERS	Members	40.20%	X	41.46	O	67.65%	X
DRUGS	Members	51.69%	X	33.71	O	55.06%	X
ELECTRONICS	Members	43.53%	X	37.43	O	74.27%	X
FINANCE	Members	60.49%	X	59.26	O	75.31%	X
FOOD BEVERAGE & SOAP	Members	59.46%	O	69.80	X	63.09%	X
FOREST & PAPER	Members	23.08%	X	41.03	O	53.85%	O
GAMING	Members	62.16%	X	75.68	O	75.68%	X
HEALTHCARE	Members	54.46%	X	57.23	X	67.69%	X
HOUSEHOLD GOODS	Members	48.84%	X	51.94	O	62.02%	X
INSURANCE	Members	74.29%	X	71.43	O	85.71%	X
INTERNET	Members	35.66%	X	41.96	X	67.83%	X
LEISURE	Members	47.87%	O	51.61	O	58.51%	O
MACHINERY & TOOLS	Members	65.06%	X	72.29	O	75.90%	X
MEDIA	Members	47.20%	O	42.40	O	53.60%	O
METALS NON-FERROUS	Members	53.52%	X	61.97	O	64.79%	O
OIL	Members	79.71%	X	86.23	X	94.20%	X
OIL SERVICE	Members	71.13%	X	82.47	X	91.75%	X
POLLUTION CONTROL	Members	51.11%	X	46.67	O	60.00%	O
PRECIOUS METALS	Members	35.29%	X	17.65	O	82.35%	O
PROTECTION & SAFETY	Members	53.85%	X	46.15	X	69.23%	O
REAL ESTATE	Members	76.33%	X	71.01	O	81.64%	X
RESTAURANTS	Members	61.29%	X	70.97	X	66.13%	X
RETAILING	Members	62.50%	X	62.19	X	75.50%	X
SAVINGS & LOANS	Members	54.20%	X	63.36	O	65.91%	X
SEMICONDUCTORS	Members	34.88%	X	26.74	X	81.40%	X
SOFTWARE	Members	44.68%	X	36.97	O	67.80%	X
STEEL	Members	50.94%	X	69.81	O	81.13%	X
TELECOM	Members	48.12%	X	41.04	O	71.54%	X
TEXTILES & APPAREL	Members	54.41%	O	54.41	O	67.65%	X
TRANSPORT NON-AIR	Members	58.44%	X	71.43	O	75.32%	O
UTILITY - ELECTRIC	Members	85.53%	O	76.32	X	85.53%	X
UTILITY - GAS	Members	84.21%	X	80.70	X	92.98%	X
UTILITY - WATER	Members	85.71%	X	71.43	O	78.57%	X
WALL STREET	Members	57.33%	X	52.00	O	80.00%	X

figure 16.3

Sector Snapshot
Sorted by R(elative) S(trength) Col(umn)

Sector	Unv	BP %	BP COL	RS %	RS Col	10-WK %	10-WK COL
BIOTECHNOLOGY	Members	39.57%	X	34.45	X	61.71%	X
FOOD BEVERAGE & SOAP	Members	59.46%	O	69.80	X	63.09%	X
HEALTHCARE	Members	54.46%	X	57.23	X	67.69%	X
INTERNET	Members	35.66%	X	41.96	X	67.83%	X
OIL	Members	79.71%	X	86.23	X	94.20%	X
OIL SERVICE	Members	71.13%	X	82.47	X	91.75%	X
PROTECTION & SAFETY	Members	53.85%	X	46.15	X	69.23%	O
RESTAURANTS	Members	61.29%	X	70.97	X	66.13%	X
RETAILING	Members	62.50%	X	62.19	X	75.50%	X
SEMICONDUCTORS	Members	34.88%	X	26.74	X	81.40%	X
UTILITY - ELECTRIC	Members	85.53%	O	76.32	X	85.53%	X
UTILITY - GAS	Members	84.21%	X	80.70	X	92.98%	X
AEROSPACE	Members	50.56%	X	52.81	O	64.04%	X
AUTOS	Members	50.00%	X	54.05	O	81.08%	X
BANKING	Members	65.99%	O	74.32	O	79.73%	X
BUILDINGS	Members	68.79%	X	68.79	O	80.14%	X
BUSINESS PROD & SERV	Members	58.70%	X	56.45	O	74.19%	X
CHEMICALS	Members	41.67%	O	67.06	O	58.82%	O
CHINA	Members	32.00%	X	56.00	O	56.00%	X
COMPUTERS	Members	40.20%	X	41.46	O	67.65%	X
DRUGS	Members	51.69%	X	33.71	O	55.06%	X
ELECTRONICS	Members	43.53%	X	37.43	O	74.27%	X
FINANCE	Members	60.49%	X	59.26	O	75.31%	X
FOREST & PAPER	Members	23.08%	X	41.03	O	53.85%	O
GAMING	Members	62.16%	X	75.68	O	75.68%	X
HOUSEHOLD GOODS	Members	48.84%	X	51.94	O	62.02%	X
INSURANCE	Members	74.29%	X	71.43	O	85.71%	X
LEISURE	Members	47.87%	O	51.61	O	58.51%	O
MACHINERY & TOOLS	Members	65.06%	X	72.29	O	75.90%	X
MEDIA	Members	47.20%	O	42.40	O	53.60%	O
METALS NON-FERROUS	Members	53.52%	X	61.97	O	64.79%	O
POLLUTION CONTROL	Members	51.11%	X	46.67	O	60.00%	O
PRECIOUS METALS	Members	35.29%	X	17.65	O	82.35%	O
REAL ESTATE	Members	76.33%	X	71.01	O	81.64%	X
SAVINGS & LOANS	Members	54.20%	X	63.36	O	65.91%	X
SOFTWARE	Members	44.68%	X	36.97	O	67.80%	X
STEEL	Members	50.94%	X	69.81	O	81.13%	X
TELECOM	Members	48.12%	X	41.04	O	71.54%	X
TEXTILES & APPAREL	Members	54.41%	O	54.41	O	67.65%	X
TRANSPORT NON-AIR	Members	58.44%	X	71.43	O	75.32%	O
UTILITY - WATER	Members	85.71%	X	71.43	O	78.57%	X
WALL STREET	Members	57.33%	X	52.00	O	80.00%	X

figure 16.4

Sector Snapshot
Sorted by R(elative) S(trength) %

Sector	Unv	BP %	BP COL	RS %	RS Col	10-WK %	10-WK COL
OIL	Members	79.71%	X	86.23	X	94.20%	X
OIL SERVICE	Members	71.13%	X	82.47	X	91.75%	X
UTILITY - GAS	Members	84.21%	X	80.70	X	92.98%	X
UTILITY - ELECTRIC	Members	85.53%	O	76.32	X	85.53%	X
GAMING	Members	62.16%	X	75.68	O	75.68%	X
BANKING	Members	65.99%	O	74.32	O	79.73%	X
MACHINERY & TOOLS	Members	65.06%	X	72.29	O	75.90%	X
INSURANCE	Members	74.29%	X	71.43	O	85.71%	X
TRANSPORT NON-AIR	Members	58.44%	X	71.43	O	75.32%	O
UTILITY - WATER	Members	85.71%	X	71.43	O	78.57%	X
REAL ESTATE	Members	76.33%	X	71.01	O	81.64%	X
RESTAURANTS	Members	61.29%	X	70.97	X	66.13%	X
STEEL	Members	50.94%	X	69.81	O	81.13%	X
FOOD BEVERAGE & SOAP	Members	59.46%	O	69.80	X	63.09%	X
BUILDINGS	Members	68.79%	X	68.79	O	80.14%	X
CHEMICALS	Members	41.67%	O	67.06	O	58.82%	O
SAVINGS & LOANS	Members	54.20%	X	63.36	O	65.91%	X
RETAILING	Members	62.50%	X	62.19	X	75.50%	X
METALS NON-FERROUS	Members	53.52%	X	61.97	O	64.79%	O
FINANCE	Members	60.49%	X	59.26	O	75.31%	X
HEALTHCARE	Members	54.46%	X	57.23	X	67.69%	X
BUSINESS PROD & SERV	Members	58.70%	X	56.45	O	74.19%	X
CHINA	Members	32.00%	X	56.00	O	56.00%	X
TEXTILES & APPAREL	Members	54.41%	O	54.41	O	67.65%	X
AUTOS	Members	50.00%	X	54.05	O	81.08%	X
AEROSPACE	Members	50.56%	X	52.81	O	64.04%	X
WALL STREET	Members	57.33%	X	52.00	O	80.00%	X
HOUSEHOLD GOODS	Members	48.84%	X	51.94	O	62.02%	X
LEISURE	Members	47.87%	O	51.61	O	58.51%	O
POLLUTION CONTROL	Members	51.11%	X	46.67	O	60.00%	O
PROTECTION & SAFETY	Members	53.85%	X	46.15	X	69.23%	O
MEDIA	Members	47.20%	O	42.40	O	53.60%	O
INTERNET	Members	35.66%	X	41.96	X	67.83%	X
COMPUTERS	Members	40.20%	X	41.46	O	67.65%	X
TELECOM	Members	48.12%	X	41.04	O	71.54%	X
FOREST & PAPER	Members	23.08%	X	41.03	O	53.85%	O
ELECTRONICS	Members	43.53%	X	37.43	O	74.27%	X
SOFTWARE	Members	44.68%	X	36.97	O	67.80%	X
BIOTECHNOLOGY	Members	39.57%	X	34.45	X	61.71%	X
DRUGS	Members	51.69%	X	33.71	O	55.06%	X
SEMICONDUCTORS	Members	34.88%	X	26.74	X	81.40%	X
PRECIOUS METALS	Members	35.29%	X	17.65	O	82.35%	O

figure 16. 5

The sectors toward the top of the list with declining relative-strength columns hold significant risk. Although their relative-strength percentage is high, the number is falling as sector members are beginning to perform worse than the broad market. You would want to avoid buying into these sectors. If you owned positions in these sectors, you would most likely want to sell.

The sectors on the bottom of the list have the lowest relative strength. For example, when this snapshot report was taken, the lowest sector in this example was precious metals; its Relative Strength chart is in an O column. You should be patient with the lowest sectors if the relative-strength column is still declining. You want to wait for these Relative Strength charts to begin advancing and to indicate they are emerging as a potential leading sector. Until the precious-metals sector reversed up, it was a lagging sector in the market. Once it reversed up, however, it was one of the best sectors to focus on for new investments.

The precious-metals Relative Strength chart reversed up into a rising column in August 2005 and rose all the way up to 90% by March 2005. The price of gold rose with it from $450 per ounce up to a high of $725 by May 2006. Precious-metals stocks soared during that time, making it a top-performing sector.

Back to *figure 16.5*, other sectors that were at the bottom of the list, but were in X columns on their Relative Strength charts, were potentially emerging as market leaders after reaching very low-risk levels. In *figure 16.5*, the three lowest relative-strength sectors that were beginning to rise were semiconductors, biotechnology, and Internet. All three produced lucrative investment opportunities in the following months.

Emerging-Sector Strategy

At this point, I would like to spend some time looking at how you can use a snapshot report to develop sector strategies. The first strategy, which I also consider the most rewarding, is the *emerging-sector strategy*. This strategy pinpoints the sectors that are beginning new relative-strength cycles and emerging as new market leaders. The goal of this strategy is to focus on sectors that can outperform the broad market for the long term.

I'll start with the sector snapshot shown in *figure 16.3*. On this report, I will focus on only those sectors that are advancing in a column of X's on their

Relative Strength charts. Next, look at the relative-strength percentage from highest to lowest. Those sectors with a relative-strength percentage reading above 60% are removed from the list. I also want to eliminate any sectors declining in an O column on their Bullish Percent or 10-Week chart. If you use the snapshot information on the Investor Education Institute's Web site and databases, you can create a report that automatically completes the above sorts and filters.

The result is a list of sectors with the lowest relative-strength percentage that are rising. These sectors also will have supportive Bullish Percent and 10-Week charts. This strategy takes the complete list of sectors, such as on *figure 16.3*, and creates a list of only four sectors, as displayed in *figure 16.6*. Interestingly, you can see that the list of sectors in *figure 16.6* has two basic industry themes—technology and health care.

Emerging-Sector Strategy Report

Sector	Unv	BP %	BP COL	RS %	RS Col	10-WK %	10-WK COL
HEALTHCARE	Members	54.46%	X	57.23	X	67.69%	X
INTERNET	Members	35.66%	X	41.96	X	67.83%	X
BIOTECHNOLOGY	Members	39.57%	X	34.45	X	61.71%	X
SEMICONDUCTORS	Members	34.88%	X	26.74	X	81.40%	X

figure 16.6

Once you discover these sectors, your next step is to drill down into the sector universe to find the members providing the best investment opportunities. Again, if you use the snapshot report on the Investor Education Institute's Web site and databases, you can click on the "Members" link for each of the sectors and get a sector-universe report. This report shows every issue in each sector. Of course, you probably don't have time to analyze every issue. Similar to the sector snapshot, the sector-universe report also has sorting and filter capabilities. Typically, you will want to reduce the entire universe to show just the stocks on a buy signal on their Point & Figure and Relative Strength charts.

Figure 16.7 is an example of a sector-universe report for the Internet sector. The report displays every Internet issue on a buy signal on both its Point & Figure and Relative Strength charts. Additionally, every issue shows that its Point & Figure trend is up, meaning the main trend line in effect for each issue is the bullish support line , and every issue is in a rising X column on its Relative Strength chart. The companies on this list are the strongest issues in the Internet sector. They have strong absolute- and relative-price movement and are your best opportunities in the sector.

Internet Sector Universe Report

| Symbol | Company Name | Exchange | Point & Figure | | | Relative Strength | | 10-Week |
			Signal	Col	Trend	Signal	Column	
NTES	Netease.com Inc ADS	Nasdaq	(Buy)	O	Up	Buy	X	Above
CNET	Cnet Networks Inc	Nasdaq	(Buy)	X	Up	Buy	X	Above
ET	E*Trade Financial Inc	NYSE	(Buy)	X	Up	Buy	X	Above
MNST	Monster Worldwide Inc	Nasdaq	(Buy)	X	Up	Buy	X	Above
AMTD	Ameritrade Holding Corp	Nasdaq	(Buy)	X	Up	Buy	X	Above
TRAD	Tradestation Group Inc	Nasdaq	(Buy)	X	Up	Buy	X	Above
GOOG	GOOGLE INC CL A	Nasdaq	(Buy)	O	Up	Buy	X	Above
GSIC	GSI Commerce Inc	Nasdaq	(Buy)	X	Up	Buy	X	Above
UBET	YouBet.com Inc	Nasdaq	(Buy)	X	Up	Buy	X	Above
RATE	Bankrate Inc	Nasdaq	(Buy)	X	Up	Buy	X	Above
ASKJ	Ask Jeeves Inc	Nasdaq	(Buy)	X	Up	Buy	X	Above
APTM	Aptimus Inc	Nasdaq	(Buy)	X	Up	Buy	X	Above
SOHU	Sohu.com Inc	Nasdaq	(Buy)	X	Up	Buy	X	Above
WEBX	WEBEX COMMUN INC	Nasdaq	(Buy)	X	Up	Buy	X	Above
EQIX	EQUINIX INC	Nasdaq	(Buy)	X	Up	Buy	X	Above
XXIA	IXIA	Nasdaq	(Buy)	X	Up	Buy	X	Above
NFLX	NETFLIX INC	Nasdaq	(Buy)	O	Up	Buy	X	Above
CKCM	Click Commerce Inc	Nasdaq	(Buy)	X	Up	Buy	X	Above

figure 16.7

At this point, we have a list of the strongest stocks in a sector that is beginning to emerge as market leader. Whether you do the analysis yourself, or you rely on fundamental analysts to provide you the information, you may want to reduce the list further through the application of fundamental analysis. The companies on this list that are both technically and fundamentally sound can be your potential investments in the Internet sector.

We already know each issue on the list is on a buy signal on both its Point & Figure and Relative Strength charts. We now want to find the strongest chart patterns and select those with a good entry point. This step is completed by looking at the charts for each issue on the list.

Shown in *figure 16.8* is the Point & Figure chart for NetEase.com, Inc. (NTES), one of the issues from the Internet sector. As you can see, these shares declined from $55 to $38 from late 2004 into early 2005. During that time, supply was in control. After declining to \$38, demand met the supply, and the price stopped dropping. After establishing a bottom, demand began to overtake supply, and the chart broke a spread triple top at \$46. At the same time, it broke the bearish resistance line, indicating that the main trend was demand in control.

NetEase.com, Inc. (NTES): Point & Figure Chart

59																					59
58																			X		58
57																			X		57
56																			X		56
55	X			.															X		55
54	12	O		X	.														X		54
53	X	O	X	X	O	.							X					6			53
52	O	X	O	X	O	X	O	X	.	Breaks Triple			X	O				X			52
51	O	X	O	X	O	X	1	X	O	Top and			X	O	X			X			51
50	O		O		O	X	O	X	O	Bearish			X	O	X	O	X				50
49				O		O		O		Resistance			4	O	X	O	X				49
48							O			Line		X	X	O			5				48
47							O		.			X	O	X							47
46							O		.			X	O	X			.				46
45							O	X		X		X	O	X			.				45
44							O	X	O	2	O	X	O			.					44
43							O	X	O	X	O	X	3		.						43
42							O		O	X	O	X	O	X	.						42
41									O		O	X	O	X	.						41
40											O	X	O	.							40
39											O	X	.								39
38											O	.									38
37											.										37
				2																	
				0																	
				0																	
				5																	

figure 16.8

Figure 16.9 is the Relative Strength chart for NTES. Here you can see that the company's relative-price movement declined from late 2003 to July 2004. After reaching a bottom, the Relative Strength chart reversed up into an X column in October 2004. In November 2004, the chart gave a new buy signal and indicated that the company's price trend should perform better than the market.

When the Point & Figure chart gave a buy signal in March 2005, both the Relative Strength and Point & Figure charts for NTES show constructive patterns. At that time, NetEase.com, Inc. was one of the strongest issues in an emerging sector, making it a good choice for new investments.

NetEase.com, Inc. (NTES): Relative Strength Chart

Price	1	2	3	4	5	6	7	8	9
31.9394									
30.1315	10				New				
28.4259	X	O			Relative				
26.8169	X	O			Strength				X
25.299	X	O			Buy Signal				X
23.867	9	O							X
22.516	X	O	X						8
21.2415	X	O	3	O					6
20.0392	X	O	2	O			X		X
18.9049	X	11	X	O	6		11	O	4
17.8348	7	O	1	4	X	O	X	O	3
16.8253	X	12	X	O	X	O	X	1	X
15.8729	6	O	X	5		7	10	O	X
14.9744	X	O				O	X	2	
14.1268	X					O	X		
13.3272	X					O			
12.5728	X								
11.8611	5								
11.1898	X								
10.5564	X								
9.9588	X								
9.3951	4								
			2				2		
			0				0		
			0				0		
			4				5		

figure 16.9

The emerging-sector strategy can be quite rewarding. This strategy helps you identify sectors that have completed a severe decline and are beginning to show signs that a positive cycle is emerging. With continued improvement, these sectors could become the highest relative-strength sectors at some point, making them excellent investment choices. Proper execution of the emerging-sector strategy can build your wealth over the long term. However, patience and risk management are key elements of a successful execution of the emerging-sector strategy.

The emerging-sector strategy requires patience. Frequently, emerging sectors go through a transitional period in which the sector moves from being viewed as a poor investment to being perceived as a potential value. The buying opportunity occurs during such a transitional period. The opportunity occurs when the indicators have signaled that a bottom is in place and a new trend is emerging. A sector that is truly emerging as a market leader may take months or years to become one of the best sectors for investments. As you may recall from our oil-sector example (*figure 14.1*), between 1998 and 2000, very few investors looked favorably upon this sector. Yet, between 1998 and 2000, the sector's Relative Strength chart hit bottom and began to turn upward. Not until 2003–2005 did the sector become a popular sector for investors.

Risk management is also important when using the emerging-sector strategy. Not every sector that initially appears as an emerging market leader will follow through in the long term. Make sure you have some risk-management strategies in place if signals change. For example, what will you do if the Bullish Percent or Relative Strength chart starts to turn down and gives new bearish signals? What if the stock you select does not follow through on its new Point & Figure or Relative Strength chart buy signal? Continuous follow-up is necessary. Do not buy and hope everything works out. Follow the sector indicators to make sure there is not a reversal in the absolute or relative trend. Follow the Point & Figure chart to make sure the strong conditions persist.

You don't have to become alarmed with every minor change. Even if the Bullish Percent chart reverses down, do not use the reversal as a signal to panic. If the chart is still in a bullish status and if the other indicators, such as the Relative Strength chart, hold up, be patient with your positions. Similarly, if you get a sell signal on a stock's Point & Figure chart, stay with the position if the Relative Strength chart holds a solid pattern. Significant changes are a different story, however. If the sector's Bullish Percent chart experiences a negative change and the stock's individual Relative Strength chart gives a sell signal, you have enough evidence this position will most likely not provide desirable results. In this case, you will want to reduce or eliminate your exposure to this investment.

Sector-Momentum Strategy

Another rewarding sector strategy is the *sector-momentum strategy*. The goal of the sector-momentum strategy is to focus on sectors currently outperforming the broad market and to ride the momentum of these sectors higher. Whereas the emerging-sector strategy is an attempt to catch the emergence of new sector leaders, the *sector-momentum strategy* attempts to invest in the most profitable sectors that are well into a mature advance. The sector-momentum strategy is typically a shorter-term approach.

Starting with a sector-snapshot report sorted by relative-strength percentage from highest to lowest (*figure 16.5*), we identify those sectors advancing in a column of X's on their Relative Strength charts. The sector-momentum strategy focuses on the highest relative-strength sectors; therefore, sectors with a relative-strength percentage reading below 60% are removed from the list. We also eliminate any sectors in an O column on their Bullish Percent chart or 10-Week chart. These eliminations leave us with a list of sectors that have the highest Relative Strength chart as well as charts that are still rising. These sectors also have supportive Bullish Percent and 10-Week charts. This strategy takes the complete list of sectors from *figure 16.5* and creates a list of only three sectors (*figure 16.10*).

Sector-Momentum Strategy Report

Sector	Unv	BP %	BP COL	RS %	RS Col	10-WK %	10-WK COL
OIL	Members	79.71%	X	86.23	X	94.20%	X
OIL SERVICE	Members	71.13%	X	82.47	X	91.75%	X
UTILITY - GAS	Members	84.21%	X	80.70	X	92.98%	X

figure 16.10

The sector-momentum strategy will emphasize the 10-week indicator more than the emerging strategy will. Remember, the emerging-sector strategy is a longer-term approach, so the longer-term indicators are highlighted. The sector-momentum strategy is a shorter-term strategy; therefore, timing will be more important. Although the sectors we are buying into using the sector-momentum strategy are market leaders, they are also at higher risk levels on their Bullish Percent and Relative Strength charts. At some point, these sectors will form a major top and begin to cycle lower. Using the 10-week indicator for these sectors allows you to enter into these strong sectors after a price correction. This strategy will increase your profit potential and reduce risk.

For the sector-momentum strategy, you want to see the 10-Week charts decline into the low-risk zone below 30%, then begin to reverse up. As long as the longer-term indicators continue to hold, the reversal up in the 10-week indicator provides you the lower-risk entry point to buy into the strongest sectors. Using *figure 16.10* as an example, notice how the 10-Week charts on the sector-momentum list are already at a high-risk level. In fact, they are above 90%. These short-term indicators imply you would not want to enter new positions at this time. An investor would be wise to be patient and wait for a price adjustment that allows entrance at a reduced risk level.

Similar to the emerging-sector strategy, once you discover the momentum sectors in which you want to invest, your next step is to drill down into the sector universe to find the individual stocks that provide the best investment opportunities. Look for the stocks in the sector where both their Point & Figure and Relative Strength charts have a buy signal.

Note that the list of stocks for the highest relative-strength sectors can be quite lengthy. After all, these are the strongest sectors and may have a large number of stocks with strong Point & Figure and Relative Strength charts. As a result, fundamental analysis may help reduce the list of issues you will consider for your portfolio.

Short-Selling Sector Strategy

While professional investors use a short-selling strategy regularly, most individual investors find this strategy confusing. In essence, selling short is an attempt to profit from a decline in a specific stock or market index.

To profit from selling an investment short, you need to first identify the sectors positioned for a decline. The idea is to isolate sectors that have completed positive cycles on both their Bullish Percent and Relative Strength charts. In other words, you want to identify sectors with indicators that are beginning a bearish phase.

To identify these sectors, we can again use the sector snapshot in *figure 16.5*. This report shows the sectors declining in an O column on their Relative Strength chart. We remove any sectors rising in an X column on their Bullish Percent chart. This elimination leaves us with a list of sectors declining on both their Bullish Percent and Relative Strength charts. A sample list is displayed in *figure 16.11*. The sectors at the top of the list have the highest relative-strength percentage; however, the relative strength is declining. This direction indicates stocks in these sectors are performing worse than the broad market. Furthermore, since their Bullish Percent charts are also in an O column, these sectors are moving down in absolute terms as well.

For a short-selling strategy, you also want to see the 10-Week charts advance into the high-risk zone above 70% then begin to reverse down. As long as the longer-term indicators continue to hold their declining O columns, the reversal down in the 10-week indicator provides you an entry point to sell short into the weakest sectors. When the 10-Week chart reaches a high-risk level, issues in these sectors will be near a short-term high; this is the ideal time to sell short in these sectors.

Short-Selling Sector Strategy Report

Sector	Unv	BP %	BP COL	RS %	RS Col	10-WK %	10-WK COL
BANKING	Members	65.99%	O	74.32	O	79.73%	X
CHEMICALS	Members	41.67%	O	67.06	O	58.82%	O
TEXTILES & APPAREL	Members	54.41%	O	54.41	O	67.65%	X
LEISURE	Members	47.87%	O	51.61	O	58.51%	O
MEDIA	Members	47.20%	O	42.40	O	53.60%	O

figure 16.11

In *figure 16.11*, you can note there are three sectors in a column of O's on their 10-Week charts. These are the sectors to further investigate. Looking at the 10-Week charts for each sector will give you further detail. *Figure 16.12* is the 10-Week chart for the leisure sector. Notice this sector is declining after reaching a high. After reaching 70% in June 2005, the sector reversed down and changed to Bear Alert status in July 2005. With both the Bullish Percent and Relative Strength charts declining for the leisure sector, coupled with the short-term sell signal in its 10-week indicator, all three indicators appear weak.

The chart in *figure 16.11* shows that the banking sector's 10-Week chart is at 79.73%, which is a high-risk level. In this sector, the 10-Week chart is still in an X column, and the sector is still advancing. In this case, you want to hold off selling short until that 10-Week chart reverses down. *Figure 16.13* is the 10-Week chart for the banking sector. You can see that the last time the banking sector's 10-Week chart reached the high-risk zone, it went to 88% before peaking. In January 2005, the chart reversed down, giving a short-term sell signal. Prior to selling short, you want to see similar action on this chart. When the chart reverses, the time is ideal to execute a short-selling strategy, assuming the long-term indicators remain negative for the banking sector.

Leisure Sector's 10-Week Chart

```
90 -  -  -  -  | -  -  -  -  -  -  -  -  -  -  -  -  -  -  -  -  -  -  -  -  -  -
            X  |
            X  O
            X  O
80 -  X  -  X  1 -  -  -  -  -  -  -  -  -  -  -  -  -  -  -  -  -  -  -  -  -  -
      X  O  X  O
      X  O  X  O
      X  C  X  O
      X  O     O
70═══════════O═══════════HIGH  RISK═══════════X═════════════════════════════
      B        O                          X  O  X
      X        O              X           X  O  X  O
      X        O              X  O        X  O  X  O
      X        O              X  O        X  O  X  O
60 -  X  -  -  O  X  -  2  O  -  -  -  -  -  X  7  -  O  -  -  -  -  -  -  -  -  -
   O  X        O  X  O  X  O                6        O  ◄── Short-Term
   O  X        O  X  O  X  O                X              Sell Signal
   O           O  X  O  X                   X
              O  X  O  X  O  X     X        X
50 -  -  -  -  | -  O  X  O  3  O  X  O  -  -  -  -  X  -  -  -  -  -  -  -  -  -
              |     O  X  O  X  O  X  O        X
              |     O  X  O  X  O              X
              |     O  X  O        O           X
              |     O              O  X        X
40 -  -  -  -  | -  -  -  -  -  -  -  O  X  O  -  -  X  -  -  -  -  -  -  -  -  -
              |                      O  X  O        X
              |                      O  X  4        X
              |                      O     O        X
              |                            O        X
30 ═══════════|══ L O W  R I S K ══════════ O ══════ X ════════════════════════
              |                            O        X
              |                            O  X     X
              |                            O  X  O  X
              |                            O  X  O  X
20 -  -  -  -  | -  -  -  -  -  -  -  -  -  O  X  O  X  -  -  -  -  -  -  -  -  -
              |                            O  X  O
              |                            5
              |
10 -  -  -  -  2 -  -  -  -  -  -  -  -  -  -  -  -  -  -  -  -  -  -  -  -  -  -
              0
              0
              5
```

figure 16.12

Short-selling is a concept many investors have trouble understanding. Most people view investing as a process of buying an asset, holding the asset while it appreciates, and eventually selling it to make a profit. "Shorting" is the opposite: an investor only makes money when a security falls in value. When an investor sells short, he or she is anticipating a *decrease* in price. This approach may sound confusing, but the strategy is actually a simple concept.

Bank Sector's 10-Week Indicator

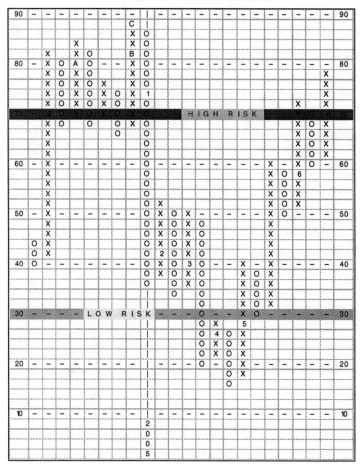

figure 16.13

When you short-sell a stock, your brokerage firm lends the stock to you, and you sell this stock. The stock will come from the firm's own inventory, from another one of the firm's customers, or from another brokerage firm. You sell the shares, and the total proceeds are credited to your account. Eventually, you must "close" the short position by buying back the shares and returning them to your broker. This action is also referred to as *covering the short position*. If the price drops, you can buy back the stock at the lower price and make a profit on the difference. If the price of the stock rises, you have to buy the stock back at the higher price; in that case, you will lose money.

Short-Selling Example

Let's say you decide to sell short one hundred shares of company XYZ. Let's say that although the stock is trading at $50, you expect the stock will decline. The transaction is straightforward, and one of two things will happen in the coming months:

XYZ Stock Falls to $50	
Borrowed and sold 100 shares of XYZ at $50:	$5,000
Bought (covered) 100 shares of XYZ at $25:	($2,500)
Your **Profit**:	$2,500

XYZ Stock Rises to $75	
Borrowed and sold 100 shares of XYZ at $50:	$5,000
Bought (covered) 100 shares of XYZ at $75:	($7,500)
Your **Loss**:	($2,500)

When using the short-selling strategy, you are essentially reversing the investment process. In the emerging- and momentum-sector strategies, your stock selection is focused on the strongest issues, expecting to profit from an advance. Usually, the investment process is to buy low and sell high. The short-selling strategy is the opposite: you attempt to profit from a stock you expect to decline. The process to sell short is to first sell high and then buy low. This process requires a different frame of mind.

More on the Short-Selling Strategy

As I mentioned with the emerging-sector and sector-momentum strategies, once you discover a sector matching your strategy, your next step is to drill down into the sector universe to find the stocks providing the best opportunities. In the short-selling strategy, you are looking for the best stocks to sell short, or stocks on a sell signal on their Point & Figure and Relative Strength charts. Rather than selecting the relative-strength leaders in strong sectors to purchase, you'll want to select *lagging issues* in the weaker sectors. Lagging issues are stocks that are on a sell signal and trading below their bearish resistance line on the Point & Figure chart and are on a sell signal, or show a deteriorating Relative Strength chart.

On April 25, 2006, the real-estate sector met the criteria to be included in the short-selling strategy. *Figure 16.14* shows the snapshot of the real-estate sector on that date. Notice how all three indicators (bullish-percent, relative-strength, and 10-week) were all in declining O columns. With the 10-week indicator for the sector still above 30%, this was a good time to sell short in the real-estate sector.

Real-Estate Sector Snapshot
April 25, 2006

Sector	Unv	BP %	BP COL	RS %	RS Col	10-WK %	10-WK COL
REAL ESTATE	Members	60.85%	O	58.02%	O	43.49%	O

figure 16.14

After you identify a weak sector, the next step in the short-selling strategy is to find stocks in the sector that have negative patterns on their Point & Figure and Relative Strength charts (i.e., lagging issues). Investigate these stocks further as potential candidates to sell short. Review each stock's Point & Figure and Relative Strength charts to find the issues best positioned for a decline. This requires a short-selling frame of mind. We already know each issue on the list has negative chart patterns. Now we want to find the weakest patterns and select those with a good entry point to sell short.

Figure 16.15 shows the Point & Figure chart for the St. Joe Company (JOE), a weak issue in the real-estate sector. In February 2006, the chart broke its long-standing bullish support line at $62. At that point, the bearish resistance line became the main trend line on the chart, indicating that the trend was down. In March 2006, the chart gave a triple-bottom sell signal at $58. Additionally, the chart fell below the low reached the previous October. Therefore, when it fell to $58, it actually broke a spread-quadruple-bottom pattern. Although it was clear that supply was already in control of this issue, breaking the quadruple bottom indicated that JOE was about to move to lower ground.

St. Joe Company (JOE): Point & Figure Chart

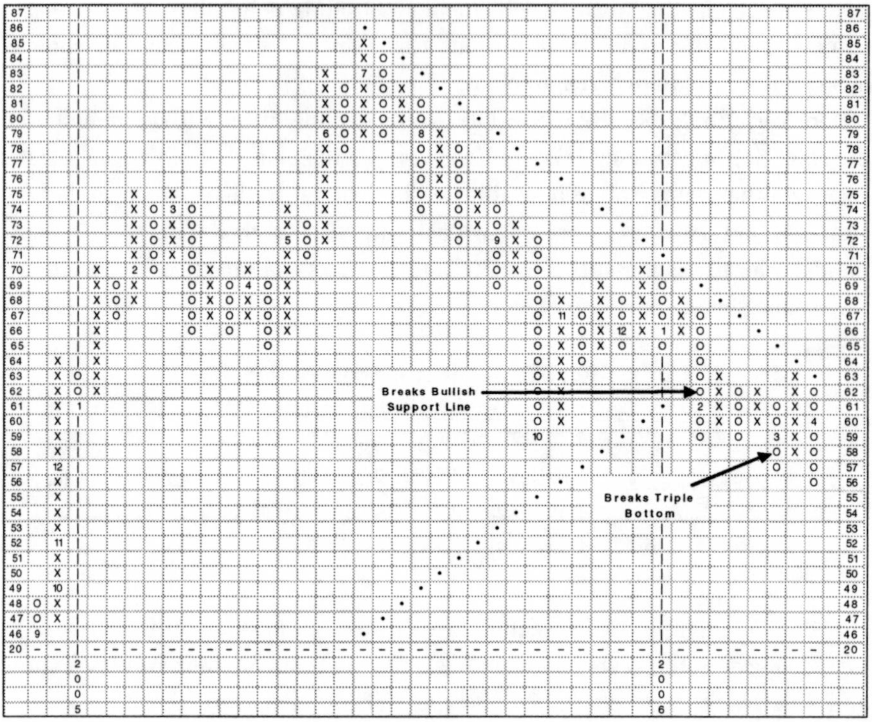

Breaks Bullish Support Line

Breaks Triple Bottom

figure 16.15

Figure 16.16 shows the Relative Strength chart for JOE. After a long-term advance, this chart peaked in June 2005. The chart reversed down into an O column in September 2005 and continued to move lower in early 2006. Although an official sell signal did not happen on this chart, the pattern indicated that JOE was beginning a period in which the stock would underperform the broad market. With both the Point & Figure and Relative Strength chart weak, JOE was a candidate to sell short in the real-estate sector.

Following the weak indicators in the real-estate sector and in JOE's Point & Figure and Relative Strength charts, the shares fell to $41 in just two months. This decline of more than 25% was a great opportunity for investors who follow the sector's short-selling strategy. Selling-short weak stocks that are in weak sectors can help you profit from declining markets, sectors, and stocks. Implementing this strategy positions you to become a truly dynamic investor. No longer will you have to rely on rising market conditions to make positive progress in your investment portfolio.

Following all three sector strategies (emerging, momentum, and short-selling) will allow you to profit from advancing sectors and stocks while also profiting from declining sectors and stocks.

St. Joe Company (JOE): Relative Strength Chart

Price														Price
31.9394														31.9394
30.1315												6		30.1315
28.4259												5	O	28.4259
26.8169												2	O	26.8169
25.299	Relative Strength ⟶											9		25.299
23.867	Chart Reverses											1	O	23.867
22.516	Down											12	O	22.516
21.2415												11	2	21.2415
20.0392												10	3	20.0392
18.9049												X		18.9049
17.8348	O			X								8		17.8348
16.8253	7	X	10	O								7		16.8253
15.8729	11	3	O	X	O							2		15.8729
14.9744	O	X	O	X	12							9		14.9744
14.1268	O	X	5		3							7		14.1268
13.3272	2				4							5		13.3272
12.5728					5							4		12.5728
11.8611					6							1		11.8611
11.1898					7	11						X		11.1898
10.5564					O	X	O					7		10.5564
9.9588					8	X	O	5		5		6		9.9588
9.3951					O		12	3	O	4	O	4		9.3951
8.8633							1	X	O	X	O	3		8.8633
8.3616							O	X	8	X	10	2		8.3616
7.8883								2	9		O	1		7.8883
7.4418											O	12		7.4418
7.0206											O	X		7.0206
6.6232											O	X		6.6232
6.2483											O			6.2483
5.8946														5.8946
	1	1			1			1			2	2	2	
	9	9			9			9			0	0	0	
	9	9			9			9			0	0	0	
	6	7			8			9			0	5	6	

figure 16.16

211

SECTION 4

MARKET ANALYSIS

CHAPTER 17

USING BULLISH PERCENT CHARTS TO ANALYZE BROAD MARKET TRENDS

> Market Bullish Percent charts will help you understand the supply-demand relationship in the overall market. This is important because you will want to be aggressive when demand is in control and defensive when supply is in control.
>
> Market Bullish Percent charts will help you understand the risk level in the broad market.
>
> Recording and interpreting broad market Bullish Percent charts is similar to the process used for sector Bullish Percent charts.

Too many investors pass by an analysis of the overall market and go right into trying to find a hot stock to buy. They feel that stocks of fundamentally sound companies will go up regardless of the market's trend. Such an approach can be a costly mistake. At times, the price movement in the overall market can be all encompassing. By using the tools introduced in this section, you will be able to identify significant trends in the broad market and position your investments accordingly.

You may be a whiz at picking stocks, but if you enter the market at the wrong time, your results can be disastrous. Think back to the year 2000. Even good stock pickers who bought in 2000 suffered major losses. A change in the broad market is often a leading indicator of changes that will soon occur in many sectors and individual stocks. If the market begins a declining trend, the trends for sectors and individual stocks that were previously positive may also change.

In a different scenario, you can have inadequate stock-selection skills, but if you enter the market at the right time, you will enjoy desirable results. For example, some novice investors who entered the market toward the end of the 2001–2002 bear market enjoyed desirable results for the next few years. The rising tide lifted all boats.

Simply stated, an evaluation of market conditions is a critical component of a disciplined approach to both investment selection and portfolio management. Understanding the tools to evaluate market conditions properly will help you become a proactive investor. A little later in the book, I'll address the implementation of four key steps for selecting investments and building a strong portfolio. At that point, you will learn that evaluating market conditions is the first step to making confident investment decisions. For now, however, let's just focus on what is included in market analysis.

As I mentioned in section 3 (Sector Analysis), when you focus your research efforts on *both sector and market* trends, you will gain a greater understanding of the investment environment. Looking first at the market, then at the sector, and, finally, at the stock is a top-down approach to making investment decisions. To be consistently successful, you have to learn to adapt to market conditions and manage your portfolio accordingly. A top-down approach helps you adapt to market trends and conditions so you can position your investments in accordance with the prevailing trends.

The good news is you can apply your previous knowledge about Bullish Percent charts, as covered in section 3 (Sector Analysis). You already have the foundation and building blocks. The only difference between sector and market Bullish Percent charts is the universe used to record the chart. For example, the oil sector's Bullish Percent chart records the percent of stocks in the oil sector that are on a buy signal on their Point & Figure charts. The universe used for a market Bullish Percent chart is every common stock that trades on the New York Stock Exchange. Market Bullish Percent charts can also include other broad market exchanges or indexes. For example, the NASDAQ Bullish Percent chart includes every stock traded on the NASDAQ; the S&P 500 Bullish Percent chart includes every stock included in the S&P 500 Index, and so on. A market Bullish Percent chart can be created for any index or exchange, even foreign markets or asset classes (growth stocks, small-cap stocks, etc.).

Given your knowledge about Bullish Percent charts, we can skip over the recording and interpretation aspects of the charts and move directly into ways to analyze and examine market Bullish Percent charts. Similar to sector analysis, you want a reliable indicator that helps you determine when demand begins to take control in the broad market to get a good handle on market trends. Market Bullish Percent charts show when a positive imbalance exists in the market's supply and demand relationship, allowing you to participate early in a positive market trend. Market Bullish Percent charts also help you identify high- and low-risk levels in the market. If the risk is high, you will want to scale back your market enthusiasm and exposure. When the market risk is low, you will want to be aggressive and apply growth strategies.

Let's take a look at a few case studies to further develop your understanding of how to use market Bullish Percent charts. To explain market analysis, we are going to work with the NYSE Bullish Percent chart.

Market Analysis and Interpretation: Real-Life Examples

Review

Throughout my explanation of market analysis, I have been referring to the New York Stock Exchange (NYSE) as an example of a market or a universe of stocks. As I mentioned in the beginning, the NYSE is just one example. Other markets include the NASDAQ, the American Stock Exchange, the S&P 500 Index, the NASDAQ 100 Index, United Kingdom, Japan, Brazil, etc. Any broad market universe with some commonality among its members can have a Bullish Percent chart.

To help bring home how to use Bullish Percent charts for your market analysis and investment decisions, I am going to show you two examples that use the NYSE. Before doing so, I want to quickly review the value of using Bullish Percent charts.

The NYSE Bullish Percent chart is an intermediate- to long-term indicator and provides guidance for setting your overall approach to the market. The chart is based on supply and demand, not on media reporting or Wall Street research about what the market is doing. More important, Bullish Percent charts are based on real-time information, not on historical information or assumptions about the future.

As I noted before—market extremes tend to cause emotional decision-making. This reaction occurs because market extremes cause extreme media reporting. Most investment decisions based on media reporting and emotional influences will be poor decisions. One of the main benefits of a Bullish Percent chart is that the chart's data helps you make objective, informed investment decisions without letting emotions cloud the picture.

Again, remember that a Bullish Percent chart is based on current stock prices, while the media and Wall Street reports are based on lagging information and pricing. As a result, when the media or Wall Street reports *bad news*, the investors who wanted to sell because of the negative news have already sold. The supply is already reflected in stock prices, and the prices are likely near lows. Although buying during times of negative news is emotionally difficult, this is the lowest-risk time to make investments. At this time, most of the available supply is removed from the marketplace. Eventually, demand will surface and prices should start to increase. A Bullish Percent chart helps show you when these points have been reached and will give you the confidence to make low-risk investments at these times.

Conversely, when the media or Wall Street reports *good news*, the investors who wanted to buy because of the positive news have already bought. That demand is reflected in stock prices, and the prices are likely near highs. The media will be reporting positive business and economic conditions during these times, and, psychologically, it will not feel right to sell. A Bullish Percent chart helps show you when the market has reached high-risk points and will give you the confidence to make sell-decisions when market risk is elevated.

Asian Financial Crisis

In October 1997, the NYSE bullish-percent indicator reversed down into a column of O's. This was the first sign that the intermediate- to long-term trend of the market was changing from demand to supply controlling market prices. At this time, the initial sign of trouble was surfacing. About one year later, this trouble became known as the *Asian Financial Crisis*.

The year 1998 was an extremely volatile year in the global stock markets. The first half of the year was an excellent time to be in the market. The third quarter was a disaster; the S&P 500 Index fell more than 20% in less than two months. The last few months of the year turned positive and produced wonderful results as the main market indexes recovered to new highs by year's end. The year was unusual since the swings were both extreme and within a short period.

The Asian Financial Crisis caused the volatility. This crises affected currencies, stock markets, and other asset prices in several Asian countries, many considered East Asian Tigers. It is also commonly referred to as the Asian Currency Crisis. The crises caused increased volatility throughout the global stock, bond, and currency markets. It led to a substantial drop in the U.S. stock market in the fall of 1998.

Remember, market analysis usually focuses on the best approach over an intermediate- to long-term period; *major* adjustments usually do not occur within such a short period as in 1998. However, when they do, you have to deal with it. Using the NYSE Bullish Percent chart for this period (*figure 17.1*), let's look at how this chart could have helped you navigate through one of the more volatile years in the market in recent times. Refer back to the information in section 3 (Sector Analysis) on how to interpret the position on a Bullish Percent chart as I show you the trends.

In mid-1997, the NYSE reflected rising prices. This demand is identified by the chart in *figure 17.1*; note that in May 1997 (as noted by the "5"), the NYSE Bullish Percent chart recorded an X at 70%. Between May and August, the chart generally recorded a rising percentage, indicating that stock prices were rising and that demand had the upper hand during this time. The chart peaked at 84% in August. Remember, once the chart rose and hit 70%, the market had moved into the high-risk zone.

The initial market decline, as noted by the column of O's, continued until January 1998. Also, as noted on the chart, the bullish-percent index fell to 60%. In the early months of 1998, demand again took over as the dominating trend, and the NYSE bullish-percent indicator reversed up into an X column. You can see that this column started in February 1998 (as noted by the "2" recorded at 66% in the second X column). The chart once again reflected generally rising percentage of stocks on buy signals during the early months of 1998, peaking at 80% in this X column. Note how the chart again rose above 70% and moved back into the high-risk zone for the second time. Remember, a reading above 70% indicates elevated risk for the NYSE. When it's above

70%, a lot of capital has *already* moved into the market, thereby limiting the amount of additional demand to push stock prices higher. When a market Bullish Percent chart is 70% or higher, you should take a cautious approach toward the market.

NYSE Bullish Percent Chart
1997–1998

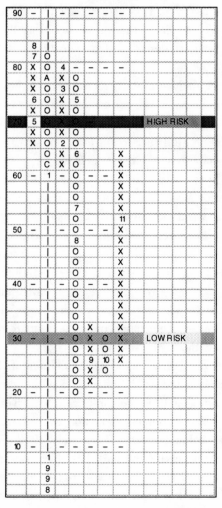

figure 17.1

Note that the second X column shown on this chart peaks at a lower percentage than the first X column, which peaked in August 1997. Interestingly, popular market averages moved to higher ground. For example, the Dow Jones 30 Industrial Average hit a high of 8,340 in August 1997. But in April 1998, the Dow reached 9,287, some 11% higher than the August 1997 high. The Dow Industrials is the most widely reported market index in the media. Many investors consider the Dow to be a broad representation of "the market," yet this average is based on *only thirty companies*. The NYSE Bullish Percent chart includes *every issue traded on the NYSE*. This market indicator is a much truer reflection of "the market."

When the Dow surged to a higher level in April 1998—the same time the NYSE Bullish Percent chart established a lower X column—this was an indication that fewer issues were working to push the market higher. This indication was a *dangerous sign* (referred to as a negative divergence). A negative divergence occurs when a broad market index (the NYSE Bullish Percent chart) establishes a lower high while a narrow, or market-capitalized weighted index (the Dow Industrials, S&P 500 Index, NASDAQ Composite, etc.), establishes a new high. Negative divergences tend to fool most investors into believing that "the market" is on solid ground because widely followed averages are reaching new highs. In reality, "the market" is not sound; more issues have a weak supply-demand relationship, as indicated by more sell signals on their Point & Figure chart.

Once the negative divergence occurred, the second reversal down into an O column in May 1998 became a strong sell signal for "the market." The reversal indicated that a significant change was taking place within the market's supply-demand relationship. The reversal into an O column indicated that supply was taking over as the dominating trend in the NYSE. Furthermore, the column reversal took place at an extremely high-risk level, making the reversal a major sell signal for the NYSE.

When a strong sell signal occurs, an investor should adopt a defensive strategy with capital preservation as the main objective. Most growth-oriented strategies will likely fail, producing loss of capital. Capital-preservation strategies could include selling and holding cash, selling partial positions, placing sell stop orders for your equity positions, buying protective put options, or hedging through the purchase of *inverse funds* or other *bear funds*. Aggressive investors can attempt to profit through short-selling strategies.

Whenever the bullish-percent index resides above 70% there tends to be a general euphoric atmosphere among the investing public. Many times, this feeling is created by optimistic reporting in the mainstream media. As I mentioned earlier, many individual investors tend to use the media as a main resource upon which to base their investment decisions. When the media is reporting nothing but blue skies in the forecast, investors tend to throw caution to the wind and buy stocks without consideration of their value. The result is a catch-22 since the approach generates the elevated level of demand that causes a Bullish Percent chart to reach the extreme high-risk level above 70%.

In 1998, when the NYSE Bullish Percent chart was indicating a major sell signal, the media's reporting was still very positive:

> ➢ On June 25, 1998, a headline in *USA Today* read, "Bull Charges Again as Red Flags Wave: The bull market just doesn't know how to quit." [1]

> ➢ On June 30, 1998, Pui-Wing Tam in the *Chicago Tribune* reported, "Wade in On the Stock Market's Dip: As the market's slipped recently, a sorry group of investors sighed in relief. These were the people who missed out on the bull market." [2]

> ➢ On July 1, 1998, David Henry in *USA Today* reported that "maybe this really is the bull market that never ends." [3]

> ➢ On July 27, 1998, James Pethokoukis in *U.S. News & World Report* reported that "we now return to our regularly scheduled bull market, still in progress."[4]

Meanwhile, the NYSE bullish-percent indicator continued to decline in an O column after giving a major sell signal in May 1998 (see *figure 17.1*). As you can tell from the media reporting noted above, there was very little warning to the average investor that the market was deteriorating; however, proactive investors who were following the NYSE bullish-percent indicator had received evidence that supply was clearly in control of the NYSE, helping them adjust their investments to protect previous gains. The percentage dropped from 80% in April to 50% in July, which means 30% of NYSE-traded issues gave new sell signals on their Point & Figure chart during that time. Such an indication clearly would have provided the confidence to adopt a defensive investment strategy and to preserve capital.

Between late July and the middle of September 1998, the Dow Industrials fell more than 20% as the news about the Asian financial crisis began to hit the mainstream media. During the same time, the NYSE Bullish Percent chart declined into the low-risk zone and bottomed at 20%. However, by mid-September, this valuable indicator already began to reverse up into an X column, indicating that demand was now beginning to become the dominant force in the marketplace. This positive reversal began a pattern on the chart that created a strong buy signal for the NYSE.

Before I show you the strong buy signal on the chart, let's go back to look at the tone of the media's reporting of business and economic conditions in the fall of 1998:

> ➢ On October 2, 1998, the front page of the *Chicago Tribune* stated, "Crises Shake World Markets."[5] The newspaper showed a picture of two traders at the Tokyo Stock Exchange, reacting to a plunge in the Nikkei Index. One trader was covering his eyes while the other was scratching his head in dismay.

> ➢ The October 12, 1998, issue of *Newsweek* magazine ran a cover story titled "The Crash of 1999?"[6] Mind you, this was still October 1998, and the story was about the coming crash of 1999.

In the September–October period of 1998, the media's reporting became overly pessimistic. Many investors read these stories and found that their "negative" emotions inhibited making rational decisions. Fear began to control decisions. Unfortunately, the media reported problems with the market *after* the damage to most investors had occurred. The Dow Industrials had already dropped more than 20%. Similar to how the media, at the top, led you to believe that this was the bull market that would never end, they also led you to believe that there was a "world crisis" and that the market was going to crash, when it was already at the bottom. The media information creates confusion, and the average investor is left asking, "What should I do?" When the news is good, an investor feels comfortable becoming aggressive; he or she anticipates that the good news will drive stock prices higher. Then, when the news turned negative, the average investor feels uncomfortable owning stocks and decides to sell; he or she anticipates more bad news on the horizon. It's a vicious cycle, buying at the top on the good news, selling at the bottom on the bad news.

Going back to the NYSE Bullish Percent chart in *figure 17.1*, a series of positive developments was starting to occur in September 1998. At that time, the first X column rose to 32%. The chart reversed into another O column in October 1998; however, this O column was short-lived and stopped declining at a higher level than the low reached in September. The first sign of a bottom was the reversal from O's to X's from below 30% in September. That reversal gives the NYSE Bullish Percent chart a Bull Alert status. The next positive clue was the higher O column established in October followed by the reversal up into the next X column. In fact, when this second X column exceeded the first, a change occurred on the NYSE Bullish Percent chart to Bull Confirmed status. (Review the status levels in chapter 11 [Bullish Percent Charts].) At this point, a buy signal was completed on the chart, and you had the indication to change your focus and develop an aggressive, growth-oriented strategy.

By the next month, November 1998, the Dow Industrials had already climbed back to a new closing high. Most investors, still shell-shocked by the speed and depth of the decline during the summer, missed this advance. By the time the media began to focus on the obvious positives, the lion's share of the gain was already factored in stock prices, and the opportunity to invest at low prices had passed

On November 24, 1998, the cover story of the *Chicago Sun-Times* was titled, "Market Mania: Merger news sends Dow to record level."[7] The vicious cycle continued as the media was once again reporting positive market developments *after* the market had already recovered to new highs.

Herein lies the true value of the NYSE Bullish Percent chart. As noted with example about the Asian Financial Crisis, the chart provides you with an indicator that directly speaks to the cause of market-price fluctuations (i.e., the relationship between supply and demand). The chart gives you the ability to ignore the media's delayed reporting of market events and helps you focus on the true trends moving the market. It helps you reduce emotional influences on your investment decisions, resulting in more informed and logical decisions. Lastly, the chart gives you the confidence to avoid following the herd and to go against the grain; to buy when the masses are selling and to sell when the masses are buying. Remember, these are the times when stock prices are out of sync with their true values. In short, the NYSE Bullish Percent chart will help you become a proactive investor rather than reactive or passive.

NYSE Bullish Percent Chart 2001 to 2006

Using a more recent example, let's look at the NYSE Bullish Percent chart from 2001 up to June 2006. The chart for this specific period is shown in *figure 17.2*.

As the calendar turned from the 1990s to the 2000s, the secular bull trend in U.S. stocks of the 1980s and 1990s came to an end, and a secular bear trend began in early 2000. I will cover stock-market cycles in depth in a later chapter.

So far, during this secular bear trend, there have been distinct periods in which market prices have declined across the board (cyclical bear markets) and there have been distinct periods in which market prices have staged a broad advance (cyclical bull markets). Bullish Percent charts are helpful during secular bull trends (as in the example we covered in 1998); however, they are priceless in helping you navigate through secular bear trends.

Let's first look at 2001. You can see that the NYSE bullish-percent index peaked at 68% in May 2001 and reversed down into an O column in June 2001. The reversal was a signal that supply was stronger in the NYSE. Cash was flowing out of the market. (Remember, when the NYSE Bullish Percent chart is in a column of O's you want to have a defensive strategy of capital preservation.) The chart remained in an O column, and the September 11 terrorist attacks brought the market to its knees. The NYSE closed for several business days as New York City and the nation recovered from the attacks. The broad market declined sharply following that horrible event.

News reports were extremely negative, and it was difficult to feel anything but pessimistic about investment opportunities. Following September 11, the NYSE Bullish Percent chart fell into the low-risk zone to 28%. It reversed up into an X column in early October 2001. This reversal indicated that demand was starting to take over; presenting a low-risk opportunity to buy. Yet, emotionally and psychologically, going against the grain and buying was difficult. Regardless, this was a profitable time, and the market experienced a short-term advance that lasted five months.

The NYSE bullish-percent index reached the high-risk zone and peaked in March 2002. That was a sign to transition your investment strategy back to a cautious approach. In June 2002, the indicator reversed down into an O column, signaling that the market trend was turning negative. The reversal was a timely sell signal. This was the time to make sure defensive measures were in place with a goal of capital preservation. The market tanked in June and July 2002, resulting in one of the worst back-to-back months in recent market history. During these two months, the Dow Industrials declined 24% from top to bottom.

NYSE Bullish Percent Chart
2001–June 2006

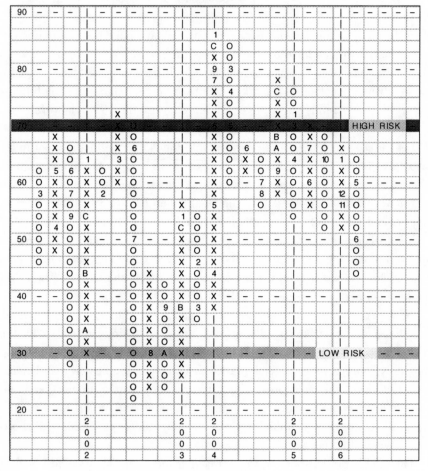

figure 17.2

Near the market bottom in 2002, the media's reporting was extremely negative:

➤ The July 1, 2002, issue of *Fortune* magazine ran a cover story titled, "System Failure: Corporate America, we have a crisis."[8] The story was about the scandals among corporate executives.

➤ In an article dated July 2, 2002, *USA Today* said, "NASDAQ at lowest point level in 5 years." The story led off with the following paragraph: "Mounting concerns about accounting scandals, the health of American businesses and sinking stock prices swept aside seemingly good economic news Monday, as the NASDAQ Composite tumbled to a five-year low."[9]

➤ The same article sited a poll conducted by *USA Today*, *CNN*, and *Gallop*. In general, the poll concluded that investors are "deeply troubled by skidding stock prices and the surge in corporate malfeasance." Key findings included the following:

1. 57% said scandals like those enveloping WorldCom, ImClone, and Enron, are a "major problem" for the nation.

2. 58% said they are "less likely" to invest in stocks because of the recent scandals.

3. 64% said stocks' recent swoon makes them "less likely" to invest.

4. 67% said the stock markets' recent slump makes them feel "less confident" about the U.S. economy.

➤ The July 20, 2002, front page of the *Chicago Tribune* reported, "Dow dives to 4-year low." The newspaper went on to say, "Sell-off deepens; people are really feeling pain now."[10]

➤ The cover of *Barron's* on July 22, 2002, featured a bull tied up in rope and in cement shoes, sinking to the bottom of the ocean.

The media's reporting was so negative that the July 1, 2002, cover of *Time* magazine stated, "The Bible and the Apocalypse: Why more Americans are reading and talking about the end of the world." I could go on and on. The media couldn't have been any more pessimistic or more damaging to investors' confidence. The result was mass liquidation of stocks at the bottom of the two-and-one-half-year bear market; according to statistics from the Investment Company Institute and Lipper, as published in the *Wall Street Journal*, investors liquidated approximately one hundred billion dollars from stock mutual funds during the second half of 2002.[11]

Looking at the NYSE Bullish Percent chart in *figure 17.2*, you can see that this index declined down into the low-risk zone and bottomed in July 2002. All of the selling caused by the negative media reporting was near conclusion, and a low of 22% occurred. At that time, everyone who had wanted to sell because of all the bad news had *already* sold. Once the market reached this level, the additional supply that was needed to push prices lower was not available. (There just isn't much supply available when the NYSE Bullish Percent chart is below 30%.)

Following the bottom in July 2002, the NYSE Bullish Percent chart began a series of higher X and O columns, giving investors the green light to begin buying. The first reversal up into an X column carried the index up to 44% in August 2002. The chart then reversed down in September and October 2002 as supply strengthened temporarily and as the chart dipped below 30% one last time.

I talked about a *negative divergence* in the example of the Asian Financial Crises. Now, the NYSE Bullish Percent chart was forming a *positive divergence* (i.e., when a broad market index (the NYSE Bullish Percent chart) establishes a higher low and a narrow, or capitalized, weighted index (the Dow Industrials, S&P 500 Index, NASDAQ Composite, etc.) establishes a new low. The NYSE Bullish Percent chart low in October was higher than the July 2002 low, while the Dow Industrials fell to 7,197 in October, below the July low of 7,532. Positive divergences are a strong sign that the supply-demand relationship is turning positive and help confirm market bottoms.

After July 2002, the NYSE Bullish Percent chart was generally in an ascending pattern throughout the rest of 2002 and most of 2003. The second half of 2002 and early 2003 was an excellent, low-risk time to commit your investment capital into the stock market as the market began to recover from the previous decline. The year 2003 turned into wonderful, money-making, cyclical bull market. These short, cyclical advances present strong growth opportunities. Relying on the media can lead you in the wrong direction because their coverage often follows the opportunity. The NYSE and NASDAQ Bullish Percent charts provide the necessary information to help you identify positive market cycles and growth opportunities before it's too late.

CHAPTER 18

SHORT-TERM MARKET INDICATORS: FINE-TUNING YOUR BUY/SELL DECISIONS

> **Short-term indicators help you find profitable cycles within longer-term trends.**
>
> **Short-term indicators help you avoid committing new funds near short-term market peaks.**
>
> **Short-term indicators help you enter the market near short-term bottoms.**

While the NYSE and NASDAQ Bullish Percent charts provide guidance for the intermediate- to long-term supply and demand relationships and risk levels for the overall market, there are a number of shorter-term indicators that will help you with decisions on a shorter-term basis. These shorter-term charts are interpreted in the same, basic way any Bullish Percent chart is interpreted.

The short-term charts help you find the cycles within the longer-term trends. Depending on your trading strategy, these indicators can be used in different ways. For longer-term oriented investors the short-term indicators will help you fine-tune the entrance and exit points for your buy and sell decisions. Even long-term investors will want to avoid buying when short-term indicators point to a heightened risk level for the overall market.

During these times, a long-term investor would want to become a little less aggressive because the market is likely to decline over coming weeks. You will want to wait for a lower-risk entry point and better prices for buying most stocks. When exiting positions, it is best to sell when the short-term indicators are at high-risk levels, changing to a bearish status, or both. Long-term investors should use the NYSE and NASDAQ Bullish Percent charts as main market indicators but should always keep the status of the short-term indicators in mind.

For shorter-term or trading-oriented investors, the short-term indicators show when there are opportunities to make investments that capitalize on short-term cycles. In fact, investors with a short-term trading style should use these charts as main market indicators while keeping the status of the NYSE and NASDAQ Bullish Percent charts in mind. For investors with short-term objectives, the short-term charts are extremely helpful in timing both buy and sell decisions; these charts also help with short-selling strategies.

I am going to cover four of the main short-term indicators used to help fine-tune investment decisions:

1. NYSE 10-Week chart
2. NASDAQ 10-Week chart
3. NYSE High-Low Index
4. NASDAQ High-Low Index

NYSE 10-Week Chart

The NYSE 10-Week Average is a short-term indicator that measures the percent of NYSE traded issues that are above their 10-week average price. The 10-week average price for any issue is simply an average closing price for the last fifty trading days (ten weeks). If the latest closing price is higher than the 10-week average, then the stock is placed in the *above* bucket. If the last closing price is not above its own 10-week average, then the stock is placed in the *below* bucket.

What is the importance of knowing if a stock is above its 10-week average price? The simple answer is that if a stock is higher than its own 10-week average price, the short-term momentum for the particular issue is rising. Conversely, if a stock is below its 10-week average price, the short-term momentum is declining.

Similar to the bullish-percent concept, if only a few isolated issues are advancing above their 10-week average price, the advance is not important to the momentum of the broad market. However, when a significant percentage of NYSE-traded issues are rising above their 10-week average price, the advance is an important indication of the momentum of the overall market. Since such an indication suggests that the momentum of the broad market is advancing, from a short-term timing standpoint, the time is ideal to buy stocks.

Conversely, when a significant percentage of NYSE-traded issues are falling below their 10-week average price, we have an indication that the momentum of the broad market is declining. During these times, you would be wise to take a step back from making new commitments in the market. You should wait until the momentum bottoms and the market risk level is reduced on a short-term basis.

The NYSE 10-Week chart is recorded and interpreted the same way as the other Bullish Percent charts as well as the sector's 10-Week charts. For details, refer to the section called "Interpretation of Bullish Percent Charts" in chapter 11 (Bullish Percent Charts). Below is a brief summary of the interpretation.

When analyzing a Bullish Percent chart or a Percent Above 10-Week chart, there are two levels of analysis:

> Direction

> Position

We are concerned with the direction the chart is headed and the position of the chart. A higher percentage is recorded with a column of X's, meaning demand is in control on a short-term basis. A lower percentage is recorded with a column of O's, meaning supply has the upper hand on a short-term basis.

Any reading above 70% places the NYSE 10-Week chart in a short-term, high-risk zone; readings below 30% mean the short-term risk is low.

Important buy signals develop on the NYSE 10-Week chart when the percentage drops below 30% then begins moving higher. This signal indicates that 70% of stocks on the NYSE have declined below their 10-week average (only 30% are left above the 10-week) and are now beginning to advance, changing the momentum of the market from down to up. At these times, short-term investors should take aggressive positions to profit from expected advances in the overall market.

Important sell signals develop on the NYSE 10-Week chart when the percentage above their 10-week average rises above 70% then begins moving lower. This signal indicates that many issues on the NYSE have advanced above their 10-week average and are now beginning to decline, changing the momentum of the market from up to down. At these times, short-term investors should sell their long positions.

Long-term investors should practice patience, wait for the lower-risk entry points, and avoid buying at the higher-risk points. However, if you are inclined to use a short-selling strategy, when the 10-week average rises above 70% then begins to decline, the time is ideal to implement short-selling strategies and profit from the expected short-term decline in the overall market. (Refer to the section called "Short-Selling Sector Strategy" in chapter 16 [Sector Strategies for Confident Decisions].)

New York Stock Exchange Percent of Issues Above Their 10-Week Average Price

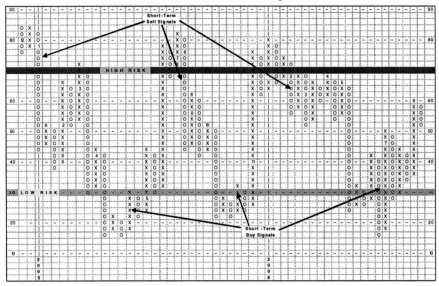

figure 18.1

Figure 18.1 shows the NYSE 10-week indicator. You can see that this indicator looks very similar to Bullish Percent charts. The extreme high- and low-risk levels are highlighted on the chart. The biggest difference between the 10-Week and Bullish Percent charts is the cycle time between the high- and low-risk levels. The Bullish Percent chart can take months or years to cycle from high to low risk or vice versa. The NYSE 10-Week chart will typically reach the high- and low-risk levels a couple of times each year. The chart in *figure 18.1* runs from December 2004 through August 2006.

You can see that the NYSE indicator reached the high-risk zone, above 70%, four times during this twenty-month period. It fell into the low-risk zone below 30% three times during the same period. The best times to buy during this period were in April 2005, October 2005, and June 2006. These were the times the NYSE 10-Week chart reached the low-risk level then reversed up, signaling that more NYSE issues were beginning to rise above their 10-week average price.

For short-term investors, these three reversals indicated an ideal time to buy in anticipation of a short-term trading opportunity. (During these times, the rising momentum carries the market higher for several weeks following the buy signals.) For long-term investors, these same patterns signaled an ideal time to commit new money to the market. You will want to use these opportunities to enter the market and buy stocks in leading sectors that have positive patterns on their individual Point & Figure and Relative Strength charts.

The most opportune times that short-term investors had to sell or that long-term investors had to avoid buying were January, March, and August 2005 and February–May 2006. Those were the times the NYSE 10-Week chart reached the high-risk zone above 70% then began to reverse down, signaling that more NYSE issues were beginning to drop below their 10-week average. For short-term investors, those four periods were the ideal time to sell investments in anticipation of a declining market. During these times, the momentum pushed the broad market lower.

Short-selling strategies can be implemented at a time like that described above. Long-term investors will want to avoid committing new money to the market at times like those. Any stocks you are considering based on the Point & Figure and relative-strength analysis will most likely be trading at lower prices in the relatively near future. Even the strongest stocks will have trouble advancing when the NYSE 10-Week chart is declining.

Along with direction and position, the NYSE 10-Week chart also has the same status levels as a Bullish Percent chart, namely, Bull Alert, Bull Confirmed, Bull Correction, Bear Alert, Bear Confirmed, and Bear Correction. These status levels are identical to the status levels on a Bullish Percent chart. Rather than repeating the description for each level, refer to chapter 11 (Bullish Percent Charts) for details. Remember, Bull Confirmed is a stronger bullish status than Bull Alert, and you should treat this signal more aggressively. Similarly, Bear Confirmed is a stronger bearish status than Bear Alert and is considered the highest-risk status.

NASDAQ 10-Week Chart

The four *main* status levels are pointed out in *figure 18.2*, a chart of the NASDAQ 10-week indicator from January 2004 to May 2005. The NASDAQ 10-Week chart showed a short-term sell signal in early 2004, followed by a general decline from January until the May–August 2004 period. During that time, the NASDAQ Composite Index declined from a high of 2152 in mid-January 2004 down to a low of 1751 in mid-August 2004, a decline of 18.63% in seven months. This was a good time to avoid making any new investments in the NASDAQ.

In August 2004, the NASDAQ Composite reached its low for that calendar year. The NASDAQ 10-Week chart bottomed in August 2004 at 20%. When the NASDAQ 10-Week chart first reversed up into an X column, the status changed to Bull Alert, meaning there was a potential short-term bottom in place for the NASDAQ. During August, the X column continued to move higher; when the index reached 36%, the X column exceeded the previous X column and caused the status to change to Bull Confirmed. This development confirmed that the low had been reached and that the NASDAQ was beginning a short-term advance because more NASDAQ traded issues were rising above their 10-week average price. Again, this was a good time for short-term investors to buy in anticipation of a rally.

Long-term investors would have wanted to buy the NASDAQ issues that were in sectors emerging as market leaders. Remember to focus on individual stocks that were well positioned from a supply-demand analysis and that were performing well relative to the broad market (i.e., stocks well positioned on their Point & Figure and Relative Strength charts).

NASDAQ Percent of Issues Above Their 10-Week Average Price

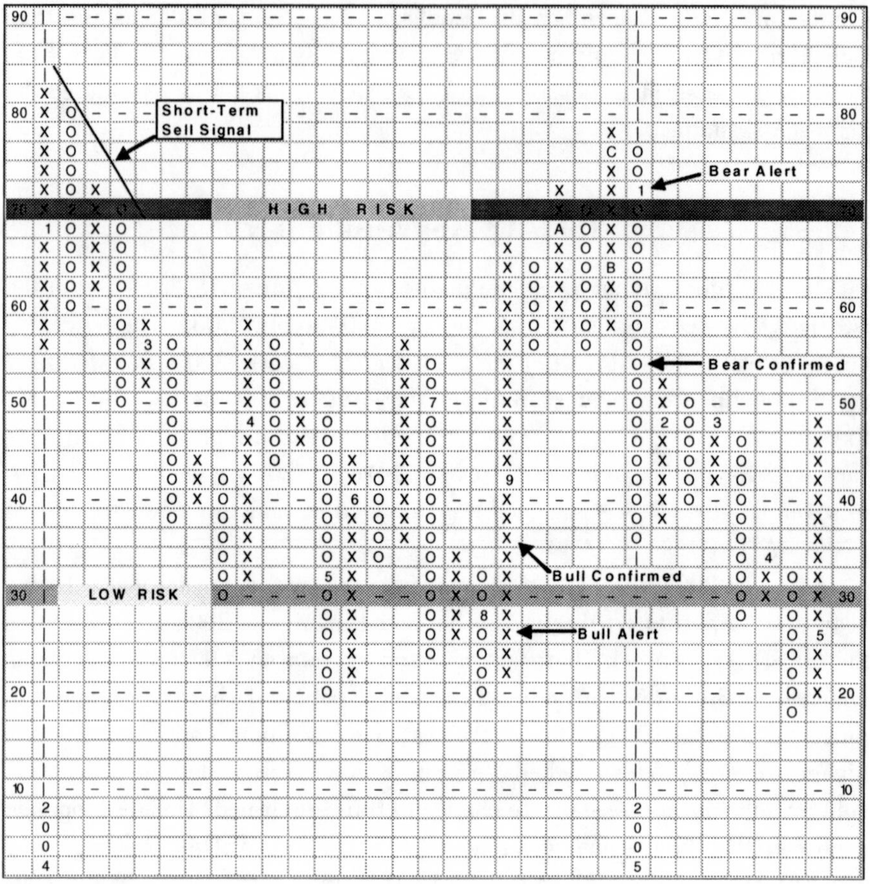

Short-Term Sell Signal

Bear Alert

HIGH RISK

Bear Confirmed

Bull Confirmed

LOW RISK

Bull Alert

figure 18.2

In August 2004, we were in the midst of a presidential election. Such elections often create rallies. The presidential-election rally unfolded, and the NASDAQ 10-Week chart advanced up to a high in late December 2004 at 78%. The NASDAQ Composite peaked on January 3, 2005, at 2,192. From the August 2004 low at 1,751, the NASDAQ advanced 25%. Again, this was a good period during which to make new investments in the NASDAQ.

Both the short-term sell signal in early 2004 and the short-term buy signal that developed in August 2004 proved to be timely signals. As the calendar turned to 2005, the NASDAQ 10-Week chart was once again positioned in the high-risk zone above 70%. (This position should indicate to you the need to adapt to a more defensive strategy on a short-term basis. Investors with a short-term trading objective should avoid making new investments. Long-term investors would want to follow the NASDAQ Bullish Percent chart for their main guidance but also take into account that the position of the 10-Week chart implies that short-term risk level is high.)

In early 2005, the NASDAQ 10-Week chart reversed down into a column of O's, changing the status to Bear Alert (*figure 18.2*). As the chart continued to decline, the O column fell below the previous O column. At that time, the status changed to Bear Confirmed. As the status changed from bullish the last few months of 2004 to bearish in early 2005, all indications were that the short-term momentum of the NASDAQ was now moving lower. The presidential-election rally was over. Any short-term positions bought on the buy signal in August 2004 should have been sold. For long-term investors, the time had come to sell any NASDAQ positions with weakening Point & Figure and Relative Strength charts while avoiding new purchases in the NASDAQ until high-risk levels subsided.

As you can see in *figure 18.2*, the NASDAQ 10-week indicator reached a low in April 2005. The period from January 3 through April 29, 2005, was a time to avoid exposure to the NASDAQ as it dropped to a low of 1890 on April 29, down nearly 14% from the high on January 3.

The greatest value of the NYSE and NASDAQ 10-week indicators is they help you avoid committing new funds to the market near short-term tops while helping you invest with more confidence near short-term lows. These indicators give you an accurate measure of risk levels and momentum or direction of the broad NYSE and NASDAQ on a short-term basis.

NYSE High-Low Index

The NYSE High-Low Index measures the number of issues making a new annual high relative to those making a new annual low. The calculation for this index is as follows:

1.   Add the total number of daily new highs and lows on the NYSE.

2.   Divide the number of new highs by the total from step one above, giving you the daily High-Low Index.

3. This percentage can fluctuate widely from day to day. As a result, a ten-day average is used to smooth out the NYSE High-Low Index. The smoothing out calculation is done on a rolling ten-day basis; perform the calculation in step two for ten consecutive trading days, add the totals, and divide by ten to arrive at the ten-day average.

For example, let's assume the daily highs and lows on the NYSE were as follows:

Daily Totals	1	2	3	4	5	6	7	8	9	10
Lows	159	362	301	174	214	187	110	71	68	47
Highs	34	56	44	35	49	35	44	35	49	35
Totals	193	418	345	209	263	222	154	106	117	82
% of Highs	0.176	0.134	0.128	0.167	0.186	0.158	0.286	0.330	0.419	0.427

Sum of % of Highs = 2.411
Ten-day Average = 0.2411 or 24.11%

figure 18.3

As you can see in the example in *figure 18.3*, the sum of percent of highs adds up to 2.411. We divide the total by ten to calculate the smoothed out percentage: 0.2411 or 24.11%. The result is the percentage we will chart. The next day, we would do the calculation again by replacing the oldest day with the new daily NYSE High-Low Index calculation.

Important buy signals develop on the NYSE High-Low chart when the percentage drops below 30% then begins moving higher. This signal indicates that the number of stocks on the NYSE making new highs is significantly less than those making new lows. Such conditions exist when the market is near a short-term low. When this percentage begins to advance from low levels, the number of new highs relative to new lows on the NYSE is beginning to improve. The advance indicates that the short-term direction of the market is turning up. At these times, short-term investors should take aggressive positions and profit from an advancing overall market.

Important sell signals develop on this chart when the percentage rises above 70% and then begins moving lower. This signal indicates that the number issues on the NYSE making new highs are significantly more than those making new lows. Such conditions exist when the NYSE is at a short-term high. When the number of new highs relative to new lows begins to decline, short-term investors should take a defensive approach to the overall market and protect their portfolios. Those so inclined can sell short at this time to profit from the expected decline in the overall market.

The NYSE High-Low Index is recorded and interpreted the same way as Bullish Percent and 10-Week charts, using direction and position as the two main levels of analysis. A rising percentage is recorded with X's and indicates that more NYSE-traded issues are making new highs relative to those making new lows. When in an X column, your short-term approach toward the NYSE should be aggressive, attempting to grow your portfolio. A declining percentage is recorded with O's and indicates that more issues are making new lows relative to those making new highs on the NYSE. When in an O column, your short-term approach toward the NYSE should be defensive, protecting your portfolio.

Extreme readings are 70% and 30%. A column reversal from the extreme levels indicates short-term turning points for the NYSE. Above 70% indicates there is a high-risk level for the NYSE on a short-term basis because a large number of NYSE traded issues are at a new high. When a large number of stocks have already reached new highs, it is generally a poor time to buy. A reversal down from above 70% is a short-term sell signal. During these times, short-term investors should manage their portfolios defensively. Long-term investors should be patient and wait for a lower-risk level prior to committing new funds to the market. Aggressive investors can apply a short-selling strategy to profit from the expected decline in the NYSE.

When the NYSE High-Low Index is below 30%, the index is indicating that the short-term risk level is low for the NYSE. A large number of stocks are now at new lows, making it a good time to buy. A reversal up from below 30% is a short-term buy signal for the NYSE. Short-term investors should manage their portfolios aggressively during these times. Long-term investors can commit new funds to the market. Most short sales should be covered when the NYSE High-Low Index is beginning to reverse up from the low-risk zone.

Figure 18.4 is the NYSE High-Low Index for June 2002 through August 2006. High-low indicators have a few different characteristics than the 10-week indicators. First, you can see that this chart can spend longer periods in the high-risk zone above 70%. The chart in *figure 18.4* shows approximately four years of the NYSE High-Low Index. Note that there are several distinct periods in which the indicator was above 70%. For an NYSE High-Low chart, a reversal down into a bearish status is important before considering that this indicator has given a sell signal. In other words, do not anticipate that a high is in place; wait for the chart to reverse before making such a conclusion.

Conversely, an NYSE High-Low Index rarely stays below 30% for a long time. Most trips down to the low-risk zone are short-lived and reverse up rather quickly.

Another difference is that the NYSE High-Low Index can reach 90% at times; 90% is a rare occurrence for the NYSE 10-Week chart.

Finally, the High-Low Index tends to move between high- and low-risk levels quickly. Once the reversal from high or low risk begins, the index can reach the other extreme in a hurry.

The NYSE High-Low Index tends to lag a reversal on the NYSE 10-Week charts. The 10-Week indicator usually will be the first to reverse up or down from the extreme levels. On the surface, the lag may appear to be a drawback from using the NYSE High-Low Index. In reality, the lag is helpful in confirming the earlier signal reflected by the NYSE 10-Week chart.

Looking at the chart in *figure 18.4*, you can see there were seven different times the index fell into the *low-risk zone* during this four-year period. When the chart reversed up, all seven occasions proved to be timely buy signals. Following the market low reached in July 2002, the NYSE High-Low Index reached 8% before reversing up into a timely buy signal. The next low was in March 2003, right at the low prior to the war in Iraq. That was followed by lows reached in May and August 2004. Every time the NYSE High-Low Index reached a low then reversed up, the result was a positive market trend.

Usually, the NYSE 10-Week chart and the NYSE High-Low Index will show similar patterns and status levels. For example, comparing the 2005 and 2006 cycles on the NYSE High-Low chart with the NYSE 10-Week chart in *figure 18.1*, you will see that both charts often reached their high and low near the same time. Ideally, these two short-term indicators are best when used together. In order to get an accurate assessment of the short-term conditions in the NYSE, you want to see both the NYSE's 10-Week and High-Low Index charts showing a similar pattern. Again, the NYSE 10-Week chart tends to lead the NYSE High-Low Index with the latter acting as a confirming indicator.

If the NYSE 10-Week chart gives a signal without a confirmation by the NYSE High-Low Index, the signal usually proves to be a short-lived trend absent of a solid moneymaking opportunity.

NYSE High-Low Index

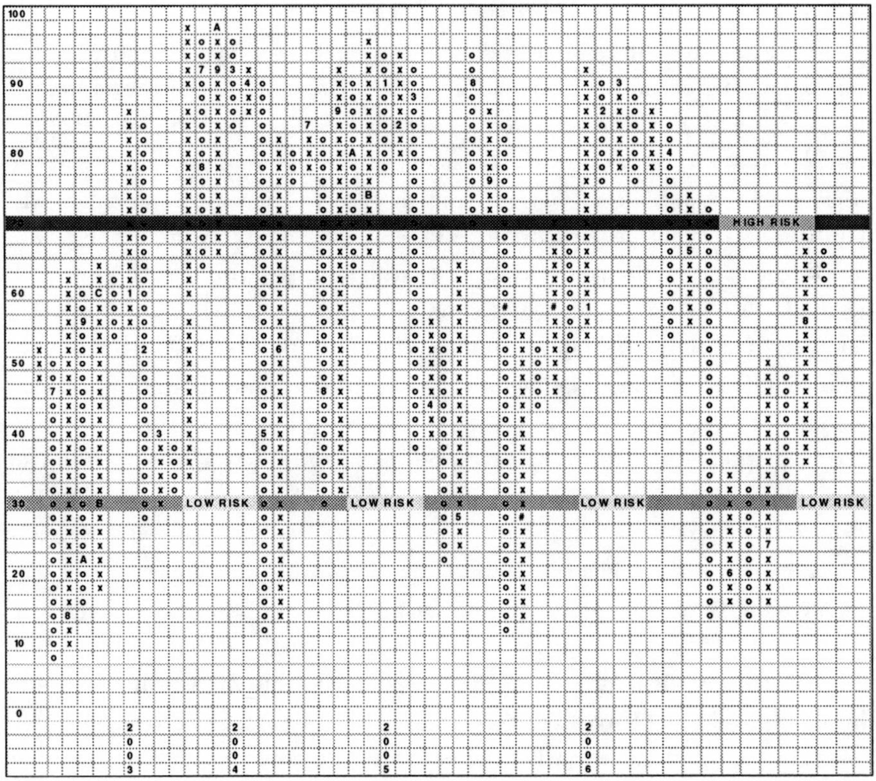

figure 18.4

NASDAQ High-Low Index

The analysis of the NASDAQ High-Low Index is identical to that of the NYSE High-Low Index. The only difference is that the universe used to record the daily highs and lows is NASDAQ-traded issues. Rather than take you through a detailed look at the NASDAQ version, you can get an up-to-date look at the current position of the NASDAQ's High-Low Index chart online at the Investor Education Institute Web site (http://www.institute4investors.com).

As with the NYSE, the NASDAQ High-Low Index and 10-Week charts should be showing similar patterns to get an accurate assessment of the short-term conditions of the NASDAQ. The best short-term trends develop when both of these indicators are moving in tandem.

A well-informed investor should know the position of the short-term market indicators covered in this chapter at all times. Using these short-term indicators, along with the Bullish Percent charts covered in the previous chapter, provides you with an accurate assessment of the risk and opportunity in the broad markets on both a long-term and short-term basis. The indicators will help you understand when market conditions are conducive for asset growth and help you adopt an aggressive, pro-growth strategy. The indicators will be invaluable when risk is high and supply is in control, helping you adopt a defensive, capital-preservation strategy. They will also help reduce the emotional influence and media effect on investment decisions, helping you make confident, better-informed and proactive decisions. In summary, these indicators help you develop winning investment strategies—even when the broad market may be unable to make significant progress for several years.

Most investors have limited time available to dedicate toward their market and investment research. Unless you are a full-time investor, you will not have the time to create, maintain, and analyze the indicators covered in this chapter. This makes online research and charting databases invaluable. You can access these charts on the Investor Education Institute Web site (http://www.institute4investors.com). For most investors, I would suggest that a weekly review of these market indicators is sufficient. When they are near extreme levels, take a look at them every couple of days. This is all it takes to stay on top of the main market trends and in front of significant changes in trend.

CHAPTER 19

STOCK MARKET TRENDS AND CYCLES

> Two major market cycles exist:
> Secular (Long-Term) Trends
> Cyclical (Intermediate-Term) Trends
>
> **Secular bear markets require unique strategies.**

I introduced stock market trends in section 1 (Background) of this book. The introduction was important for setting the stage, defining market cycles, and explaining the need to be a proactive investor. At this point, I would like to delve further into market cycles because they are critical in a complete analysis of market conditions. To start, I want to review the general information already presented about market cycles.

Secular Trends in the Stock Market

History shows that the market enters prolonged periods of generally rising equity prices called *secular bull trends* and prolonged periods of generally declining, or stagnant, equity prices called *secular bear trends*. Prior to transitioning from one secular trend to the other, an extreme market condition will always occur. In reviewing the historical chart for the Dow Jones Industrial Average in *figure 19.1*, you will note extended periods of down to sideways moving equity prices (a secular bear trend) and extended periods of advancing equity prices (a secular bull trend). Note that the chart also shows that during each secular trend, there were shorter periods of rising or declining equity prices. These short periods are cycles within the larger secular trend.

Secular market trends typically last between five to twenty years. There have been only six completed secular trends in the past 104 years: three secular bull markets and three secular bear markets. The chart in *figure 19.1* shows that a secular bear trend began near the turn of the twenty-first century. As of mid-2006, the current bear trend is about six and one-half years old.

Let's take a more detailed look at the Dow Jones Industrial Average from 1960 through May 4, 2005. The chart seen in *figure 19.2* (which was accessed May 4, 2005 from http://www.stockcharts.com) gives us a closer look at the last two completed secular trends. During secular bull trends, such as the period from 1982 to 2000, a buy-and-hold investment strategy works quite well. While a buy-and-hold approach does not necessarily maximize returns, the strategy usually allows you to make money during a bull market. The reason a buy-and-hold strategy works during a secular bull trend is that such markets are an excellent time to own equities; you do not need to have very much knowledge or experience investing in the market. The rising market will bail you out of many mistakes you might make. All you really need to do is own good stocks and mutual funds, and the market trend will reward you. Investors utilizing a buy-and-hold approach during the three secular bull markets noted in *figure 19.1* would have realized an annual return of 14.83%.

Secular Market Trends—Dow Industrial Average

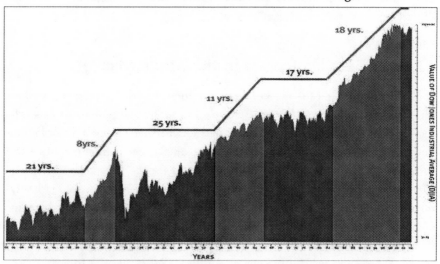

Rydex Investments, *Where Do You Think We're Headed?* (www.rydexinvestments.com.) Chart. <u>Dow Jones</u>: 12 January 2005. (http://www.dowjones.com.)

figure 19.1

Dow Jones Industrial Average—Secular Trends

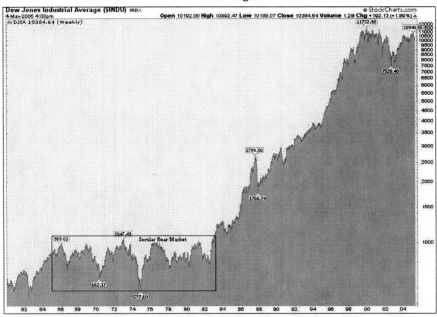

Chart courtesy of StockCharts.com

figure 19.2

Unfortunately, the market does not always accommodate us as it does during secular bull market periods. The last completed secular bear trend was the sixteen-year period from 1966–1982. During those years, a buy-and-hold strategy did not work well. In fact, these years were disastrous for most investors in stocks and mutual funds. For investors who bought and held in 1966, it took sixteen years before they made any significant earnings progress. Diversified investors utilizing the "pie chart" strategy also suffered, making virtually no progress for a full sixteen years. Investors utilizing a buy-and-hold strategy during the three secular bear trends noted in *figure 19.1* would have realized an annual return of just 0.21%. These three secular trends covered sixty-three years.

The chart in *figure 19.3* (which was accessed May 4, 2005 from http://www.stockcharts.com) shows the NASDAQ Composite from 1978 to May 4, 2005. You can see the massive secular bull trend in the NASDAQ during most of this period. The culmination of this secular bull trend was the technology and telecom bubble, which burst in 2000. Several more years will likely pass before the NASDAQ is able to claim a new high.

NASDAQ Secular Trends

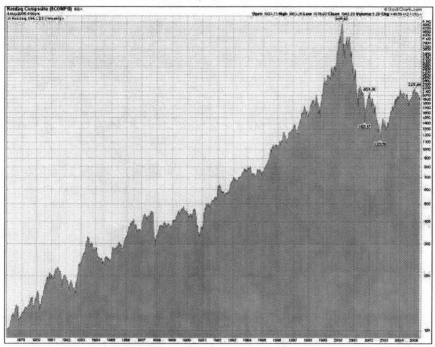

Chart courtesy of StockCharts.com

figure 19.3

If you utilize a buy-and-hold strategy, your success will depend on whether you enter the market at the beginning of a secular bull trend or near the end of the trend. History has shown that most investors do not have the conviction to start investing in equities at the beginning of a bull market trend. Typically, the previous secular bear market has convinced most investors that equities are not a good asset class to own for the long-term; as a result, most investors begin a buy-and-hold program well into a bull market trend. Unfortunately, the risk of buy-and-hold strategy is elevated near the end of the secular bull trend. The beginning of secular bull market, such as 1982, was an excellent time to start investing with a passive strategy. During secular bear trends, a passive investment strategy will only deliver disappointing results

It is important to note that while one market may experience a secular bear trend, other markets or other asset classes (i.e., natural resources) may experience a lucrative secular bull trend. For example, just think of the progress made in many foreign stock markets, particularly the emerging-country markets, while the U.S. markets have struggled to make meaningful progress. Many commodities and natural resources (oil, gold, copper, etc.) have soared during the same period. A proactive investor should recognize this dynamic and shift a portion of their assets away from the United States to focus on the markets and asset categories that offer the best growth potential.

There will also be many opportunities in certain sectors of the market even when the broad market may be in a secular bear trend. The secular bear trend may be the result of some sectors declining while others are advancing, keeping the broad market averages from making much general progress. However, if you can isolate the sectors that are leaders in the market and avoid the lagging sectors, you can still make money in secular bear trends. Using the tools presented in this book in section 3 (Sector Analysis) gives you this benefit.

Finally, within any long-term secular bear trend, there will be cycles in which the broad market indexes rise for several months, even years, at a time, allowing you to generate positive results in the U.S. market. These cycles are referred to as cyclical bull trends.

Cyclical Trends in the Stock Market

During secular bear markets, there will be periods of three to thirty-six months in which the broad market can advance. During these times, you need a handful of proven and trusted indicators that provide the necessary information for you to confidently take advantage of these windows of opportunity. A proactive investment strategy using market Bullish Percent, 10-Week, and High-Low Index charts provide you the guidance to participate in the cyclical bull trends while avoiding the problematic cycles during a secular bear trend.

Cyclical trends usually begin when they are not expected. In the case of cyclical bull markets, they will begin when the public believes stock prices will continually decline. At this time, business and economic news is typically bleak. When the majority of investors have sold, it eliminates the available supply needed to push stock prices lower. A cyclical bull market opportunity is created for proactive investors looking for undervalued stocks.

During secular bear markets, this opportunity is what a proactive investor should be watching for. The NYSE and NASDAQ Bullish Percent charts will be your guide to spotting these opportunities. While investors who are driven by emotion have sold their stock, investors who are driven by a supply and demand analysis see an opportunity to purchase stock at low prices. These investors generate the demand needed to reverse the trend, causing the cyclical bull market.

Figure 19.4 (which was accessed May 4, 2005 from http://www.stockcharts. com) shows a closer look at the period of 1966–1982 for the Dow Industrials. Although the secular trend was bearish during this sixteen-year period, you can clearly identify several shorter periods in which stock prices were advancing. For example, look the periods 1967–69, 1971–73, 1975–77, etc. These are the cyclical bull trends during the longer-term secular bear trend. During these cycles, which seem to have repeated every two years, there are opportunities for proactive investors to grow their portfolios. Unlike the buy-and-hold investors who had to wait sixteen years before general progress was made, proactive investors benefited from these short-term bull markets. The 1971–73 cyclical bull market advanced 58% from low to high. The advance during the cycle of 1975–77 was even better.

During this same secular bear market, it was imperative to avoid holding through the cyclical bear trends. You can see the negative cycles taking place in 1969–71, 1973–74, 1977–79, etc. Proactive investors that use the tools (NYSE and NASDAQ Bullish Percent, 10-Week, and High-Low Index charts) in section 4 (Market Analysis) of this book can identify these problematic cycles beginning to protect previous gains. Aggressive investors can implement a short-selling strategy during cyclical bear markets to profit from the declining trend.

Cyclical Trends During the 1966–1982 Secular Bear Market

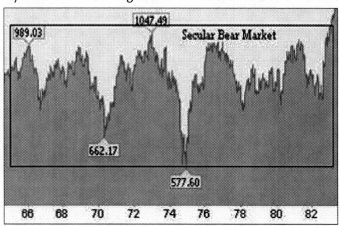

Chart courtesy of StockCharts.com

figure 19.4

How do you navigate through the cycles of a secular bear market? The proper use of the NYSE and NASDAQ Bullish Percent charts will help you identify the changes in the cyclical trend. These charts help you understand when the market's risk level is low and when demand is beginning to take control, leading to a cyclical advance and an opportunity to grow your assets.

For example, let's take another look at the NYSE Bullish Percent chart (*figure 17.2*) introduced in chapter 17 (Using Bullish Percent Charts to Analyze Broad Market Trends). You will see that this indicator moved down to the low-risk zone below 30% during the second half of 2002. At the same time, the Dow Industrials made the low for the 2000–2002 bear market. This low is shown on the chart of the Dow Industrials in *figure 19.5* (which was accessed May 4, 2005 from http://www.stockcharts.com). You can see that the 2002 monthly low of 7,592 (the intra-day low was 7,198 in October 2002) occurred while the NYSE Bullish Percent chart was also establishing a major low. When the NYSE Bullish Percent chart began to advance off its bottom, first into Bull Alert status and then into Bull Confirmed status, a buy signal occurred for the broad market. This signal helped proactive investors confidently buy near the market low at the same time that uninformed investors were dumping their stocks from fear created by negative media reports at the time.

249

Cyclical Trends from 2000–May 4, 2005

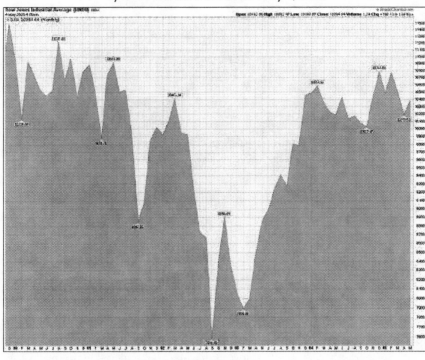

Chart courtesy of StockCharts.com

figure 19.5

As the NYSE Bullish Percent chart worked its way higher, a profitable cyclical bull market unfolded. By following the NYSE Bullish Percent chart, you will never get in at the exact low or out at the exact high to capture the full gain or move, but you will receive the lion's share of the trend as the indicator moves from one extreme to the other. During the secular bear trend that began in 2000, the cyclical bull market that began in 2002 has been the only significant U.S. market opportunity to grow your investment portfolio.

Strategies for Secular Bear Markets

The market indicators discussed in the previous two chapters are invaluable in identifying the start of new cyclical bull trends. Profiting during a secular bear trend is not an easy task. It requires dependable indicators that are unbiased and that provide clear, concise guidance to help make your decisions based on logic, not emotions.

Equally, if not more, important to identifying the beginning of new cyclical bull market trends is your ability to identify the end of the cyclical bull market. When the secular bear trend resumes, the declines can be intense. At such times, you need to protect your investments by quickly adopting a defensive approach. By a defensive approach, I mean quickly identifying and accepting market changes as well as quickly selling stocks that begin to show negative patterns on their Point & Figure and Relative Strength charts. Also be quick to sell positions in sectors that begin negative cycles. Sell these positions regardless of their profit or loss status.

Investment strategies you use during secular bear trends should be quite different than during secular bull trends. Here are a few guidelines to follow:

- **Focus on absolute returns rather than relative returns.** During secular bull markets, a proper measure of your portfolio's performance is based on relative returns (i.e., how your portfolio is performing relative to the market indexes). During secular bear trends, relative performance should take a back seat to absolute returns. By absolute returns, I mean you want to make money, regardless of the performance of market indexes. This may require periods in which you hold plenty of cash in your portfolio, waiting for the opportunities to come to you. Whether it be in the form of a new cyclical bull trend beginning or a significant sector opportunity, patience is a requirement during secular bear trends. Don't feel the need to always have your portfolio fully invested unless market conditions warrant a fully invested position.

- **A flexible, dynamic strategy will work better than a buy-and-hold approach.** As I've explained at length, a buy-and-hold approach will produce disappointing results during secular bear trends. You will have to be able to adapt to the market conditions, sometimes growing your portfolio and sometimes preserving your capital. The bullish-percent and sector indicators will help you adjust according to the dominant forces in control of the market.

- **Wealth preservation first, wealth accumulation second.** When in a secular bear trend, always manage your risk and preserve the wealth you accumulated during the last secular bull market. Capital preservation should be first and foremost. In secular bull trends, wealth accumulation takes the front seat. Risk management, which never should be completely ignored, takes on less importance. It is best to try to keep your portfolio fully invested during secular bull trends because the market will generally rise.

➢ **Consider alternative asset classes that may be in a secular bull market.** While the U.S. stock market may be entrenched in a secular *bear* trend, there will be some asset categories that are in a secular *bull* trend, offering greater growth opportunities. For example, in the 1970s, when the U.S. stock market was in a secular trend, stock prices in Japan were soaring. International stock markets are likely to perform better than the U.S. market during the current secular bear market too. In recent years, the stock markets in the emerging countries of Asia, Latin America, and central and eastern Europe have soared. Could these markets be in a secular advance while the developed markets like the United States and those of western Europe offer less opportunity? Something to consider.

Also rising during the 1970s were natural resource and commodity prices. For example, the price of gold rose throughout most of the 1970s and made an all-time high in 1980 near eight hundred dollars per ounce. The price of oil and other commodities was also strong during the 1970s. Commodity prices were in a secular bull market, while stock prices were stagnant for sixteen years.

During the 1980s and 1990s, stock prices soared, while commodities became stagnant. Hard assets and financial assets switched secular trends. In 2000, when the secular trend in stocks changed once again, commodities, such as energy and metals, as well as other natural resources, began a secular advance.

CHAPTER 20

OTHER IMPORTANT MARKET PATTERNS

> Combining market patterns with Bullish Percent charts can lead to
> profitable investment decisions.
>
> Two such patterns have stood the test of time:
> Four-Year Presidential-Election Cycle
> The Best and Worst Six-Month Periods of the Year

Combining the proper use of Bullish Percent charts, an understanding of secular and cyclical market trends, and knowledge of two important market patterns will help you develop strategies for profitable investment decisions. These two additional patterns are (1) the four-year presidential-election cycle, and (2) the best and worst six-month periods of the year. Although most market participants are aware of these two patterns, in this chapter I will delve into each concept and help you understand the importance of each one.

The Four-Year Presidential-Election Cycle

It has been said that there is a distinct cycle in the stock market that coincides with the U.S. presidential election. The theory states that during the first two years of a president's term, tough decisions are made that may have a negative short-term effect on business and economic conditions; these decisions tend to create difficult years for the stock market. The last two years of a presidential term tend to be more prosperous and reap the benefits of the tough decisions made in the first two years.

One needs to look no further back than the first term of President George W. Bush. The first two years of his first term were 2001 and 2002. Those years were marked with recession and a major bear market. The last two years of his first term, 2003 and 2004, were entirely different. Prosperity and a bull market prevailed. During the last two years of any president's term, the stock market has produced results three-times higher than the first two years. Is this mere coincidence, or is there really something behind the four-year presidential-election cycle?

According to the *Stock Trader's Almanac 2004*,[1] 170 years of statistics validate the presidential-election stock market pattern. Here is a quote from the publication:

> It is no mere coincidence that the last two years (pre-election year and election year) of the 43 administrations since 1833 produced a total net market gain of 717.5%, dwarfing the 227.6% gain of the first two years of these administrations.

> Presidential elections every four years have a profound impact on the economy and the stock market. Wars, recessions and bear markets tend to start or occur in the first half of the term; prosperous times and bull markets, in the latter half.[2]

These 170-year statistics are impressive. Once these statistics are broken down further, the cycle becomes even more prevalent. There have been forty-three presidential administrations over the last 170 years. The first year (post-election year) of those forty-three administrations has produced the worst results in the stock market. The market gained only 67.9% during the first year of presidential terms over the last 170 years. Furthermore, the first year was the only year that showed more declining than advancing years, with nineteen *up* years, twenty-three *down* years, and one year with no change.

The third year (pre-election year) was the best for the stock market, gaining 457.6%. Advancing third years outpaced declining years by nearly three to one—thirty-two *up* years and eleven *down* years.

While there is a clear pattern that coincides with the presidential-election cycle, an investor would be foolish to use this analysis in isolation. However, *combining* the use of Bullish Percent charts with knowledge of the four-year presidential cycle can be invaluable. For example, in 2002, when the NYSE and NASDAQ Bullish Percent charts were forming bottoms in the low-risk zone (see the NYSE Bullish Percent chart in *figure 17.2*), it was the second year of President George W. Bush's first term. The Bullish Percent charts began to give major buy signals just as we were entering into the third year of his term (the best in the presidential cycle), and the stage was set for a strong stock market during the second half of Bush's first term. The first two years of his term showed a loss on the Dow Jones Industrial Average of 23.9%, and the second two years showed a gain of 26.7%.

You will also notice remarkable results when you *combine* the use of the four-year presidential cycle with secular trend considerations. During the last secular bear trend from 1966–1982, the first two years of presidential terms were disastrous for the stock market. Of the eight years representing the first half of an administration's term, seven were *down* years while only one was *up*. The total combined loss for those eight years was 103.1%. The second half of the same administrations' terms during the 1966–1982 secular bear market showed all eight years higher. The total gain was 115.5%.

These statistics are remarkable given they occurred during the same secular bear trend and under the watch of the same presidential administrations. Yet being in the market during the second half of a president's term produced wonderful results, while a term's first half produced significant losses.

Will the use of the four-year presidential cycle be effective during the secular bear market that began in 2000? Early indications look promising. As stated above, the first two years of President Bush's term (2001 and 2002) showed a loss on the Dow Jones Industrial Average of 23.9%; the second two years (2003 and 2004) showed a gain of 26.7%.

The Best and Worst Six-Month Periods of the Year

There is an old adage on Wall Street: "Sell in May and go away; buy in November and you will remember." As simple as this adage may seem, these have been words to live by for more than fifty years. Going back to 1950, the six-month stretch beginning on November 1 and ending on April 30 has produced remarkable profits for stock investors. On the other hand, the six-month period starting on May 1 and ending on October 30 have not been kind to stock investors.

The November through April period has been deemed "the best six months" by the *Stock Trader's Almanac 2004,* page 50. Over the last fifty-five years, the "best" six months gained 10,765 points in the Dow Jones Industrial Average. Considering the Dow is currently trading close to the 11,000-point level, those are unbelievable statistics. During the "worst" six months of the year, the May–October period, the Dow *lost* 786 points. These findings mean that for the last fifty-five years, all of the market gains have occurred during the "best" six months and losses have occurred during the "worst" six months.

Putting this strategy in dollar terms, a $10,000 investment account based on the Dow Industrial Average bought on November 1 and sold on April 30 every year since 1955 would have made $489,933 in profits. The same account bought on May 1 and sold on October 30 each year since 1955 would have *lost* $502. Wow! The difference between making nearly a half-million bucks or losing money is only because of the months you are "in" or "out" of the market. In percentage terms, the difference is a profit of 4,899% on your investment during the "best" six months and a loss of 5% during the "worst" six months.

It's hard to argue with this data. There is a clear pattern, showing that the stock market has rewarded investors during the "best" six months. However, an investor would be foolish to use this strategy without the aid of other market indicators. When combining the "best" and "worst" six-month-period strategy with the use of Bullish Percent charts, you have a wonderful combination of seasonality and supply-demand analysis of market trends and cycles. For example, in 2003, the "worst" six-month period produced a solid profit of 15.6%. Again, using the NYSE Bullish Percent chart in *figure 17.2*, you will see that this indicator was in an X column and a Bull Confirmed status. When the NYSE Bullish Percent chart is rising, you have an opportunity to grow your assets, regardless of the time of year. When the NYSE Bullish Percent chart is giving a positive indication, you want to override the "best" and "worst" six-month strategy.

The years 2001, 2002, and 2004 were different stories. The NYSE Bullish Percent chart was near or above the high-risk zone at 70% in May of each of these years. In 2001 and 2002, the chart reversed down into an O column in June; the chart was already in an O column as we entered May 2004. When in an O column, the market is at risk of producing losses; you want to manage risk and preserve capital at these times. All three of these years produced losses of 15.5%, 15.6%, and 1.9%, chronologically, during the "worst" six-month period.

Along with the combined use of the "best" and "worst" six-month strategy and bullish-percent indicators, you can also combine the secular trend analysis into the mix. During the last secular bear trend from 1966–1982, the "worst" six-month period produced losses in ten out of sixteen years. The combined loss was 70%. Meanwhile, during the 1982–2000 secular bull trend, the numbers were quite different. The "worst" six-month period produced only six out of eighteen losing years, with a combined *profit* of 63.3%

The "best" six-month period produced profits during the 1966–1982 secular bear trend, but they paled in comparison to the profits produced during the 1982–2000 secular bull trend. The secular bear trend statistics are ten out of sixteen profitable years, with a total gain of 79%. The secular bull trend showed only one losing year, seventeen out of eighteen profitable years, with a total combined gain of 215%.

The four-year presidential cycle and the "best" and "worst" six-month period seem too simple and random to work. However, you can clearly see from the data presented in this chapter that there is something to both of the patterns that is more than mere coincidence. When combining their use along with the bullish-percent indicators, dynamite results can be produced.

SECTION 5

THE FOUR-STEP PROCESS TO MAKING CONFIDENT DECISIONS

CHAPTER 21

OVERVIEW

> **A Disciplined Investment Approach:**
> First: evaluate market conditions
> Then: evaluate sector conditions
> Next: select individual stocks
> Finally: manage risk and your portfolio

In the previous sections of this book, I have built the foundation for making confident investment decisions. I want to quickly recap some key concepts:

➤ Utilize an active decision-making process as opposed to a passive "buy-and-hope" strategy.

➤ Carefully watch supply and demand trends in the market, sectors, and individual stocks and appropriately respond to changes.

➤ By utilizing an active decision-making process and carefully watching supply and demand trends, you will be a proactive investor. This is noticeably different than using media coverage or Wall Street research. Being proactive and informed means using unbiased information to monitor opportunities in the market and to invest in current trends, not "after-the-fact" trends. Filter out noise that comes from the media. The media only reports current and past business and economic conditions. There is a delay between events and media coverage, and the past provides little value to investors. Future conditions will influence market direction. Simply stated, using the media for investments means you are making reactive, not proactive, decisions. Additionally, the media tends to play on investors' emotions, especially greed and fear.

➤ When selecting individual stocks, the root cause of price movement is the relationship between supply and demand. When demand is in control, prices increase, and there are opportunities to buy. When supply is in control, prices decrease, and you should sell or pursue other opportunities.

➤ Filter out noise from minor changes in the market. Don't respond to every change in the market; look for significant changes that indicate new trends. If a price movement is minor and irrelevant to trading, avoid any unnecessary or costly reaction. Remember, minor changes may just be market noise and not important to the overall trend of the stock.

➤ Employ a top-to-bottom approach (i.e., analyze and understand the overall market and industry sectors before selecting individual stocks). As I mentioned earlier, this approach is opposite of how most people tackle investment decisions. Understanding the price movement in the market and sector, before understanding the movement in the individual company, will produce better overall and long-term investment results and returns.

➤ Disciplined investing is only successful if you are *consistently* disciplined. You must set a course and follow it. Changing investment strategy will not maximize returns and will lead to confusion and frustration.

These concepts are meaningful, but without collective application, they do not help you. The four-step process to disciplined investments takes these concepts and provides a collective approach to investment management. The four-step process is a top-down approach; you start with an analysis of the biggest picture and funnel down until you are directed toward individual stocks with the best potential for delivering desirable results.

Is now the time to buy stocks, or should you wait for better prices? Based on the current economic conditions, should you invest in energy companies, or are health-care stocks the better choice? Or is it technology? Which stocks are the true leaders within each industry? When should you sell? The answers to these questions depend on when they are asked and will certainly change over time. This four-step process is designed to help you answer such questions and help you become a proactive and confident investor.

When selecting investments, the sheer number of securities to choose from can appear overwhelming. There are nearly ten thousand publicly traded stocks and several thousand more mutual funds from which to choose in the United States alone. When considering the international markets, the number of potential investments is staggering. The four-step process is designed to help you adapt to the market dynamics in control at any given time.

CHAPTER 22

FIRST: EVALUATE MARKET CONDITIONS

> **Benefits of First Looking at the Market:**
>
> **The overall market trend is a strong influence
> on stock-price movement.**
>
> **An accurate assessment of market conditions helps you apply
> capital-appreciation and capital-preservation strategies
> at the appropriate times.**

What is the importance of starting with an evaluation of market conditions? Simply put, sometimes the price movement in the overall market can be all encompassing. Using the tools introduced in section 4 (Market Analysis), you will be able to identify significant trends in the broad market and position your investments accordingly.

Commonly, investors do not feel a need to be concerned about the overall market because they feel stocks of fundamentally sound companies will go up regardless of the market's trend. You may be a whiz at picking stocks, but if you enter the market at the wrong time, your results can be disastrous. Many investors thought they could pick good stocks toward the end of the last secular bull trend (1999–2000). But many of those investors suffered huge losses.

In a different scenario, you can have inadequate stock-selection skills, but if you enter the market at the right time, you may enjoy desirable results. For example, some novice investors who entered the market in 2003, just as a cyclical bull trend was beginning, have enjoyed desirable results.

NYSE and NASDAQ Bullish-Percent Indicators

The best tools I have found to help you evaluate domestic market conditions are the NYSE and NASDAQ Bullish Percent charts. These two tools will help you identify opportunities to employ a capital-appreciation strategy. They will also help you employ a capital-preservation strategy when appropriate.

The two main points of consideration on the NYSE and NASDAQ Bullish Percent charts are direction and position. A rising bullish percentage is recorded with an X column on the chart, meaning that more stocks are giving buy signals on their Point & Figure charts and indicating that overall demand for stocks is strong. When demand is stronger than supply, the market is providing an opportunity for growth; a capital-appreciation approach is appropriate. A declining bullish percentage is recorded with an O column on the chart, meaning that more stocks are giving sell signals on their Point & Figure charts and indicating that overall demand for stocks is weak. When supply has the upper hand, a capital-preservation approach toward the market is appropriate.

The extreme risk levels are at 70% and 30%. When the NYSE or NASDAQ Bullish Percent chart is at 70%, much of the available demand has already been exhausted in the market; most investors have already purchased, capital is limited, and demand is not available for additional growth. At this level, risk is high, and you should avoid new commitments into the market. When at 30%, most of the available supply has already been exhausted in the market; most investors have already sold, and capital is available. At this level, risk is low and stock prices represent good value and opportunity.

Obviously, when the market is in a declining pattern, you do not want to sit back and wait for a change. A key to surviving a bear market is to abandon the buy-and-hold strategy. When a market is in a decline, you want to reduce or eliminate your exposure in sectors and stocks that are experiencing a decline.

Conversely, when the market is in a growth pattern, you do not want to sit back and assume that every stock will grow. Again, you want to look for pockets of opportunity. Some sectors will be leading the broad market advance, while others will be laggards. Investors are known for being a bit lax during bull markets. This is a dangerous attitude for two reasons—first, you may not be maximizing returns, and, second, certain stocks and sectors can experience a negative cycle even when the overall market is rising.

When the NYSE or NASDAQ Bullish Percent charts reverse columns from extreme levels, it could indicate major turning points in direction. These reversals are strong buy and sell signals for the overall market. When a market reverses up from below 30%, you have the best buying opportunities, and you should position yourself for aggressive growth. When the market is reversing down from above 70%, a major sell signal is in effect; you would want to conserve and protect your assets.

Another consideration for the NYSE and NASDAQ Bullish Percent charts is the status level. Bullish status levels are opportunities to grow your portfolio; bearish status levels indicate to proceed with caution.

Bullish Percent charts occasionally give clear-cut buy and sell signals that make them extremely helpful tools. Sometimes, the signals can be less clear. In an ideal scenario, the NYSE Bullish Percent chart would reverse down from the high-risk zone, change to Bear Confirmed status, give a strong sell signal, and eventually decline down into the low-risk zone, setting up a great buying opportunity once it reverses up. These actions would provide a clear and complete bearish cycle. The market will not always, however, accommodate our wishes.

Sometimes the chart declines somewhere near a neutral position, never reaching the low-risk zone at 30% prior to reversing back up. These are the times when in-depth analysis is necessary. A complete analysis of the situation might tell us that the direction is moving higher once again and that overall demand for stocks is gaining strength, or it might tell us that the status has not yet turned bullish because the new X column has not exceeded a previous X column. At these times, sector rotation can be very important. The broad market may be trading without a strong trend, but there are positive trends in certain sectors. Some sectors are rising at the same time that others are falling, creating equilibrium in the broad market. At these times, your overall market analysis should take a back seat, and you should focus your research on sector analysis. Finding low-risk sector opportunities and avoiding exposure to high-risk sectors will be the key to success while the overall market is in search of a trend.

Short-Term Market Indicators

Use of the NYSE and NASDAQ 10-week and high-low indicators will help you fine-tune your market analysis. These valuable indicators will help you in these ways:

> ➤ Find profitable cycles within the longer-term trends

> ➤ Avoid committing funds near short-term market peaks

> ➤ Enter the market near short-term market bottoms

> ➤ Provide a sell discipline near short-term market peaks

The interpretation of these two indicators is similar to that of the Bullish Percent chart. Of course, the short-term indicators will cycle from high to low risk, and vice versa, faster than the Bullish Percent charts. The best short-term signals occur when the 10-Week and High-Low Index charts for a market are giving similar indications. When the position of both the 10-week and high-low indicators are in the high-risk zone, scale back your enthusiasm—even if the Bullish Percent charts are indicating that the longer-term trend is positive. Eventually, the short-term market indicators will reverse down, and a lower-risk buying opportunity will occur in the coming weeks or months.

Secular Trend Analysis

While the NYSE and NASDAQ Bullish Percent charts will help you ana-lyze the cyclical (intermediate-term) market trends, you should also gain a perspective on the secular (long-term) trends. Asset allocation and portfolio management are impacted by whether the market is in a secular bull or bear trend. If the domestic market is in a secular bear trend, you may want to shift a larger portion of your assets into international markets. If so, you want to look for international markets in a secular advance. During these times, you will find the use of international Bullish Percent charts a big help. There are many useful international indicators to assist with this analysis.

Yet another asset class worth consideration is natural resources and com-modities. The secular trend of such assets tends to move counter the secular trend of financial assets. During the 1980s and '90s, stock prices soared, while commodities became stagnant. In 2000, when the secular trend in stocks began to decline, commodities (such as energy and metals), as well as other natural resources, began a secular advance.

Other Important Market Patterns

Other patterns, such as the four-year presidential-election cycle and the "best" and "worst" six-month periods of the year should also be part of your market analysis. If we are in the first two years of a president's term and entering the "worst" six-month season, and the NYSE or NASDAQ Bullish Percent chart is showing a strong sell signal, don't fight the evidence. Don't try to be a hero and think your ability to select stocks can override what is likely to be a few tough months, at a minimum, for the market. Exercise patience, and you will likely find a more attractive entry point for your stock selection down the road.

Of course, the opposite scenario can also occur. If we are in the last two years of a president's term and entering the "best" six-month season, and the bullish-percent indicators are showing a strong buy signal, don't hesitate to position yourself aggressively.

Tactical Application from Evaluating Market Conditions

Evaluating market conditions means first looking at the overall market for guidance on your next investment step. Market analysis helps you set a direction for your asset allocation and for further analysis of sectors and individual stocks. Market analysis allows you to know when the market is conducive for capital-appreciation or capital-preservation strategies. Based on your market analysis, you have several options for seeking out investment opportunities. Below are some basic options available, based on trends you identify in the overall market.

If the market indicators are *positive*, proceed as follows:

➤ Look for sectors with the strongest Bullish Percent and Relative Strength charts. Sectors that meet the criteria to be included in the *emerging-sector strategy* are a good place for you to focus. Avoid weak or neutral sectors.

➤ Invest in individual stocks in strong sectors. The stocks you select should have strong patterns on their Point & Figure and Relative Strength charts. Stick to *relative-strength leaders* or *emerging issues* in the sectors you choose.

➤ Shift investments from weak sectors and stocks to stronger sectors and stocks.

If the market indicators are *negative*, proceed as follows:

➢ Hold a cash position in your portfolio; protect your assets during a declining market and build liquidity for purchases when the market indicators improve.

➢ Sell stocks in weak sectors (i.e., those giving sell signals on their Point & Figure and Relative Strength charts or those that have made significant gains for you during the positive market cycle). For example, stocks can be sold if they reach your target-price objectives when the market indicators begin to turn negative.

➢ Look for sectors moving contrary to the overall market's movement. These tend to be defensive sectors, such as food and beverage, precious metals, drugs, and utilities. If your sector analysis shows one or more of these sectors beginning to emerge as a leader, focus a portion of your investments in these sectors. Of course, you want to pick the strong companies within these sectors.

➢ If you are so inclined, you can implement the *short-selling strategy*.

➢ Focus on international or alternative markets. If the indicators for the U.S. market are negative, solid market opportunities may be available in other markets.

CHAPTER 23

THEN: EVALUATE SECTOR CONDITIONS

Benefits of Looking at Sectors:

The sector trend has a strong influence on stock prices. Individual
stocks tend to move in the same direction as their sector.

Trend changes for a sector are a strong indication for you to change
sectors and your exposure to individual stocks.

The market indicators, such as the NYSE or NASDAQ Bullish Percent
chart, are rarely at 70% (high risk) or at 30% (low risk). When the market is at
extremes, sectors tend to be distributed on the same side as the market indicators. For example, when the NYSE bullish-percent indicator is above 70% (in
the high-risk zone), most sector Bullish Percent charts will also be reflecting a
high-risk position. You should use this information to steer away from the high-
risk market and sectors. A similar parallel holds true at the opposite extreme.
When the NYSE bullish-percent indicator is below 30% (the low-risk zone),
most sectors will also have Bullish Percent charts that reflect a low-risk position. When you see this indication, it is a green light to aggressively buy into
the low-risk market and sectors.

The market is not always positioned at one of the extremes. More commonly,
the broad market Bullish Percent charts are in the neutral zone between 30%
and 70%. During these times, you have a mix of sectors and stocks showing
demand in control, while others reflect supply in control. In these scenarios,
sector analysis takes on a higher level of importance. Sector analysis helps you
find the pockets of opportunity when the market is in middle ground.

Sadly, most investors do not spend any meaningful time analyzing sectors,
yet price movement in sectors accounts for the largest cause of individual
stock-price movement. Regardless, investors often skip over market and sector

270

analysis in search for the golden company. Such an approach is risky; a bit like Russian roulette.

I strongly recommend that you spend a large portion of your research effort in sector selection. To be a consistently successful investor, you have to be accurate on your sector analysis. The payoff for such effort is significant. If you are in the right sector, the individual stock selection becomes much easier.

Sector Bullish Percent Charts

The ability to analyze and recognize supply-demand imbalances in a sector can be very profitable. As with market analysis, when interpreting sector Bullish Percent charts, focus on the chart's direction and position. When the chart is advancing, demand is stronger than supply in the sector. When the chart is declining, supply is in control. Ideally, you would want to focus on sectors reversing up from below 30%. A sector does not have to be below 30% when you buy, but it is desirable if it has recently dropped into the low-risk zone and is now experiencing an advance. The combined drop and advance assures us we are entering into a sector early in an emerging trend.

Avoid buying into declining sectors with a bearish status. Make sure you steer clear from sectors that are declining after reaching the high-risk zone. If you own stocks in such sectors, you will most likely want to reposition these assets into stronger sectors. *Staying out of a bearish status sector is a simple and straightforward strategy and is one of the single most important steps you can take to reduce your risk dramatically. Do not skip over this step.*

As a sector moves higher, take a less aggressive approach toward the group. As I have illustrated with market analysis, the closer a market or sector is to 70%, the higher the level of risk. When a sector's Bullish Percent chart is near 70%, you can anticipate that a change will eventually occur. A high-risk position does not mean you should sell all of your holdings in the sector (certainly not as long as the directional movement is higher), but the time is not right to place new money in the sector.

Sector Relative Strength Charts

When your portfolio is focused in the top-performing sectors, you can build wealth at a desirable clip. Sector Relative Strength charts are invaluable tools in helping you isolate leading sectors. Equally important, sector Relative Strength charts help you avoid the weakest sectors.

When the broad market movement is advancing, many sectors may also be advancing from the market momentum. At such times, a large number of sector Bullish Percent charts may be moving in a positive direction, and you may have difficulty determining the best sectors for investment decisions. When both the market and sectors are advancing, sector Relative Strength charts come into the picture. Only the sectors that are outperforming the broad market will be advancing on their Relative Strength charts. Those moving up just because the general market is advancing will show a neutral Relative Strength chart. Of course, those advancing at a slower pace than the market, or those declining while the market is rising, will display a weak Relative Strength chart.

Sector Relative Strength charts are long-term indicators and move slower than Bullish Percent charts. As a result, you should primarily focus on the direction of the chart. If the chart is moving higher, more stocks in the sector are performing better than the market. Declining charts mean weak relative strength. The position is also important, but secondary, to the direction of the chart.

Combining the Use of Sector Bullish Percent and Relative Strength Charts

Your best sector opportunities are when movement on both the Bullish Percent and Relative Strength charts is positive for a sector. Both charts moving together indicates that sector members are experiencing strong *absolute*- and *relative*-price movement. A portfolio focused in such sectors should experience strong growth.

If the Bullish Percent chart is strong—but the Relative Strength chart is weak—you may have an indication that prices are moving up with a broad market advance but that the sector is not as strong as the overall market. In this case, you would want to focus in other sectors that are leading the market.

If the Bullish Percent chart is declining—but the Relative Strength chart is rising—you may have an indication that the sector is moving down with a broad market decline. However, the rising Relative Strength chart indicates that the sector is not dropping as much as the overall market. This sector should stay in your focus since the sector could be one of the leaders during the next market advance. Your key to act is when the Bullish Percent chart reverses into a rising X column.

You want to avoid sectors displaying weak Bullish Percent *and* Relative Strength charts. If both charts are moving down, make sure you eliminate any exposure you may have in such sectors. These sectors will provide the best opportunities for selling short.

Sector 10-Week Indicators

Even when the longer-term indicators (Bullish Percent and Relative Strength charts) are positive, you will want to avoid entering into a sector after a substantial move has occurred in recent weeks. The sector's 10-Week chart will help fine-tune the entrance and exit points for your buy and sell decisions. When a sector's 10-Week chart points to a heightened risk level above 70%, or when the chart is declining in a bearish status, you will want to wait for a better time to buy into the sector. Most likely, the sector will decline in the coming weeks, providing better prices for you to buy in the sector. When exiting positions, you should sell when the sector's 10-Week charts are at high-risk levels or in a bearish status.

Long-term investors should use the sector's Bullish Percent and Relative Strength charts as their main sector indicators but should always keep the status of the sector's 10-Week chart in mind. Short-term or trading-oriented investors could use the 10-Week charts as their main sector indicators while keeping the status of the Bullish Percent and Relative Strength charts in mind.

Sector Strategies

A complete sector-analysis strategy encompasses all three indicators listed above: the bullish-percent, relative-strength, and 10-week. Using all three enables you to focus on the best sector opportunities at any given time. Remember a sector-snapshot report can help tremendously when viewing all these indicators simultaneously. You can refer to the sector-snapshot report located on the Investor Education Institute's Web site:

> ➢ *Emerging-Sector Strategy:* The emerging-sector strategy uses a sector-snapshot report to pinpoint the sectors that are potentially beginning new relative-strength cycles. These sectors may be emerging as

new market leaders. The goal of this strategy is to focus on sectors that can outperform the broad market for the long term.

> *Sector-Momentum Strategy:* The goal of the sector-momentum strategy is to focus on sectors that are outperforming the broad market and to ride the momentum of these sectors higher. This strategy focuses on sectors already experiencing a mature advance. As a result, you would not expect to hold these investments for the long term. Given the shorter horizons for these investments, timing is important. The 10-week indicators are the key for buy and sell decisions using this strategy.

> *Short-Selling Sector Strategy:* The short-selling sector strategy isolates sectors that have completed positive cycles on both their Bullish Percent and Relative Strength charts. Once the sector's indicators provide evidence that a bearish phase is beginning, you want to attempt to profit from the decline in the sector. Although the combined use of Bullish Percent, Relative Strength, and 10-Week charts gives you the tools to analyze and identify declining sectors, selling short is not a strategy everyone may feel comfortable implementing.

CHAPTER 24

NEXT: EVALUATE INDIVIDUAL STOCKS

> Use Point & Figure and Relative Strength charts to select stocks
> with strong patterns.
>
> Look for stocks where demand is in control and the stock has just
> broken out of a supply and demand balance pattern.

Once you have evaluated market and sector conditions, you will have your general market approach (capital appreciation or preservation) and know which sectors to focus on and which to avoid. At this point, you need to choose the strongest individual stocks in the leading sectors.

Let me emphasize this point:

> ➤ If you jump right to the stock-selection step in the process without understanding the position of the broad market and evaluating your sector strategies, you will get disappointing results. *Do not cut corners.* Do not waste your time looking at individual stock Point & Figure and Relative Strength charts without first gaining a market and sector strategy.

When selecting an individual stock, you should use both Point & Figure *and* Relative Strength charts to select the stocks with strong patterns. Relative Strength charts will help you find the strongest stocks within a sector. Point & Figure charts will help you further look at those stocks for important supply-demand patterns. The pivotal points are when supply and demand are not in balance. Understanding the key patterns is important since they help you determine if a stock should continue in a growth direction or is at risk of a downward change in direction.

Below are some characteristics you want to see when selecting stocks:

Point & Figure Charts

➢ Demand should be in control on the Point & Figure chart. The chart should clearly show that the main trend line in effect is a bullish support line.

➢ Look for strong buy signals on the Point & Figure chart. Ideally, the stock should begin to break out of a balance pattern. When balance patterns are broken, the strongest price movements follow.

➢ Avoid buying stocks that are extended on their Point & Figure chart. If a balance pattern was broken several months ago and a significant price movement has already occurred, be patient with the stock. Either look for different opportunities in the sector or wait for the stock in question to consolidate the recent gains and to break another balance pattern.

➢ Avoid stocks where supply is in control. No matter how tempted you may be to buy a stock trading at a new low, always keep in mind that it is impossible for a stock to begin a long-term advance unless a strong supply-demand relationship exists. In other words, wait until you know that the bottom has occurred and that an advance is beginning.

Relative Strength Charts

➢ The relative-price movement should be positive for stocks you are buying. Ideally, the Relative Strength chart is on a buy signal and is in an X column.

➢ When selecting stocks in the emerging-sector strategy, it is okay to look at stocks yet to give a new relative-strength buy signal if two other conditions are present—first, if the Relative Strength chart has experienced a significant decline and, second, if the chart shows a reversal up and is now rising in an X column, indicating that the recent relative-price movement is gaining strength.

➢ Avoid buying stocks that are both on a sell signal *and* in an O column on their Relative Strength charts. Stocks with this pattern are weak and will deliver poor returns.

Combined Use of Point & Figure and Relative Strength Charts

The best stocks to own are the issues that have strong patterns in Point & Figure *and* Relative Strength charts. Your portfolio should be concentrated in relative-strength leaders. Such issues have a Point & Figure buy signal, are trading above their bullish support line, have a relative-strength buy signal, and are in a rising X column on their Relative Strength charts. These characteristics are indicative of the ***strongest stocks*** in the market.

CHAPTER 25

FINALLY: MANAGE THE POSITION AND RISK

> Investment management is a dynamic process.
> You must always be prepared for changes.
>
> Use changes in the market, sector, or stock as opportunities,
> not obstacles.

Once you have selected your investment, the job is not complete. You need to evaluate your positions continuously. This means reviewing market and sector indicators along with the Point & Figure and Relative Strength charts of the stocks you own. If there is a meaningful change in the position of the market, sector, or stock, that change is your signal to make a change to your portfolio.

For example, if the sector indicators begin to show signs of weakness, you may need to manage risk by moving your investments out of the sector. If a Point & Figure or Relative Strength chart for one of your stocks begins to show signs of weakness, you will likely want to manage the risk in the stock by selling. If your market and sector analyses are still positive, shift those dollars into a stronger issue within the sector. At times, the overall market indicators turn extremely negative, and you need to manage risk on the market level. At these times, you will want to raise your cash position, selling the questionable sectors and individual stock positions.

With the tools provided in this book, you can now analyze risk on many different levels—the overall market, industry sector, and individual stock. If risk is present, you want to take action to minimize the impact. Losses are a part of investing. For many people, managing risk within the market seems to be the most difficult aspect of investment management. When a small loss occurs, many rational people get nervous and react emotionally. The result is often a huge loss rather than a minimized loss. *Minimizing your losses is the key to becoming a hugely successful investor.*

Psychological influences are an obstacle for many people. Most investors cannot handle the emotional baggage that comes with selling a stock for a loss; however, taking the small loss is often the best decision you can make. When faced with the decision of taking a loss, even a small loss, most investors look to the sky in search for a silver lining. Any small piece of positive news or abbreviated rise in the shares will give them cause to hope that the stock price will eventually "come back up." So they close their eyes and hope for the best. If you find yourself in this situation, get out of the position. Live by the motto, "When in doubt, get out!" This perspective will help you stay out of trouble.

On the other side of quickly getting out of your losing positions is being patient with your winning positions. Don't be too quick to take your profit. Again, here is where psychological influences come into play. For most investors, selling a stock that had a small profit is easy. Selling a profitable stock verifies that you made a correct decision. It also feels good to ring the register. The saying, "You can't go broke taking a profit," may be true, but you need to replace that profitable position with another profitable investment. Stocks will go to extremes, both when they are rising and falling. If you have a winner, hold on tightly with both hands and take all the profit the stock wants to give. Of course, you will never be able to get out at the very top, but the objective is to stay with the positive trend.

Use the market, sector, and stock charts to help you decide when to sell. When the weight of the evidence in the charts and indicators begins to weaken, the time has come to sell. Most investors will sell their winners too quickly and hold onto their losers to long. Learn to do the opposite, and you will greatly improve your results. Sell out of your losers quickly and hold onto your winners until chart evidence indicates that the time has come to sell.

Nobody has the capital to buy every investment opportunity that comes along. For this reason, portfolio management is important. For many reasons, you want to diversify your exposure. As a result, you may find that selling partial positions in stocks that made significant gains is appropriate. For example, if you make investments in a particular sector using the emerging-sector strategy and the sector begins a long-term advance, these positions can become a large part of your stock portfolio. In other words, due to gains, the overall percent of your portfolio represented in that sector may be too high. As new sectors show up on the emerging-sector strategy list, you may want to participate in the new opportunities. If you do not have the cash in your portfolio, you may want to sell partial positions in your profitable holdings to participate in the new, emerging opportunities. Using this portfolio management strategy will reduce your risk in two ways. First, you will have reduced your exposure in sectors that have already made a significant move. And secondly, you will be repositioning your assets into lower-risk sectors.

CONCLUSION

As I mentioned in the introduction, my main reason for writing this book is to help you make confident and proactive investment decisions. After reading the strategies discussed in this book, I hope you take away valuable information for managing your investments and making confident, proactive decisions. Your next logical step is to put these strategies to practical use for your financial gain. The tools available online, such as those found on the Investor Education Institute's Web site (http://www.institute4investors.com), will be a tremendous help to you as you begin application.

While every investor's goal is financial gain, I realize your investments represent far more than just financial earnings—they represent your plans to achieve security in retirement; they represent your plans to provide high levels of education for your children; they represent your plans to pass on a legacy; and they represent your desire to *enjoy life.* I hope my book has shown you new and effective strategies to manage your investments. I hope you will never again blindly rely on media reports or Wall Street research for your information source. I hope you will no longer rely on passive strategies such as buy-and-hold, or blind diversification as a strategy. I hope you learned how proactive participation could help you achieve your personal goals.

The charting methodologies I have covered in this book are not new—Point & Figure, Relative Strength, and Bullish Percent charts have been around for many years and were created by successful investors. Yet with computer technology and database management, what once was a laborious strategy is now simplified. Furthermore, computer technology has allowed us to fine-tune and elaborate on some of the core concepts and develop some new, proprietary strategies. The ability to scan the market for sectors that are emerging as leaders and then to easily find a list of the strongest stocks in those sectors is an invaluable tool to help you find new investment opportunities. To be able to completely review the technical position of all your portfolio holdings on one computer screen and to be alerted to any meaningful changes will aid your portfolio- and risk-management efforts.

I firmly believe the information I presented in this book will be invaluable as you move forward with your investment plans. My twenty-two years of experience as an investment manager and advisor substantiate my belief that the approach addressed in this book provides strong results; however, no approach will be successful unless you apply it consistently and with discipline.

ACKNOWLEDGEMENTS

Investor Education Institute

Every successful investor starts with an *education* and follows a *discipline*. The Investor Education Institute consists of a consortium of professional investors, money managers, buy-side analysts, and investment strategists that provide unbiased educational materials and market information designed to empower you to be an informed and confident investor.

Our higher purpose is to help you take control of your *financial destiny*, get more out of your investments, achieve security in retirement, and enrich your life. How do we accomplish this? We help you learn to identify important market trends, isolate leading sectors, quickly drill down to find the strongest stocks, and manage your risk.

Many investors struggle to get the complete investment picture. Many are frustrated with lackluster results and little in the way of financial progress. The reason is that they are not getting the right education and information.

Our mission is to provide you with an educational experience that is second to none and to help you take the appropriate steps to put it to work for your personal benefit.

Our role is to help you connect the dots, give you a plan to operate, protect you from bad decisions, and help you do it in an easy way.

Should you have any questions about the strategies you learned in this book, please feel free to contact our professional members by phone at 1-800-504-8505 or by e-mail at inquiries@institute4investors.com.

Free Ninety-day Membership

As an additional learning tool, with the purchase of this book, you are entitled to register for a free ninety-day trial membership on the Investor Education

Institute's website. To activate your free membership, please visit http://www.
institute4investors.com and sign up for your free registration.

I encourage you to use the research database on our website regularly to
access the current charts, indicators and reports. In addition to finding these
various tools helpful as you read the book, they will also help you assess current market and sector trends. Such real-life assessment makes the information
in this book more interactive and relevant to your investment management
plans.

If you have any problems gaining access, please contact the Investor
Education Institute for assistance at 1-800-504-8505. The Institute wants you
to fully utilize our charting system and truly welcomes your questions and
requests for assistance.

In addition to the charts, indicators, and reports available on our website,
you may also find the article published to our blog helpful. The professional
members of the Institute post new articles several times each week, helping
members understand market and sector trends. You can find our articles at
http://blog.institute4investors.com.

Arlington Capital Management

Arlington Capital Management is a premier, private wealth-management
advisory firm that offers investment-management and wealth-planning solu-
tions. Arlington Capital Management maintains a leadership role in the investment-management and advisory profession by utilizing proven investment
tools and further developing them into a proprietary investment methodology.
The investment strategies and information provided on the Investor Education
Institute's website (http://www.institute4investors.com) and within this book
reflect the foundation of Arlington Capital's investment methodology. Further
information is available online at http://www.arlington-capital.com, by phone
at 847-670-4030, or by email at inquiries@arlington-capital.com.

About the Author

Joseph F. "Joe" LoPresti is the founder of the Investor Education Institute. He has twenty-two years of professional-investment experience, assisting investors since 1985. Joe is also the president and chief investment officer for Arlington Capital Management, an investment-management firm located in Arlington Heights, Illinois. Joe leads the firm's investment committee in determining the allocations and investment decisions for client portfolios. Prior to his career in the financial-services industry, Joe studied economics and finance at Millikin University in Decatur, Illinois. He also publishes *Empowered Investing Flash Report*, a market newsletter. Joe has written articles that have appeared in *BusinessWeek* magazine and is the host of a weekly investment talk show. In addition to managing assets for his personal clients, Joe works closely with other investment advisors and financial planners, who look to him to manage their clients' portfolios. As an educator, Joe teaches a number of investment courses, including Technical Analysis of the Stock Market, Investment Portfolio Management, Managing Your Retirement Assets, and Empowered Investing at various colleges. Joe lives in northwest suburban Chicago with his wife, Angela, and three daughters, Christina, Marissa, and Breanna.

NOTES

Chapter Three

1. Chartered Financial Analyst Institute, http://www.cfainstitute.org (accessed April 7, 2005).

2. Market Technicians Association, http://www.mta.org (accessed April 7, 2005).

Chapter Ten

1. Tomas J. Dorsey, *Point & Figure Charting*, pg 141, (New York, NY: John Wiley & Sons, 1995).

Chapter Seventeen

1. David Rynecki, "Bull Charges Again as Red Flags Wave," *USA Today*, June 25, 1998, MONEY section.

2. Pui-Wing Tam, "Wade in On the Stock Market's Dip," *Chicago Tribune*, June 30, 1998, YOUR MONEY section.

3. David Henry, "Bull Market Dodges Obstacles," *USA Today*, July 1, 1998, MONEY section.

4. James M. Pethokoukis, "The Two Warring Faces of Wall Street," *U.S. News & World Report*, July 27, 1998, 22.

5. "Crises Shake World Markets," *Chicago Tribune*, October 2, 1998.

6. "The Crash of 1999," *Newsweek*, October 12, 1998, cover.

7. "Market Mania," *Chicago Sun-Times*, November 24, 1998.

8. "System Failure: Corporate America, we have a crises," *Fortune*, July 1, 2002.

9. Adam Shell, "NASDAQ at lowest point in 5 years," *USA Today*, July 2, 2002.

10. Ameet Sachdev, "Dow dives to 4-year low," *Chicago Tribune*, July 20, 2002.

11. Christopher Oster, "Investors Rush to Stock Funds," *Wall Street Journal*, August 29, 2003, C1.

Chapter Nineteen

1. Rydex Investments, *Where Do You Think We're Headed?* www.rydexinvestments.com. Chart. <u>Dow Jones</u>: 12 January 2005. http://www.dowjones.com.

Chapter Twenty

1. Yale Hirsch and Jeffrey A. Hirsch, *Stock Trader's Almanac 2004* (Hoboken, NJ: John Wiley & Sons, 2004).

2. Hirsch and Hirsch, *Stock Trader's Almanac 2004*, 127.

BIBLIOGRAPHY

Barron's, July 22, 2002, Cover.

Chicago Sun-Times, "Market Mania," November 24, 1998.

Chicago Tribune, "Crises Shake World Markets," October 2, 1998.

Fortune, "System Failure: Corporate America, we have a crises," July 1, 2002.

Henry, David. "Bull Market Dodges Obstacles." *USA Today*, July 1, 1998, MONEY section.

Hirsch, Yale, and Jeffrey A. Hirsch. *Stock Trader's Almanac 2004*. Hoboken, NJ: John Wiley & Sons, 2004.

Newsweek, "The Crash of 1999," October 12, 1998.

Oster, Christopher. "Investors Rush to Stock Funds." *Wall Street Journal*, August 29, 2003.

Pethokoukis, James M. "The Two Warring Faces of Wall Street." *U.S. News & World Report*, July 27, 1998, 22.

Rydex Investments, *Where Do You Think We're Headed?* www.rydexinvestments.com. Chart. <u>Dow Jones</u>: 12 January 2005. http://www.dowjones.com.

Rynecki, David. "Bull Charges Again as Red Flags Wave." *USA Today*, June 25, 1998, MONEY section.

Sachdev, Ameet. "Dow dives to 4-year low." *Chicago Tribune*, July 20, 2002, Front Page

Shell, Adam. "NASDAQ at lowest point in 5 years." *USA Today*, July 2, 2002, Money section.

Tam, Pui-Wing. "Wade in On the Stock Market's Dip." *Chicago Tribune*, June 30, 1998, YOUR MONEY section.

INDEX

978-0-595-67469-5
0-595-67469-0

Printed in the United States
95149LV00004B/190-213/A